About the Author

FIN DWYER is an Irish historian and creator of the popular *Irish History Podcast*, boasting millions of downloads and a global listenership. He has worked on projects for RTÉ and his first book, *Witches, Spies and Stockholm Syndrome: Life in Medieval Ireland*, was published to critical acclaim in 2013.

FIN DWYER

A Lethal Legacy

A History of Ireland in 18 Murders

Harper
North

HarperNorth
Windmill Green
24 Mount Street
Manchester M2 3NX

a division of
HarperCollins*Publishers*
1 London Bridge Street,
London SE1 9GF
UK

www.harpercollins.co.uk

First published by HarperNorth 2023
1

A catalogue record for this book is available from the British Library.

ISBN: 978-0-00-855599-3

Typeset in Sabon by Palimpsest Book Production Ltd, Falkirk, Stirlingshire

Printed and bound in the UK using 100% Renewable Electricity
by CPI Group (UK) Ltd

In Memory of Finbar Cafferkey

Contents

Introduction

One of the most enduring aspects of the human condition is our fascination with murder. From Cain and Abel in the Old Testament, to *Making a Murderer* on Netflix, our obsession with the act of killing – its motivations, its ramifications – has permeated culture since the dawn of history. Understanding this fixation is complex, but one thing is clear: the level of our interest in murder appears to have little relation to the prevalence of the act in our society. Few people ever witness a murder; they are much rarer than we imagine and have been for centuries. And yet we surround ourselves with depictions of this crime. In the 1990s the Cultural Indicators Project reported that children were exposed to 8,000 murders through television by the age of twelve. Our nineteenth-century ancestors had their own similar concerns about the frequent graphic depictions of violent murders that appeared in the newspapers of the time.

Whatever the case, our cultural obsession remains and

has seamlessly transitioned into contemporary online culture, where descriptions of violence abound and true crime has established itself as one of the most popular entertainment genres.

Why are we drawn to murder? The reasons behind our seeming insatiable interest in the crime is not immediately obvious. Part of our fascination is undoubtedly rooted in the act itself. Across continents and time it is a universal taboo; the ultimate transgressive act, a point of no return. How such a crime should be punished and whether it can ever be justified remain topics of relentless debate. But our continued interest in murder in the twenty-first century is complicated by the fact that it has been on the decline for centuries. Murder is becoming less common and less of a problem for society, yet our interest appears to only increase. In the twenty-first century, murders in Ireland are relatively rare. Perhaps this is what partly fuels modern interest – violence is something we actually encounter less and less.

When murder does occur it is often a personal act, rooted in the interactions of just two people. And yet, personal and intimate though the act may often be, it can just as often have historical implications. With this in mind, I've chosen to traverse over 200 years of Irish history by focusing on eighteen murders. While these individual acts of violence are rarely the decisive turning points of history in and of themselves, through an understanding of them I believe it's possible to illuminate the darker recesses of the past, and gain a greater understanding of the context in which they took place. What is often most fascinating for an historian is that, in the aftermath of a murder, history tends to slow down – its lens focuses on people frequently relegated to the footnotes of history or forced off the margin altogether – and people who lived entirely normal, even banal lives, are momentarily cast centre stage in the record of their times.

The violent act of murder is not by definition useful to the historian, although the interest contemporaries take in the events surrounding a murder are often extremely insightful. To fall victim to a murder, or to stand accused of one, generally means an individual is subject to intense scrutiny. The subsequent investigations, reports, records and commentary provide the minutiae so often lacking in historical records. For example, prisons in nineteenth-century Ireland recorded height, eye colour, hair colour and in some cases even tattoos. More importantly, trials often record the broader historical context; their background and relationships between the victims and the accused as well as their families, friends, neighbours, and wider society. They are picked over and, crucially, recorded in great detail. This level of detailed documentation can leave historians with a ringside view of major events in the past, a perspective frequently obscured by the noise of battlefields or the focus on politicians and those at the centres of power.

Given that murder is predominantly perpetrated by men, and that women are more frequently the victim, a focus on murder risks created a two-dimensional view of the past. It quickly became apparent that if I focused chapters solely on the killer and their victims, this could create an illusion whereby women were bystanders in the historical process. The reality, it goes without saying, is very different.

Therefore the book consciously avoids structuring the chapters exclusively around the relationship between the murderer and their murdered. Some focus on the victim, others look at the killer; many examine the events from the perspective of siblings or parents of those killed.

Defining what exactly constitutes a murder was, perhaps surprisingly, one of the more challenging aspects of preparing the book. Using court convictions of murder as a distinction raises significant problems. Charges of murder are often reduced to manslaughter solely to ensure a conviction, while Irish history is littered with cases of people who were never charged with murder despite overwhelming evidence. I also followed the generally accepted definition of combat deaths, which holds that members of military organizations are killed, not murdered. This is a useful distinction, particularly in terms of understanding the past and especially military conflicts. I therefore excluded all cases where the victim was a member of the British Crown Forces, the Irish Republican Army, Ulster Volunteers, or associated organizations. This doesn't preclude murders committed by members of these organizations. I used a broad definition when considering an act as murder, one where intentional violence resulted in the death of a civilian.

Finally, choosing where to start and end any work of history is a challenge: the interrelated 1798 Rebellion and the Acts of Union, which came into effect in 1801, mark a useful break with the past and act here as our starting point. The abolition of the Irish Parliament and creation of a union between Great Britain and Ireland set the stage for the following two centuries of history, up to the present day. But if choosing a starting point is tricky, deciding where to end a history book is nothing short of a minefield. Yet the 2018 Repeal of the 8th Amendment (which banned abortion in the Republic of Ireland) was unquestionably significant, and from the perspective of the historian this was a key moment in terms of understanding the decades that preceded it. It stood, like pivotal events before it, as a natural line in the sand between eras in our island's history.

Fin Dwyer
Waterford, 2023

CHAPTER 1

A United Kingdom?

1821

> What shall therefore the lord of the vineyard do?
> He will come and destroy the husbandmen,
> and will give the vineyard unto others.
>
> (Mark 12:9)

December 1821, in the midst of one of the worst winters in living memory, and the County Tipperary magistrate Samuel Jacob was growing more concerned by the day. The sound of approaching horses, once a source of news, was now the drumbeat of growing anxiety and fears. Every day Jacob received more reports from his spies across the county, each one more alarming than the last. Rebellion was in the air once more.

Born in 1754, Jacob had lived through some of the most turbulent decades in Irish history. He had seen sixty-seven winters come and go and witnessed violent revolts and uprisings first-hand, and knew well the warning signs. He could vividly recall the impact the French Revolution of 1789 had and how it had transformed his world, its tentacles stretching from Paris to his native Tipperary.

The revolution initially had provoked excitement amongst many across Europe, including Ireland, and the changes it triggered provoked cautious enthusiasm. But the execution of King Louis XVI in 1792 and the increasingly radical revolution polarized attitudes. While conservative men like Samuel Jacob were horrified, the French revolutionaries maintained considerable support among those who had been agitating for change in Ireland.

By 1793 the rising tensions between revolutionary France and Britain finally led to an outbreak of war. Although the conflict would be fought on far-flung battlefields, back in Samuel Jacob's native Ireland, the war had initially, at least, been a welcome development. The conflict disrupted trade between Britain and the Continent, and Irish agricultural goods commanded soaring prices in the British markets. While the fallout of the revolution had seen profits rise it did in time led to turmoil at home.

The revolutionaries' message of liberty, equality and fraternity resonated among many in Tipperary and across Ireland. The Society of United Irishmen, a revolutionary movement, argued that an independent Irish republic modelled on the French experiment was a way to resolve some of the Ireland's long-standing problems. Drawing support from members of all religious communities they demanded universal manhood suffrage and an end to Catholic persecution. Believing these could never be achieved under British rule, they had come to the conclusion that the only strategy to effect their goal was an armed insurrection to establish an independent Irish Republic –

and in 1798 the United Irishmen organized one of the largest rebellion in Irish history.

Samuel Jacob, then in his forties, could vividly remember that terrifying summer when the rebels rose up, and the bloody repression that soon followed as government forces prevailed. Tens of thousands had been massacred in the following months. While this counter-revolutionary terror subdued large parts of the population, another rebellion had erupted in 1803 – although this one was a pale imitation of the first, and government forces easily crushed the rebels. While republicanism had been suppressed, peace did not return. The Ireland of Samuel Jacob's time was bitterly divided, just as it would be in the century to follow. Between the two rebellions, the passage of the Acts of Union resulted in Ireland's amalgamation with Britain into a United Kingdom. United in name, the kingdom was anything but united in nature. Inequality and widespread poverty in Ireland stoked discontent.

While social upheaval fermented beneath the surface, in 1815 Jacob's spies had forewarned him of what appeared to be another uprising beginning to take shape, as the ghosts of the French Revolution returned to haunt Ireland. That year, Napoleon's defeat at the Battle of Waterloo marked the end to the decades of war ignited by the French Revolution. In Ireland this ushered in an economic depression of an unprecedented scale. For over twenty years Irish farmers had enjoyed booming prices, but the end of the war saw European trade resume and prices fall through the floor.

In that winter of 1815, as the poor faced hunger and eviction, they fell back on long-established traditions of resistance. In clandestine gatherings they swore oaths and banded into secret societies commonly called the Whiteboys. They pledged to stand by each other and to take collective action: this saw letters and notices threatening violence on those contemplating forcing the poor from their homes. Where such measures failed, more persuasive tactics such as property destruction, assault and occasionally murder were employed. In response to the outbreak of social upheaval in 1815, the government called out a militia, the Yeomanry, who were able to re-establish control for a time.

The memories of these violent rebellions were still all too fresh for Jacob when, in the winter of 1821, some of his most reliable spies returned to warn him that yet another revolt was in the offing. They reported the same signs – rising food prices were once again driving the poorer population deeper into poverty. Yet again clandestine meetings were called; oaths were sworn. Farmers threatening to evict poor labourers who couldn't pay rent faced menacing letters. Violence would follow.

So convinced was Jacob that this would lead to outright rebellion that he wrote to William Saurin, the Attorney General for Ireland, pleading for action. Stating his credentials as a man experienced in predicting revolts, Jacob informed Saurin that his native South Tipperary was on the brink: 'With regret I take the liberty of stating to you that we are again threatened with insurrection . . . Preparatory steps were being taken now with more secrecy and system than heretofore. Instructions were given to be ready to rise.'[1] Indeed by late 1821, Jacobs no longer needed his network of spies to understand what was happening. The pot was starting to boil. Raids on the houses of wealthy farmers to secure weapons were happening almost every day. Anyone who might dare threaten to issue eviction notices to the poor was likely to receive a death threat in response.

For Jacob, this was a well-rehearsed drama, one he had seen play out all too often in his sixty-seven years, but things were beginning to feel different this time. In late November 1821 terrifying names were being whispered across South Tipperary, adding a new layer of fear to this most recent swell of agitation. Those names were Ned and Mary Shea. Once entirely innocuous, the Sheas' names had begun to turn up in letters and posters threatening violence against big farmers,[2] invoking such terror that even the most determined landlords heeded the warnings – yet that they would play such a role in history would have come as a surprise to most, not least the couple themselves.

Ned and Mary Shea had lived modestly. Their births were not recorded in any surviving document. The couple had scarcely been known beyond their native community of Gurtnapisha on the north slopes of the hill of Slievenamon in South Tipperary. The Sheas owned a farm in a country where the vast majority of people worked in agriculture. They were neither the richest nor the poorest in their community. They didn't live in the one-room cabin of the poor farm labourers, nor was the family home one of the sprawling mansions of the Irish landlords that dotted the landscape. Theirs was a substantial dwelling that accommodated sixteen people including Ned and Mary, their children and several of their employees.

One of the crucial aspects of his life that *did* distinguish Ned Shea from those around him were his politics – Ned had been a member of the Yeomanry, the highly unpopular militia used to maintain government control. While it may have set him apart, it hardly made him exceptional. All told, Ned and Mary were unremarkable people who lived unremarkable lives; not the type of people whose names would strike terror across the country.

Yet in the weeks following their deaths in November 1821, the pair were on a path to worldwide infamy. By Christmas, London's theatre critics mused that their story would provide better entertainment than what was offered up in the city's playhouses.[3] In the following months, their unwanted fame spread across the world. By February 1822 they were being discussed as far west as Louisville, Kentucky,[4] and by the early summer the East India Company nabobs were reading about the lives – or perhaps more accurately the deaths – of Ned and Mary Shea as they sipped their gin in Kolkata.[5] Though it had been a less than auspicious year until its closing chapters, the violent events of 1821 would come to symbolize the terrible ends brought about by the inequality that underpinned Irish society in the early nineteenth century.

Through the first half of 1821, there was little reason to believe the year would be remembered in later decades. The weather was good, which meant an anticipated bountiful harvest heralded the prospect of social peace – something that had often proved elusive in Ireland in previous decades. In the summer, Ned Shea and the magistrate Samuel Jacob, both loyalists and supporters of the

British administration in Ireland, received further positive news when it was announced that the new monarch, George IV, planned to visit Ireland in August.

The fact that the King would be the first monarch to set foot in Ireland since 1690 – and perhaps, more importantly, the first to do so without an army at his back – presented the possibility of a new era in Anglo-Irish relations. The *Windsor and Eton Express* voiced the views of loyalists on both sides of the Irish Sea when it hoped the visit would be 'a pledge that the oppressions under which Ireland once groaned have given place to the gradual power of justice and liberality; it is a solemn ratification of the Union of the sister kingdoms, giving the assurance of an identity of interests and feelings'.[6] Indeed, in the opening days of the visit, the bitter division in Irish society seemed to melt away, as King George was greeted by crowds of well-wishers wherever he went.

Yet the prospects of a new chapter in Anglo-Irish relations and a good harvest were both illusory. Hopes that King George might lend his support to growing demands to end the continued legal discrimination against the island's Catholics, some 80 per cent of the population, were dashed. On leaving Ireland, the King revealed his deeply held sectarian view of the world and his opposition to Catholic emancipation.*[7]

By the final days of the royal visit, Irish attentions were already being drawn toward even more pressing matters.

---

* As the King departed Ireland from Dún Laoghaire harbour, the Catholic leader Daniel O'Connell presented him with a laurel wreath. The King snubbed O'Connell in a move that revealed his strident opposition to Catholic emancipation.

The royal visit had been marred by a shift in the weather. It had rained almost continuously after King George had landed at Howth outside Dublin on 12 August and his departure from Dún Laoghaire (still known as Kingstown at the time) nearly four weeks later was delayed by a day as the adverse weather continued. Although the royal party sailed on 5 September, the improved weather was but a brief respite. The relentless rains continued.

This was the moment in which the stage was being set for Ned and Mary Shea's entry into Irish history.

Despite the inclement weather, the initial prognosis for the harvest of 1821 remained optimistic. There were fears that grain might be affected, but crucially the potato crop, which underpinned the entire economy, was predicted to hold up. While grain prices affected people in the pocket, the potato was the staple of the poorest. If the potato failed, people would starve. And, as Samuel Jacob knew all too well, when the poor were hungry, bloody civil unrest was sure to follow.

As the weeks dragged on, the autumnal rains did not relent. By November the *Freeman's Journal* carried distressing reports from across the island that the potato crop was so poor it was hardly worth saving.[8] As the poorest in society began to starve, events took a predictable course. The brittle rural Irish economy started to fracture, and societal bonds were once again tested to the limit as the poor struggled to survive and the rich protected their interests.

But this was not a simple struggle of landlord and tenant. The world of Irish land ownership was byzantine. High agricultural prices during the war with revolutionary

France had led to a dramatic rise in rents, which incentivized sub-letting. By the early nineteenth century landlords rented to middlemen, who in turn rented to farmers, who themselves rented small potato patches to labourers in return for work. This resulted in competing interests at all levels in society. Farmers and labourers would frequently engage in violent struggles that were far removed from the landlord, who ultimately owned the property.

The conflict between these competing groups invariably flared up after bad harvests. Wealthier farmers organized into secret societies known as 'Shanavasts', engaging in violent clashes with a similarly clandestine organization called 'Caravats', a group drawn from the ranks of poorer labourers and small farmers.[9] While these secret societies that perpetrated much of the violence were largely the preserve of men, women like Mary Shea faced their own threats. Abductions of women, with a view to forcibly marrying them, was often used by poorer labourers as a means to secure social advancement. Such abductions could involve brutal sexual assaults in an effort to ensure silence on the part of the woman.

These assaults were rooted in the transactional view of marriage at the time. Women were considered a financial asset of a family, to be traded for influence and power in an advantageous marriage. This exposed them to the dangers of being abducted by those seeking advancement but lacking the means or standing to secure a marriage they desired.

The sheer levels of unrest between the various classes in Irish society was obvious to visitors at the time. Georg Kohl, a German who visited, observed the tinderbox that was Irish society in the early nineteenth century: 'conspiracies are constantly formed among the poor farmers and labourers; and as these conspiracies are said to be as plentiful as the grievances complained of, they must, indeed, be numberless'.[10]

Despair spread across the countryside as the harvest rotted in the fields. Tensions began to rise dramatically. By early November 1821, the situation in County Cork was already extremely volatile. Newspapers began to report on the violent mood in the county: 'The terror of assassination disturbs the mind of every respectable inhabitant, and already, four families have withdrawn from the neighbourhood alluded to, to seek shelter in populous places.'[11] Even though the violent unrest was clearly rooted in the fears of famine and starvation, the authorities refused to acknowledge this reality. Back in South Tipperary, where a similar situation was developing, Samuel Jacob, who gave voice to men of property, made little reference to the actual causes of discontent, but instead emphasized the rebellious nature of the Irish.[12]

As the tectonic plates of Irish society built up greater and greater pressure below the surface, Ned Shea found himself squeezed between the factions. Being a farmer in a time of rising food shortages always presented choices, and he chose poorly.

In mid-November Shea was presented with a dilemma many farmers and landlords were facing – his tenants were refusing to pay their rent. This was one of the first ways that food shortages affected communities in Ireland at the time. As the poor lost their primary food supply, potatoes, they had to decide: pay rent and starve or buy other food and default on their rent. The decision was a straightforward one. Time and again through the centuries, this dilemma has been posed to the poor and understandably people opted to eat and worry about their rent at a later date. Land was of no use to a dead person, yet while they were unable to pay rents due to circumstances beyond their control, the poor did remain determined to hold on to their small farms and plots of land, the loss of which would only impoverish them further.

The desperation and tenacity of the local poor was abundantly clear to the Sheas; the family home had already been targeted earlier in 1821, in a botched raid for guns, as the secret societies sought to arm themselves. Nevertheless, Ned Shea pushed ahead and evicted his tenants for non-payment of rent on 17 November 1821. Callous as such an act was, this behaviour was not unusual in the nineteenth century. The relationship between richer farmers and the poor who rented their lands was fraught at the best of times. Many farmers like Shea felt little obligation or loyalty to the poor. However, in the climate of late 1821, when starvation faced thousands, it was inevitable his action would provoke a response, but the scale of what unfolded took many by surprise.

Shea's action stoked up the deep feelings of resentment that surrounded the man. Even before he had evicted the tenants, he was not liked by many in his community. His membership in the Yeomanry only heightened bitterness towards the man. The reaction for his eviction of his tenants was predictable, swift and brutal.

On the night of 20 November Philip Dillon, a neighbour, heard screams echoing across the fields from the Shea house. Arming himself with a blunderbuss, Dillon and his son-in-law went to investigate. Through the darkness, he could see the Shea household was ablaze but he had arrived to catch the perpetrators in the act. As the house came into view Dillon could see the silhouettes of well over a dozen men moving around a building consumed by the flames. It was clear this was no accident.

The attackers were intent on destroying the Shea house by igniting a pile of fuel heaped at one end of the building. They then surrounded the building, ensuring no one escaped. As the fire spread, a hay rick to the rear of the building caught fire and as the flames leapt into the night sky the inferno was visible across the region. Desperate to save his neighbours inside the burning building, Dillon discharged his blunderbuss at the men surrounding the Shea house, but the primitive gun – unreliable at the best of times – had little effect. Emboldened, the attackers refused to move, instead taunting Dillon to 'advance if you dare'.[13] Helpless, Dillon and his son-in-law had no option but to withdraw. The Sheas were consigned to their fate: burning alive inside their farmhouse.

Meanwhile, another neighbour who witnessed the terrible glow of the flames sent for Ned Shea's brother, Nicholas. When Nicholas Shea arrived at Gurtnapisha around 2 a.m., only a few hours after the house had been attacked, he found a scene of utter devastation. The intense conflagration had died down. In the intensity of the blaze the roof of the house had collapsed, leaving little but a mass of ash and scattered personal possessions.

The attackers had vanished but what perhaps unnerved him most was the silence. The occasional crackle of burnt timber was all that remained of the once noisy household. There was neither sight nor sound of Ned or Mary Shea, nor of the fourteen people who lived with them. All life had been extinguished.

It would be another seven hours before Nicholas Shea was able to enter the smouldering ruins of his brother's house. Amidst the debris it was possible to decipher what had transpired. At the door they found the charred remains of two men. Ned Shea was first to be identified, due to one of his legs being shorter and because he had a missing tooth. The other was later identified as a servant, Peter Mullaly. Both men had gunshot wounds and the husks of weapons with them. It was surmised that they had come out to defend the house but had been shot by the attackers.

Further into the charred house were fourteen other bodies. Mary was easily identified – she was heavily pregnant – as were the couple's five children, aged from two to ten. As was common for the time, the household had not consisted solely of the Sheas but also of servants, and another woman who happened to be visiting on the night of the attack.[14] In total, there were sixteen bodies within the smoking shell of the house.

When an inquest was convened, the jury was brought to the house to witness the scene. One of their number would later write a detailed account of what had faced them: 'No pen could describe the scene that presented itself on entering the yard. The dwelling was burnt to the ground. Not one of the inmates escaped to tell the tale or to describe the horror and agonies, pursued by the devouring flames.'[15]

As the bodies were laid out in the yard, many members of the inquest jury broke down, unable to take in the scene before them. The horror was encapsulated in the fate of the Sheas' two-year-old child who Mary Shea, in a desperate bid to save her infant, placed in a pail of water – a desperate but ultimately futile gesture.

Almost immediately, the authorities launched a major investigation, determined to find those responsible for the attack, described by one local magistrate, Francis D'Espard, as, 'the most sanguinary and atrocious acts, the most hellish imagination could devise.'[16]

Fearing that the dire harvest would drive others towards a similar course of action, they were desperate to find those responsible. A huge sum of money, two thousand pounds, was offered as a reward for information leading to arrests and convictions within six months. Such a vast sum at the time was certainly enticing. With that amount of money a person could leave Ireland and emigrate to North America where they could start a new life, far from Tipperary.

Yet the outrage of the authorities was not universal among the poor. Even though the Sheas lived in what was described as a 'thickly populated part of the neighbourhood',[17] no one came forward to offer information. Furthermore, given the local geography it was obvious that more neighbours could have come to the family's aid but didn't.

The silence that the authorities faced in late 1821 left them with a very limited understanding of what actually transpired on the night. Even though the sums of money on offer could have easily saved individual families, the looming famine appears to have only hardened attitudes in the community. To some at least, the attack and brutal murder of the Shea family was to one degree or another bound up in the wider struggle between farmers and labourers in the community.

One of the magistrates at the inquest informed the authorities in Dublin Castle that 'a spirit of insubordination was spreading through the community' towards anyone who dared to rent the farm where the previous tenant had been evicted.[18] Horrific as it was, in the minds of some Ned Shea was the author of his own demise.

In the following weeks refusal to co-operate began to develop into active resistance to the investigation. William Chaytor, a member of parliament for County Tipperary, wrote to the Lord Lieutenant, Lord Anglesey, informing him of the growing opposition he and others faced when they tried to investigate the Sheas' murder.[19] Once posters advertising the rewards were put up around the locality they were, in Chaytor's words, 'ripped down in the hour'.[20] Writing about sentiment in his native Clonmel, he said, 'I have never known such a similar circumstance before and I think it strongly indicates the feeling of the lower orders of this town.'[21] Sixty-seven-year-old Samuel Jacob, who saw this as clear evidence that an armed insurrection was imminent, wrote, 'Since the massacre of the Sheas, houses have been attacked for arms, and arms taken.'[22]

His fears, though warranted given his experiences in the past, were exaggerated. In the following months across the south and west, raids, attacks, threats and murders continued, though the insurrection he foretold did not materialize.

This was in part due to government intervention. In 1822 £500,000 was provided for famine relief, on the condition that it was matched by similar grants from the wealthy on the ground in Ireland. While this staved off a full-blown famine, the fact that relief in some regions was withheld from communities where protests over food shortages took place proved a brutally effective form of limiting resistance.[23] In the longer term, the emergence of this strategy of collective punishment employed against whole communities served to erode the legitimacy of the British authorities on the island. This would be repeated over the following two hundred years during the Great Hunger of the 1840s, the Land War in 1880s, the War of Independence in the 1920s and in the Troubles in Northern Ireland. It created a vicious cycle whereby people affected by inequality were unjustly punished for actions they had no hand or part in. This often served to radicalize the communities in question and the response from the authorities was further repression. At every step this eroded the legitimacy of the British presence in Ireland among large sections of the population.

Meanwhile, the authorities in South Tipperary in the 1820s remained determined to secure prosecutions against those involved in the attack on the Sheas. In May several local men were arrested for the initial raid for weapons on the household in the weeks preceding the fire. Although the men were found not guilty, the arrests provoked a response from those fearful the authorities might be closing in on the killers.

In a stark warning to would-be informers, the house of Phillip Dillon and his son-in-law, both of whom had tried to intervene on the night of the attack, was raided that same month. Luckily for both, neither was home at the time. This continued violence took place in the midst of deepening tensions between farmers and tenants. The food shortages and high prices that followed the poor harvest of 1821 only worsened into the winter.[24] A few days after the attack on Dillon, a secret society raided the house of another farmer in the area. On this occasion, by contemporary standards, the farmer was lucky – rather than burning the building to the ground, it was levelled by sawing the roof timbers.

Tensions continued to increase until finally the harvest of 1822 eased the situation across Tipperary and the wider crisis across Ireland began to subside. But the authorities remained resolute they would find and dispense the ultimate punishment to the guilty, and the easing of famine conditions appears to have loosened tongues in the local community. Unbeknownst to most at the time, the approach of the first anniversary of the murders provoked a key witness to come forward.

Ultimately, it was a guilty conscience rather than money that motivated Mary Kelly to break her silence. Kelly had been a neighbour of the Sheas and, unsurprisingly for such a small, tight-knit community, she was related to some of the victims. But she had also been party to some of the early planning for the attack. In a confession to a local Catholic priest she revealed that it had begun as an attempt to raid the Sheas' house for weapons.

A week prior to the attack, William Maher, an acquaintance of her son, had come to her house and manufactured home-made bullets by melting a spoon. These were to be used in an upcoming raid on the Sheas to procure weapons. However, a few days later Ned Shea had evicted his tenants and this had transformed the nature of the attack. With local animosity towards Shea at a fever pitch, Mary Kelly claimed William Maher had been able to enlist others.

Crucially she also claimed to have seen around fifteen people – including William Maher and his brother Darby – set off for the Sheas' property on the night in question. She then heard the exchange of gunfire at the house; the shots that killed Ned Shea and Peter Mullaly and then the other shots discharged by Philip Dillon, the neighbour who had tried to intervene.

In her confession Kelly, carefully distancing herself from the murderers, told the priest she had been outraged when what she thought was a raid for weapons led to the burning of the house. In the immediate aftermath of the attack she had not come forward but she did ask for an explanation from William Maher. In Kelly's version of events Maher told her that after reaching the house he and the others had demanded the weapons and when Shea refused, the house was burnt. Kelly then claimed William Maher had since regularly intimidated her into silence with threats.

While she kept her counsel for twelve months, in 1822 Kelly had first approached a local priest, who encouraged her to reveal what she knew to the magistrate, Francis D'Espard. Kelly provided the magistrate with essential information as to the identity of the group who had attacked the house claiming she had seen them pass her home. However, from the outset Kelly was a somewhat problematic witness given she had poor eyesight.

Nevertheless D'Espard, with few other leads, pressed ahead but the case moved slowly. It was a further two years before he succeeded in bringing forward prosecutions but eventually William and Darby Maher were arrested and brought before the courts. The accused both had alibis on the night in question, but Mary Kelly provided a sensational and damning testimony, claiming to have seen them in a group of men heading towards the Shea house. When the brothers were found guilty, William Maher hung his head and covered his face with his hands. He knew his fate.

The judge donned the traditional black hat signalling William and his brother Darby would face the ultimate punishment – execution. In an age of swift justice, the Maher brothers were hanged a few days later. In a final act of punishment, the two men were denied a normal burial – their bodies were instead given to medical science.

D'Espard, spurred on by this successful prosecution and armed with the identity of another man centrally involved, William Gorman, continued his investigation. Gorman was the tenant evicted by Ned Shea and was widely assumed to have been involved in the attack. In June 1825 he was seized on the street in nearby Carrick-on-Suir, but in a display of the general hostility towards the authorities, a crowd of bystanders sprang to his defence and freed him.

From there, William Gorman went on the run. Although he would evade the authorities for nearly two years, he never left his native Tipperary. For a time he was able to live in a cave near Francis D'Espard's home of Killaghy Castle, illustrating the sympathy the accused maintained among sections of the population. Although unable to live a normal life, Gorman, who maintained his innocence, plotted vengeance against those who hunted him.

Having identified D'Espard as the key figure behind the case, Gorman resolved to assassinate the magistrate. Although his audacious plan failed in 1825, he still evaded capture. It was only in 1827 when the authorities finally surrounded him in a new hide-out in a disused quarry in the area and Gorman was finally apprehended. Somewhat predictably his trial was little more than a formality.

Mary Kelly was again the key witness. Although she was now blind, she remained adamant she had seen William Gorman in the party heading towards the Shea house. Like the Maher brothers, Gorman also produced an alibi, but this did little to convince the jury. Found guilty, he became the third man to be executed for the attack when he was hanged on 1 April 1827. Next, the South Tipperary magistrates arrested Patrick Walshe, another of those implicated by Mary Kelly. Walshe, however, was a man of far greater means than his co-accused. With the considerable resources of his father-in-law, who offered a five-thousand-pound bail, he mounted a robust defence. His legal team focused on the fact the key witness Mary Kelly was blind and could not be considered reliable. They successfully proved she could not possibly have identified the attackers on the night in question.

The final trial took place in 1829, eight years after the burning of the Sheas' home, when two further members of the raiding party – Philip Gorman (brother to the executed William) and Richard Brown – were apprehended after years on the run. Ultimately, though, Kelly's reliability as a witness had been fatally undermined during Patrick Walshe's trial and the two were also acquitted.

The fact that the defence case was based on Kelly being 'long notorious for bad sight' also brought to an end any hopes that the remaining attackers would be convicted. It also called into question the previous convictions. Kelly's claims to have been able to identify those present on the night of the attack were highly questionable. Reporting on the Patrick Walshe's trial in 1827 the newspaper, *Finn's Leinster Journal* reported: 'it was proved her sight was so bad she could not distinguish an object at a distance of a few yards'.[25] By that point her evidence had secured the conviction and subsequent execution of three men.

The last mention of those involved in the fatal attack was a report not from Ireland, but from the Caribbean. In 1830 a Tipperary man, William O'Brien, a soldier in the British garrison on Tobago, admitted to having participated in the attack. He never stood trial.

While Ned and Mary Shea's murder dominated South Tipperary for a decade, it had little impact on wider society. No action was taken to alleviate the underlying poverty that provoked regular outbreaks of violence. Yet the attack bore disturbing similarities with another, infamously brutal incident that took place in County Louth. In 1816 – another year of economic instability – Wildgoose Lodge, the house of farmer Edward Lynch, had been raided by a local secret society looking for weapons. After Lynch went to the authorities, the house was burnt to the ground, killing all eight people inside. This would gain enduring notoriety when the writer William Carleton encountered of remains of several of those executed in the aftermath of the attack, inspiring the book *The Burning of Wildgoose Lodge*.

Yet the authorities refused to countenance that poverty and inequality were the reasons driving this violence in Irish society. Instead, those in power tended to view it as part of the Irish character. Robert Peel, the Chief Secretary for Ireland in 1822 and later Prime Minister of the United Kingdom claimed that the only solution was 'an honest despotic government for Ireland'.[26] Charles Whitworth, a Lord Lieutenant of Ireland, commented that 'the great object is not to lose sight of the distinction between England and this part of His Majesty's dominions' considering 'the character and spirit are completely different'.[27]

The underlying tension that led to the murder of the Sheas continued to foment further violence throughout the nineteenth century. During the years 1831, 1835, 1839 and 1842 the spectre of starvation haunted Irish society and desperation led to outbreaks of violence – yet this only served to convince the authorities that the Irish character was as volatile as harvests were undependable.

CHAPTER 2

Sectarianism

1834

> Now I beseech you, brethren, by the name of our Lord Jesus Christ, that ye all speak the same thing, and that there be no divisions among you.
>
> (1 Corinthians 1:10)

In the early morning of 3 October 1834 a simmering tension pervaded the town of Moira, in north-west County Down, nestled between Belfast and Lough Neagh. A sense of impending violence crackled in the air – a bare-knuckle brawl was set to unfold between two local men, Stanhope Fleming and William Carroll. Little did either man know that after the dust settled on their fight, one person would be murdered and two others arrested, facing a potential murder charge and the death sentence that carried with it.

In recent years there had been little to excite the small community of Moira, or its people. The town had lost its former vigour, having fallen victim to the Industrial

Revolution. In an all-too-familiar experience for early nineteenth-century communities, machines had rendered Moira's cottage industry obsolete. Industrialization may have led to a dramatic increase in production but this came at the expense of towns and villages where cottage industries had sustained life for generations. Moira was a case in point. Its linen industry was in terminal decline. One visitor in the 1830s remarked that Moira: 'was at one time celebrated for the manufacture of linen, large quantities having been made, sold and bleached in the town, but it has long been on the decline and little is done in the market'.[1]

The town of Moira offered its inhabitants little opportunity or diversion, yet what played out in the wake of the brawl that fateful Friday morning would deliver far more than a temporary distraction from the town's economic malaise. People would still be discussing the matter over a decade later.

Few details survive of the origins of the dispute that provoked the fight. In the commonly accepted version of events, the incident began at a local dance in Moira in late September 1834. Over the course of that evening, some form of argument broke out between Fleming and Carroll. Whether a blow was struck or an errant word had caused offence was never recorded, but Fleming left the dance feeling he had been wronged.[2]

Fleming refused to let the matter lie. He had been publicly humiliated and, as the hours passed into days, he became more and more determined to gain satisfaction. On Thursday 2 October he assembled a group of friends and proceeded to William Carroll's lodgings. There in the street, he publicly demanded that the matter be settled in a fight. But as William Carroll looked at the crowd standing shoulder to shoulder with Fleming, he thought better of the offer and retreated back inside.

Still the matter did not rest. The following morning Fleming returned to Carroll's lodgings at 7 a.m. and again called on him to accept his challenge. With accusations of cowardice now in the air, William Carroll felt he was left with little choice. His landlord Archie Dayling, and Dayling's wife, intervened, pleading with their lodger not to pursue such a reckless course of action. While their protests prevented Carroll fighting in the heat of that moment, he agreed to settle the matter once and for all later that morning. His only condition was that Fleming would guarantee him fair play.

Around nine o'clock in the morning, William Carroll arrived at Stanhope Fleming's workplace and the two men made their way to a meadow known locally as the Clover Field.[3] Word of the impending fight has spread like wildfire around the town, and was now an eagerly awaited contest that saw ploughmen and local quarry workers leave their work and make for the meadow. The crowd surrounding the two men began to swell.

Inside the makeshift ring of onlookers, Stanhope Fleming and William Carroll, in accordance with custom, stripped down to the waist and the fight began. Recollections of what transpired in the following minutes diverge. Two versions emerged, each one heavily influenced by the loyalties of the witnesses. No one denied that William Carroll and his supporters were heavily outnumbered, and he may only have had a single individual, a man named McAlister, with him. Meanwhile, several dozen friends, supporters and workmates of Fleming's had arrived in the Clover Field, and more continued to arrive after the fight began.

As informal as the bout was, the two bare-chested fighters nevertheless fought in rounds, allowing them to catch their breath at regular intervals. As the fight reached its third round, Carroll was clearly coming off the worst. While some accounts implied Fleming was simply the better fighter, others would claim that Carroll's initial fears that he would not receive fair treatment had materialized as the fight dragged on. In his own version of events, Carroll claimed that on one occasion after he fell, Fleming's supporters had punched and kicked him as he tried to stand up.

While the veracity of these claims would be contested, no one disputed the fact that the fight was transformed by the appearance of William Carroll's brother John after the third round. John Carroll was seen entering the Clover Field accompanied by another man, John Boyle. As the pair crossed the field to the fight, Boyle was witnessed handing something to John Carroll along with words of encouragement along the lines of 'go on'.[4] As the pair reached the crowd assembled around the fight, John Carroll made his way directly to Fleming, who was resting between bouts.

Carroll immediately began to attack Fleming. The two exchanged a few punches, but as Fleming moved to strike Carroll, cries of 'knife' went up from the crowd as they spotted the glint of metal in Carroll's hand. Boyle had handed him a blade as they had crossed the field, and when Stanhope Fleming lifted his arm to punch Carroll, he exposed his side. John Carroll took full advantage and plunged the blade into the side of his opponent's chest. Fleming fell back; the knife had penetrated his ribs.

A moment of shock followed. As the crowd began to react, the fast-thinking Boyle, who had accompanied John Carroll to the Clover Field, realized the situation would turn ugly very quickly. Hauling his friend from the fight, Boyle led the way from the field but as they escaped, they left the very man they had come to support – John's brother William – behind.

Realizing the stakes of the fight had been raised from a matter of honour to one of life and death, William Carroll also took flight. Remarkably, Fleming, seemingly oblivious to the fatal blow he had suffered, gave chase. He caught up with William Carroll at the edge of the Clover Field and the two men fell into a ditch and started to exchange blows once more – but the full effect of the knife wound now began to take effect. Stumbling, Fleming fell forward onto Carroll, blood oozing from the wound in his side. He then started to ask for water, saying he would die of thirst.

As William Carroll made good his escape, doctors were summoned.[5] The local surgeon, Dr Reid, arrived on the scene and although Stanhope Fleming was still alive, there was little that could be done to save his life. Within minutes the injured man expired.

As shock rippled through the community of Moira, an inquest was convened. The proceedings were little more than a formality. How Fleming had died and who had killed him were not in doubt. The town doctor was able to determine a precise cause of death – John Carroll had severed Stanhope Fleming's coronary artery.

But while Fleming's family and friends seethed with rage at the injustice of his murder, such deaths were an all-too-frequent occurrence in the early nineteenth century. The settling of disputes through violence was disturbingly common, even acceptable: the leading Irish politician of the age, Daniel O'Connell, killed his rival John D'Esterre in a duel in 1815. In fact, Fleming's murder was just one of the 250 homicides recorded in 1834, a figure that was almost certainly an underestimate of the true figure.[6] As news spread of the killing, it began to gain a surprising degree of traction. At first just the victim of a petty local dispute, which started at a local dance, Fleming quickly became a *cause célèbre*.

His funeral was one of largest in Ireland that year. Though the population of Moira was just eight hundred people, thousands descended on the town to march behind the coffin of a man most had never met or even heard of before. They had little or no interest in Fleming personally, but rather the cause that had quickly attached itself to his murder.

While the incident and his funeral received considerable coverage in newspapers, the various stories provided little by way of detail on Fleming himself. There were no biographical details: his age was never recorded, nor was his profession. Even the original cause of the dispute that had led to the murder was never detailed, beyond the fact that it had taken place at a local dance. Instead, coverage pivoted around one aspect of the affair in particular: the religious background of those involved.

While it does not appear to have been the source of the original argument, time and again publications focused on the fact that Fleming was a Protestant and a member of the Orange Order while John Carroll – who had wielded the knife – his brother William, and John Boyle were all Roman Catholics. Reports on the murder and the surrounding events increasingly focused on the impact on and reactions of the wider community, rather than the wrong done to Fleming and his family. This appears to have been in direct conflict with local interpretations of what transpired: in the twelve verses of the local ballad that recorded the event, neither man's religion was mentioned.[7] The emphasis on religion appears to have been due to powerful external forces, ensuring that Fleming's murder would come to adopt wider and more significant connotations than it initially held.

Even though he may have been killed as a result of a minor local feud, Fleming's murder happened as relations between Irish Protestants and Catholics were reaching a critical juncture. Religious tensions, particularly in the north-east, had been heightened since the 1780s. This had been underpinned by wider social and economic changes, which threatened the traditional Protestant domination of life, particularly in the linen trade. Catholics were increasingly involved in an industry hitherto largely dominated by Protestants. These tensions had resulted in violent clashes since the 1780s.

While Fleming had been an active participant in stoking these rising tensions, they would ultimately relegate him to second-place status at his own funeral in 1834.

When Stanhope Fleming was born is unknown; surprisingly, in the midst of such a high-profile case, no one ever bothered to record any personal information about him. Many of those who would take a posthumous interest in Fleming were interested in one aspect of his life – his murder and, in a particular, who murdered him. What we can ascertain though, given he had a family and appears to have been widowed, is that he must have been born in the decades either side of the turn of the nineteenth century.

As an Irish Protestant Fleming was in the minority in wider Irish society. By 1834, while 80 per cent of the population were Roman Catholic, only 20 per cent were Protestants like Fleming. Yet despite being heavily outnumbered, Protestants dominated economic, social and political life on the island. This complex situation originated back in the cauldron of violence that had been the late sixteenth and seventeenth centuries in Ireland. When successive English governments of the day had dispossessed Catholic landowners, they had replaced them with English and Scottish Protestant settlers, dramatically altering the Irish religious landscape.

Heavily outnumbered, this community maintained their control of what became known as the Protestant Ascendancy through a series of laws that built an explicitly sectarian society, where access to power, wealth and status was predicated on religion. A series of laws conferred exclusive rights on members of the Protestant Church of Ireland, prohibiting Catholics, Presbyterians and Quakers from voting or holding office, limiting their private property, and forbidding them firearms. They were also banned from the armed forces.

While some had been able to effectively work the system, such as Daniel O'Connell's wealthy Catholic family in

Kerry, they were an exception that proved the rule. By Fleming's birth around the turn of the nineteenth century, nearly all wealth and power was concentrated in the hands of the Protestant community. That said, not all Protestants were wealthy or powerful. Fleming himself was a man of very limited means, and after his death his dependants faced destitution.

Yet the Ascendancy offered benefits to poorer Protestants like Fleming. Increased legal rights bestowed prestige, status and a sense of superiority over their Catholic neighbours. In fact, attempts to reduce this inequality at the heart of Irish society would lead to an increase in sectarian violence.

Modern sectarianism, as Fleming understood it, had emerged in the villages and towns around his native Moira in the 1780s through tensions over employment in the linen trade. The later decades of the eighteenth century had seen increasing numbers of Catholics enter the trade, which had been central to the economy of the north-east. It had traditionally been the preserve of Protestants, and the rising competition for work affected poorer Protestants like Fleming in particular. It also threatened the limited sense of prestige afforded to them by the Protestant Ascendancy.

Protestants, organizing into a secret society known as the Peep O'Day Boys, reacted by attacking Catholic homes and wrecking their weaving looms. They also seized weapons – a Protestant monopoly on violence was seen as a symbol of their dominance.[8] This violence escalated as Catholics responded in turn by forming their own secret societies, known as Catholic Defenders, or Ribbonmen.

But it was the French Revolution of 1789 that proved to be a major catalyst for the outbreak of sectarian tensions during Fleming's lifetime. The revolution resulted in the outbreak of war between Britain and revolutionary France in 1793, a conflict that transformed both Britain and Ireland.

As the demands for troops dramatically increased, the British government was more and more alarmed by political developments in Ireland. The Society of United Irishmen, a republican organization sympathetic with revolutionary France, began to gain traction.

Realizing that the discrimination and disenfranchisement of Catholics was creating a well of support for republicanism, the authorities began to review the value of the Ascendancy. Therefore in 1793, in an effort to curry favour with Catholics, they forged agreements with the Catholic Church, while the ban on Catholics joining the armed forces was removed. Wealthy Catholics were granted the vote that same year. The catalyst for these changing attitudes in London were the international tensions arising from the French republican revolution. When France declared war on Britain in early 1793, the British government was fearful about the loyalties of Irish Catholics. Therefore, after the outbreak of war the British government sought an accommodation with Irish Catholics to avoid the nightmare scenario of a war with revolutionary France and a republican uprising in Ireland.

Limited as the reforms were, many in the Protestant community feared where this would lead. Seeing the Ascendancy under threat, they formed the Orange Order, aimed at maintaining the status quo. The Order organized provocative parades each year to mark the victory of William of Orange over his Catholic rival James II at the Battle of the Boyne in 1690. Commemorating this battle, seen by many as the starting point of the Ascendancy, was designed to be provocative, and the parades were frequently marred by violence.

While the 1790s had been a decade of growing tensions, these exploded into extreme violence in 1798, when the long-anticipated republican revolt eventually erupted. Facing the most serious revolt in Ireland since the seventeenth century, the British government enlisted the aid of the Orange Order to maintain control. Tens of thousands were killed in a wave of violence. After the Rising was resoundingly crushed, many members of the Order assumed this would end Catholic aspirations for a generation. However, while supporters of the Ascendancy were dominant in their own community and nationally after the Rebellion was put down, the tide of history was running against them even in this moment of strength.

So much so, that Stanhope Fleming would grow up in a radically different Ireland than his forefathers. In the aftermath of the 1798 rebellion, the entire nature of British control over the island underwent a dramatic reorganization. The Acts of Union was passed in 1800 and enacted the following year. The Irish parliament was dissolved and Ireland now ruled directly from London. To secure the backing of the Catholic Church for what was a controversial measure, the British government intimated it would pave the way for an end to all legal discrimination against Catholics.

While the government would later renege on this commitment, it created rising expectations in Catholic Ireland that the nineteenth century would be one of change. New Catholic confidence found expression in a vibrant movement that by the 1820s was demanding full emancipation. In response, support for the Orange Order surged in Protestant communities. It was no surprise that Stanhope Fleming himself joined the Order, given it claimed a membership of around two hundred thousand men.[9]

All the while, sectarian violence between the Ribbonmen and the Orange Order further escalated, becoming a regular feature of life at the time. But the winds of change gaining strength in London were moving in one direction only. Irrespective of their personal view of Catholics, there was growing support among politicians in London for Catholic emancipation as a necessity in order to stave off further revolts in Ireland.

For Fleming and his contemporaries in the Orange Order, the 1820s and 30s were extremely disorientating, as many of their long-held assumptions began to shatter. A close relationship with the British authorities had deteriorated in the decades since the Act of Union. By the 1820s, those in high office in Britain began to view the Order as a disruptive, even subversive, force. Increasingly an obstacle to the passage of Catholic emancipation, the Orange Order, along with other similar organizations, was effectively banned in 1825 in an effort to calm the political climate in Ireland.

This move would leave Protestant leaders divided on how to move forward. Meanwhile, the demand for change among Irish Catholics continued to gain pace. When the Catholic leader Daniel O'Connell contested and won a parliamentary seat in 1828, the government's hand was forced, and full emancipation was granted the following year.

This measure did little to dampen the sectarian divisions in Ireland. In fact, fears about what this change would mean for Irish society had been one of the main drivers of violence in recent years, so it was little surprise that it continued. The untangling of sectarian animosity could not simply be administered from Westminster. Almost every facet of life remained divided along sectarian lines. A perusal of contemporary newspapers underscores this. Most publications adopted an editorial line directed towards either a Catholic or a Protestant readership. This, more often than not, translated into bitter sectarian diatribes against the opposing faith.

Even when faced with shared economic hardships, the response of the Protestant and Catholic poor could frequently be hamstrung by the sectarian divide between them. Although in the winter of 1830–31 renewed food shortages saw demonstrations near Moira where 'Orangemen, Catholics and other sects burn the symbols, and raised a common and tricoloured flag',[10] this was notable because it was unusual – in the run-up to the annual Orange demonstration the following July, Catholics attacked Orangemen in Moira,[11] while later in the year, when Orangemen raided the house of a Catholic in nearby Portadown, one of their number was shot and killed.[12] For the most past, the lines of sectarian division ran deeper than class affiliations.

For the Orange Order, the years before Stanhope Fleming's murder brought a series of further setbacks that would shape how it reacted to his killing. Although the Order had been effectively banned in 1825, this measure had lapsed by 1828. But new legislation, the Party Processions Act of 1833, effectively thwarted the Order by banning parades and demonstrations commemorating historic and religious events. This effectively outlawed their traditional 12 July marches. At the same time, prominent allies of the Orange Order were being demoted from positions of authority. Back in the 1820s, William Saurin had been replaced as Attorney General for Ireland while in 1833, in Fleming's native County Down, Colonel William Blacker was dismissed as a commissioner of the peace in the county for his continued allegiance to the Order. For a community who considered it their right to dominate Irish society, this trend was deeply alarming.

It was the backlash to these broader historical events that would frame Stanhope Fleming's funeral in October 1834. In July of that year, even though their parades were effectively prohibited, the Orange Order in Moira defied the ban and pushed ahead with a traditional event on the Twelfth. The authorities responded by summoning several of those who had participated in the parade before the courts, but the Order continued to flex its power. On the morning of their hearing, the door of the court was daubed with the sectarian slogan, 'Jew, Turk, or Atheist, may enter here, but no papist.'[13]

Less than two months later Fleming was murdered outside Moira. There was no evidence that the initial altercation had been motivated by sectarianism. The ballad written by Patrick Reynolds framed the incident in local terms: '*It was at a dance where this anger took root / There Fleming and William Carroll did dispute.*' However, when it reached the wider community, the framing focused on the fact that a Catholic had killed a member of the Orange Order. In the fraught political and religious climate of North Down in the early 1830s, it was inevitable that the Orange Order used this as a chance to flex its power.

The Order decreed that Fleming had been the victim of a sectarian killing and began to mobilize members to attend the funeral of what the *Newry Telegraph* called their 'slain brother'. The funeral also provided the local Orange Order in Moira, which had been banned from parading, with the chance to demonstrate. When Fleming's funeral took place, it was in effect an Orange Order demonstration. His funeral procession allowed them to follow the letter if not the spirit of the law. They did not wear their badges, but identified themselves with hats and scarves.

Meanwhile, the two men deemed responsible for Fleming's killing, John Carroll who had stabbed him, and the man who had supplied the blade, John Boyle, had been arrested and were later sent forward for trial. In a somewhat surprising turn of events, both men received the more lenient conviction of manslaughter rather than murder. This was particularly surprising in the case of John Carroll, given he had actually stabbed Fleming. While the lesser sentence saved the two from the gallows, they were transported for life. This punishment saw the pair shipped to the far side of the world, where they would serve their sentences in penal colonies in Australia. The two men left Ireland on board the convict ship, the *Lady*

McNaughton, which raised anchor in Dublin Bay on 23 June 1835. Given the term of their sentence was life, they were banned from ever returning to Ireland, even after they secured pardons in Australia.

Patrick Reynolds's ballad about Stanhope Fleming's death could still be heard in the North Down area as late as 1845, although the widespread posthumous fame he had enjoyed beyond his local community did not have similar longevity. Viewed as a pawn in the wider sectarian conflict, it was inevitable that focus would shift away from his memory to new flashpoints, which continued with depressing frequency.

As the Orange Order persisted in its fight against the changes that followed Catholic emancipation, sectarian violence continued. In March 1835 Ribbonmen rioted after a horse called Protestant Boy won at the Fermanagh races. In the ensuing fracas William Lang, a Protestant, was killed.[14] The following month, another sectarian dispute at the Drumcree Fair saw a Catholic, Hugh Donnelly, killed in a dispute with Orangemen. In the face of a new government ban in 1836, the governing body of the Orange Order moved to dissolve it before it would suffer the ignominy of being suppressed by the government. With each new murder, Stanhope Fleming's memory and uses to the sectarian forces faded as a new name and a new case served as a potent catch cry.

While the outbreaks of violence in the 1830s spoke volumes to the fears that Irish Protestants, particularly in Ulster, had about emancipation, these had always verged on the paranoid and conspiratorial. In the short term, the Catholic emancipation of 1829 did not dramatically change Ireland. Many of the legal bars had already been removed, while decades of state discrimination had left Catholics disproportionately impoverished to a degree that could not simply be undone with the passing of an Act. Many did not have the resources required to take advantage of the opportunities that emancipation technically opened for them.

The ending of official discrimination towards Catholics in Ireland did pose major questions about the longer-term direction of Irish history and the future of sectarian relations on the island. Protestants had enjoyed over a century of near total supremacy, which was no longer underpinned by law. Catholics could now aspire to political office and careers in professions previously banned to them. Unfortunately the potential this offered for a new chapter in history was firmly shut by the conservative forces, which continued to dominate society. Sectarianism would remain a defining feature of life even if it was no longer underpinned by law.

CHAPTER 3

Hunger

1846

> They that be slain with the sword are better than they that be slain with hunger: for these pine away, stricken through for want of the fruits of the field.
>
> (Lamentations 4:9)

Each morning as Thomas Christian rose to look over the picturesque town of Dungarvan, Co. Waterford, he could reflect on the correct decisions he had made in his career. The port may only have been home to 8,700 souls in 1841, but they served Christian's needs well enough. As a doctor and surgeon, the town docks created a steady stream of varied work.

He could regularly be found tending to men injured while unloading ships on the quay but more often than not he was in more refined surroundings. Dungarvan streets were lined with the houses of wealthy merchants who lived long lives and could afford regular and expensive medical treatment. Tending to the merchants' maladies and ailments may not have been challenging work but it afforded Christian respect and standing in the community.

It was certainly better than the alternative. Many surgeons plied their trade in the ships of the Royal Navy. Working under the harsh navy regulations – the Articles of War – the work was hard. The injuries sustained by the crews in peace time could be horrific. The prospect of being caught up in a naval conflict was an ever-present fear. The chaos a bombardment from an enemy vessel could wreak on a navy ship was terrifying. Explosions sent enormous splinters of decking hurtling through the air, impaling anyone unfortunate enough to be in the way. If the surgeon wasn't hit, he had to tend to the injuries they inflicted. In contrast Dungarvan, if somewhat predictable, was more enticing.

This would all change for Christian in the autumn of 1846. Tensions had been building in the town in recent weeks, but when the doctor received a knock on his door on 28 September asking him to tend to injured men, he ventured into a war zone.

Taking his bag, the surgeon navigated his way cautiously through what seemed like an alien environment. His native Dungarvan had changed. The quiet commerce that defined daily life had given way to chaos. The streets of the town were strewn with shattered glass, makeshift weapons, stones, bricks and the occasional puddles of blood. As Dr Christian stepped through the debris, he passed the smashed-up bakeries of the town, whose windows were now broken across the cobblestones. Over the course of the previous afternoon Dungarvan had become a battlefield – now Dr Christian had been drawn from the safety and security of his home to tend to the casualties.

Civil unrest, which had started earlier in the day as a protest, had soon descended into a riot. As the afternoon dragged on, the riot had turned lethal when soldiers opened fire on civilian crowds, who in turn grabbed what weapons they could and fought back. While the crowds had dispersed, for the time being at least, nervous soldiers could still be seen milling around Dungarvan's streets. Runners dashed back and forth from the town courthouse, which had been converted into a temporary barracks for the troops.

Arriving at a local school situated on the southern fringes of the town, Dr Christian found two civilians shot and bleeding. There had been reports of others who had sustained flesh wounds during the violent fray, but John Mulcahy and Michael Fleming appeared to have been the only two who couldn't walk.

With darkness encroaching on the eastern horizon, Dr Christian had the two men carried from the school to the safety of the nearby workhouse, where they were brought to the infirmary. There, in the candlelight and shadows, Dr Christian set about his work. It didn't take long before the surgeon recognized that one of the men in particular, Michael Fleming, would require the full extent of his expertise if he was to survive his wounds.

Fleming's leg was shattered from the shot. While a broken leg would not kill the man, the musket ball lodged in the wound would. Whether Dr Christian would save Fleming's leg was a secondary concern: if the ball was not removed, the wound would fester and almost certainly turn septic. In such an eventuality, the doctor would be powerless to stop the infection spreading through Fleming's body, and his life would be on the line. Nevertheless, working tirelessly through the hours of darkness, Dr Christian managed to remove the musket ball as Fleming writhed in pain. He had saved Fleming's life and leg, for the time being at least.

In the following hours all he could do was watch, wait, and try to keep Fleming's wound clean. His patient was by no means out of the woods. This was an age when half the soldiers who suffered similar wounds did not survive. The shock of the operation killed many. Patients were only given the most rudimentary of anaesthetics. Opium for those who could afford it – or in the case of Michael Fleming, more likely alcohol – was the extent of the pain relief offered.

As Fleming gritted his teeth through the pain that night, Dungarvan Workhouse remained on edge.

Many assumed it was only a matter of time before even more serious rioting broke out. Reports were circulating that while those engaged in the protests had withdrawn from Dungarvan, they were now raiding farms in the locality for weapons. They had already put up staunch resistance armed with nothing more than what they had found on the street. If they had guns, that would make it a far more even fight with the military. The gravity of the situation was lost on no one; the increasingly nervous Dungarvan magistrates despatched furious letters to the British administration in Dublin Castle, pleading for aid.

That said, though the outbreak of violence in Waterford was sudden and fierce, it was in many respects predictable and, to a degree, inevitable. When asked by Maurice Charles Kennedy, a workhouse clerk, why he had been rioting,

Fleming responded by saying he was merely following others. Evasive as his answer was, the reasons for the riot were self evident to most.[1] By 1846 Dungarvan was not the only Irish port consumed by violence.

Tensions had been on the rise throughout the previous twelve months. The failure of the potato crop in the autumn of 1845 was far from an unprecedented event at that time, although the cause had been different from previous years, and began to deeply unsettle the populace. While crops had often failed in years past due to adverse weather or droughts, in 1845 the situation was different. Many knew they faced a new and deadly threat and, as blight, a previously unknown fungus, spread on the wind like a biblical plague of old, the infected plants began to wilt. The previously healthy stalks and leaves blackened in the fields and an obnoxious stench signalled decay. Initial hopes that the potato, which grew beneath the soil, would be protected were quickly dashed. When farmers began to lift the crop they found the potatoes on infected plants had been reduced to an inedible pulp.

That the potato above all things was being attacked by a new disease immediately triggered huge concern. That one simple vegetable had become the lynchpin holding wider Irish society and the entire economy together. Throughout the nineteenth century, food exports had become an increasingly important aspect of the Irish economy. By the 1830s Ireland was supplying 80 per cent of Britain's grain[2] as well as producing a large amount of dairy and livestock. In this economy, the potato had become crucial as, due to its prodigious nature, it allowed the rapidly growing Irish population to provide for themselves from small plots of land while the rest of the land was used to produce the foods that propped up the export economy.

Despite the average farm size decreasing, the Irish population had actually doubled between 1750 and 1820. This extraordinary increase was only possible because of the potato. An extremely nutritious vegetable, the potato grew in the most inhospitable soils. This allowed the poor to thrive in marginal land while the wider agricultural economy remained focused on grain production and animal husbandry.

While the rate of growth had started to ease by 1830, the population nevertheless increased by a further 25 per cent, standing at around 8.5 million people in 1845.* This left Irish society balanced on a knife edge. The export economy functioned only because nearly one-third of the population – three million of the poorest people – were sustained by a single crop – the potato.

The potentially devastating threat posed by this new disease was immediately recognized in Britain and Ireland and the government in London hurriedly despatched a scientific commission to Ireland to identify the infection in the crop. However, as the months passed, many in Ireland demanded more urgent measures. In October the Lord Mayor of Dublin, Daniel O'Connell – the first Catholic to hold the office in centuries – had called for a ban on the export of certain foodstuffs from the island, an effective measure, which had already been employed

* The precise population in 1845 is the subject of debate. A census conducted in 1841 registered 8.14 million. While this is generally considered to be an underestimation, the population continued to grow over the following four years. A figure of roughly 8.5 million is accepted by most historians.

by the British government on occasions to mitigate against the Famines in Ireland notably between 1782–1784 [3]. But this call faced powerful opposition.

In London, the newly prevailing *laissez-faire* ideas of free trade demanded as little government interference in the economy as possible. Limiting exports was anathema to this world view. In this position, politicians in London were supported by a small but influential group within Irish society. At ports like Dungarvan, the Irish merchant class, along with wealthier farmers, were also opposed to the restrictions on exports. They did not face starvation, and benefited considerably from the export of food to Britain – in the autumn of 1845, many of those engaged in the export trade around the Dungarvan area were intransigent in their opposition to famine relief measures that would affect their business. The poor, meanwhile, had more immediate concerns. Aware that the continued export of crops would lead to an increase in the price of food at home they demanded a port closures.

When merchants, landowners and large farmers from the surrounding area gathered in the town workhouse on 21 October that year, their discussions on possible solutions were limited, to say the least.[4] The matter of an export ban was not even raised. When Baron de Decies, an influential local landlord and politician, suggested they call for the removal of taxes on grain imports, which maintained an artificially high price for farmers,[5] not a single person in the room would second him. Much of the meeting was taken up with largely pointless tests on diseased potatoes. It broke up in disagreement as to whether or not the details of the meeting would be published.

*

While merchants, big farmers and those with the ultimate responsibility – the British Government – remained committed to the export of food, the crisis had not yet reached breaking point in 1845. The failure was only partial, and the poor, inured to the vagaries of the unreliable potato harvest, had strategies to deal with limited failures. On an individual level, some defaulted on rent, while others pawned whatever they could. Intervention on a national level from the British government helped keep the price of food below starvation levels, for the time being at least, but nevertheless, the poor had endured a brutally difficult winter that year. The local dispensary in Dungarvan recorded an increase in patients falling ill from eating rotten potatoes. More concerning was the appearance of dysentery in the population. By the early summer of 1846 the situation across County Waterford was dire. In May, the House of Commons in London heard reports of: 'a mountain district, seventeen miles long by four to seven broad, containing a population of from 12,000 to 15,000, in which there were not above 100 families that had the means of subsistence from day to day'.[6]

In the following weeks this crisis became a catastrophe. The Great Hunger had begun.

The hopes of the population were desperately pinned on the harvest of 1846. If the potato harvest was satisfactory, the crisis would subside as it had in previous years. But when the stalks began to blacken and the crops started to rot once more, all hopes began to fade. The disease, later identified as the fungus *hytophthora infestans* had appeared on the crop yet again, spelling total disaster. A near-total crop failure ensued. The poor, who had desperately struggled through the previous winter, now faced starvation.

As this scale of the catastrophe made itself clear, it was immediately obvious that the ports along the south coast, such as New Ross, Waterford, Youghal, Cork and especially Dungarvan, would become flashpoints if merchants and large farmers attempted to export food as normal to Britain.

The poor would not simply stand idly by as large quantities of food were shipped overseas. The hope for at least some intervention from the government in London had also vanished. The Conservative Party of Sir Robert Peel had fallen from power. He was replaced by Lord John Russell, the leader of the Whigs. Russell himself lacked the charisma and personality for the role and Charles Wood, the Chancellor of the Exchequer, and others, were able to exert significant influence over state affairs. Wood was deeply wedded to the policy of non-intervention.

That summer the entire political class seemed uninterested in the plight of the poor. When a by-election was called for the parliamentary seat of Dungarvan, the issue of the looming famine scarcely featured. Electoral politics at the time was a rich man's game, as the franchise was limited to freeholders of property valued at £10 or more. Irish nationalists remained focused on repealing the Act of Union and supported the Whigs, who they saw as more amenable to their cause. This would see Richard Lalor Sheil – an ally of Lord John Russell – stand in Dungarvan unopposed. The poor were shut out of the decision-making processes that would dictate their fate.

While the potato had failed abysmally in that summer, the harvest of other crops was largely unaffected. Likewise, the livestock and meat trade, along with that of the dairy farmers, continued to produce large quantities of food. The destination of this food became the focus of the growing tensions in the country.

By early September 1846 there was no denying the desperate situation facing the poor – by the middle of the month, newspapers were already reporting famine-related deaths in the Dungarvan area.[7] Despite the fact that escalating tensions were almost certain to lead to violent conflict in Irish towns and ports, the government refused to take decisive action. They established a public works programme, but as prices soared the wages on offer could not feed a family with even the cheapest of food. By late September the *Ballyshannon Herald* in County Donegal reported that the price of Indian meal, a type of meal ground from dried maize, had risen from £12 to £17 per ton in the space of a week.[8]

As the government remained adamant that it would not halt the export of grain, meat or other produce from Irish ports, it was clear that vast quantities of food would continue to leave Ireland, despite the fact that one-third of the population faced starvation.

Throughout that September large quantities of flour – the early produce of the harvest of that year – began to make its way through the Irish countryside for the ports of the south. This incensed and incited the population. By the last week of September the British administration in Dublin Castle was receiving a flurry of letters from the Dungarvan area warning of the growing tensions. At night, bonfires were seen on the hills surrounding the port town. Such fires were often lit to celebrate good news, but in September 1846 no one doubted that this ominous warning was a call to arms.[9]

In the town itself, the attitudes of the wealthy and the town authorities towards the poor began to harden, indicating that a clash of one kind or another was imminent. Little else could explain the provocative actions of the police as they harassed a celebration of a local landlord who had reduced rent, when they threw a tar barrel that had been lit in his honour into the river.[10] By the end of the month, the nature of opposition to the export of food was changing rapidly, and escalating in intensity. Isolated robberies began to give way to more strategic interventions. The poor were banding together and directly stopping food leaving Irish ports by any means necessary.

On 26 September one of a series of letters from Dungarvan saw the constabulary report how a large crowd of around 500 men armed with sticks were travelling across the countryside warning farmers in the locality not to sell their grain for export. The crowd made it clear that if landlords distrained the crop – took the grain in lieu of rents the tenant farmers couldn't pay – then the armed crowd would deal with them in time.[11]

On the same day Baron de Decies reported to Dublin Castle that a crowd of 200 men armed with bludgeons and sticks had turned up at the house of Lewis Fitzmaurice, a large farmer and property owner in Dungarvan, demanding he hand over money he had received for selling grain. These growing tensions exploded in the riots that engulfed the town on 28 September.

How events that day began remains unclear. The Dungarvan magistrate P.C. Howley, like everyone, was aware that tensions were building in the area. He had travelled to the nearby town of Tramore and from there to Kilmacthomas to perform his duties as magistrate, but remained concerned about the rising tensions in Dungarvan, fearing an outbreak of disturbances in the town. Such were his fears that he mustered a a troop of mounted soldiers known as dragoons in Kilmacthomas and set out for Dungarvan.

As was customary, Howley also hired labourers to carry the soldiers' baggage on their journey to the port town. These labourers included none other than Michael Fleming, who worked for the local merchant William Walsh. According to Howley, the dragoons and their baggage train covered the thirteen miles from Kilmacthomas to Dungarvan in just four hours. When they reached the town, Howley's worst fears were already materializing. Unemployed labourers had been marching through the streets and were said to be demanding that others in work join them on their protest. Among their grievances were the pay on offer in the town, which were deemed to be starvation wages, a rate that a family could not possibly survive on.

The situation escalated after bells in a local church were tolled to summon people from the surrounding countryside. As Howley reached Dungarvan, thousands of peasants were streaming into the port. The mixture of fear, anger and hunger proved a lethal combination. As they had on other occasions, the swelling crowd began to target those they deemed responsible for the export of food.

The crowd, now numbering several thousand, went to the offices of the Liverpool Shipping Agent, a firm that was about to ship grain, butter and other foods from Dungarvan, and issued a stern warning not to ship the grain from the port. They also visited Messrs P. Dower & Son, who had large quantities of Indian meal. Here they demanded that they receive money, or be fed. Dower told the mob that he agreed with their plight but thought the 'line of conduct they were pursuing would only mar any substantial good done for them, and probably lives would be lost'.

This appeal, coming from a well-fed man, was never likely to work on a crowd facing death from starvation. Over the following hours, individuals went to various bakeries demanding to be fed. Only one baker, Mr Fisher, refused, and for his troubles his shop was ransacked. Others were, unsurprisingly, more amenable to the demands of the crowd.

While the demonstration had involved limited planning, a leader emerged over the course of the day: Patrick Power (referred to as 'Crooked Power' in a letter from the magistrate, Howley), who rode a white horse through the crowds. Power made a speech outlining the desperation of the people and what they needed from their richer neighbours:

> That the farmers are not to thrash or send out any corn to market, no milk should be given to their pigs, but kept and given to the labourers without any charge for same. No bailiffs are to be allowed to distrain for rent . . . All able-bodied labourers should get two shillings a day and the old men and boys ten pence provided meal was one shilling a stone and if higher the wages increased and every person to be employed or paid if allowed to remain idle. [12]

One of the final demands underscored the uncompromising mood of the crowd: 'No person should be served for any debt, on pain of the plaintiff's ears being cut off.'[13]

In the face of a looming famine measures along these lines – to control the movement of food and the price of essentials – were needed. Interventions like this and the wider demand of port closures did carry risks. If the measures were allowed to continue indefinitely they could disincentivize production and disrupt wider trade, including imports. However, the British government in the late eighteenth century had become adept at introducing targeted and effective port closures as part of famine relief measures.

By the 1840s economic orthodoxies had shifted and the notion of intervening in the market through price controls or port closures was considered anathema to the prevailing free market ideas in the corridors of power in London.

While the protests of the poor ran contrary to their financial interests, they also embodied the worst fears of the magistrates, merchants and farmers of Dungarvan (and likely of the rest of the country). Having grown up in a world where violent conflict with the poor had flared on a regular basis in years of hardship, they viewed the protests as a threat to order rather than as a desperate demand for aid.

Howley, having identified what he assumed were the ringleaders, had the police move in and seize several men from the crowd, including Patrick Power, the rider of the white horse. This was followed by negotiations between what Howley called the 'better-disposed part of the crowd' and the authorities[14]. A petition explained the grievances of the people. They reiterated that the price of the cheapest food, Indian meal, was rising while their wages were falling. They were willing to take a further cut in wages as long as cheaper food was made available. In their own words: 'Our only object is to get employment and a rate of wages that will support us and our families.' [15].

But the course of events had enraged some and they now added that the prisoners Howley had seized should also be released. Faced with what was an undeniable crisis, Howley and other town magistrates retired to consider their options. After their deliberations, they remained resolute and refused to release the prisoners. Instead, they told the crowd that if they left Dungarvan and returned to their homes in the countryside, the magistrates would consider solutions in the coming days. This appears only to have incensed the crowd further. As negotiations collapsed, Howley gave directions for the police to clear the streets. This was the point at which the violence erupted. As the police attacked, the crowd responded by throwing stones. Under a hail of missiles, the police had little option but to withdraw.

Howley at this point sent in the dragoons, the mounted soldiers he had brought with him from Kilmacthomas. They took up position in front of the police. This only angered the furious crowd still further – tensions between the military and the public in the area were already running high. According to Howley, shouts of 'Kill them!' were heard from the people as the dragoons appeared[16]. An attempted cavalry charge failed, and Howley proceeded to read the Riot Act, warning the crowd that if they did not disperse he would instruct the army to open fire. He received an answer in the form of a rock, which struck his horse, nearly knocking him into the throng. There was only one thing likely to satisfy the starving crowd at this point, and that was the distribution of food.

Over the course of that afternoon, while the events playing out in the streets of Dungarvan escalated, Michael Fleming had in effect changed sides. His day had started like any other, working for his employer in Kilmacthomas. The military had then hired him from Walsh for the day. Although he had carried their baggage to Dungarvan, on reaching the town he joined the protests. While later he was said to have claimed that he was rioting because others had been, Fleming undoubtedly related to the demands of the demonstration. The situation in his native Kilmacthomas was no better than in Dungarvan. If the price of food continued to rise and wages to fall, it was precisely people like him who would starve.

As that afternoon dragged on, the nature of the conversations taking place behind the lines of soldiers and police facing them began to change. Magistrate Howley claimed that it was the commander of the dragoons, Captain Sibthorp, who first demanded he be allowed to open fire, and that Howley had initially urged caution. Howley later claimed he only gave Sibthorp permission to open fire when he was left with no option, in a matter of life and death. This decision was in effect a death sentence for the demonstrators who were tightly packed in the streets.

The course of events that followed was confusing. While the firing would last for four hours, the military would later claim that only twenty-six shots were discharged. The circumstances surrounding the shooting of Fleming was unclear. There was no doubt he had been shot by the military but whether they it was 'a matter of life and death' was dubious.

The crowd had been forced well back from the centre of the town when he was shot; the school where Dr Christian found him was at the very edge of Dungarvan, where the hinterland of the town gave way to open countryside.

The authorities remained convinced the crowds would return better armed the following day. Demands for more military reinforcements to aid in the defence of Dungarvan were despatched to the barracks in Clonmel. The following day Magistrate Howley presented a siege-like situation in Dungarvan to the Lord Lieutenant in Dublin: 'The peasantry are enraged at being fired on. I am informed they meditate further hostilities. I learned there are about 5,000 people assembled at Whitechurch about six miles from the town.'[17]

He went on to plead for additional police to protect the town and the ships leaving the harbour, where local fishermen were now threatening a blockade. This was followed the next day with a request for cavalry, to facilitate communications between the town and surrounding barracks.[18] The government responded by sending four companies of the 47th Lancashire Regiment of Foot along with a steamer.

The Great Hunger had reached a critical juncture. An indefinite closure of Irish ports would unquestionably have had massively detrimental effects on the Irish economy and been counterproductive in that it would by extension have impacted imports. A temporary closure, though, in the desperate situation of late 1846, could have been effective. However, the government remained resolute and they went to considerable lengths to protect Irish merchants, who were keen to continue exports.

At Youghal, another port down the coast, the Navy steamer HMS *Myrmid*on had to be despatched to patrol the estuary of the Blackwater, where the peasantry were stopping grain being shipped down the river. In late September and early October there were major disturbances at Kilworth, Fermoy, Castlemartyr and Limerick.

Meanwhile in Dungarvan, the soldiers' use of what would prove to be deadly force had the desired effect. Despite the magistrates' fears, the crowds did not return; instead an eerie silence descended upon Dungarvan the day following the riots. The authorities took the opportunity to reinforce the town, as hundreds of police and soldiers augmented the existing garrison.

In the workhouse, the situation facing Michael Fleming was grave. As he lay in the infirmary, the workhouse was slowly filling up as the growing numbers of destitute poor were left with no option but to seek aid in the institution. While days passed into weeks, Fleming lingered on in a precarious state. His chances of surviving the gunshot wound were never more than fifty-fifty, and by the middle of October his fate was sealed when the wound became infected.

Even though he was in a hospital of a kind, there was little understanding of how disease spread and no ability to counteract it. As the hours passed on, his temperature continued to rise. Unimpeded by medical intervention, the fever spread from his infected wound and coursed through his body. Having seen the process play out time and again

Dr Thomas Christian could recognize the signs of imminent death. Three and half weeks after he had first entered the workhouse, the patient's breathing became increasingly laboured. Michael Fleming had entered his final hours and, on 23 October, he drew his last breath.

The inquest into his death was sadly a somewhat farcical affair where Dr Christian would play his final role in the saga. The witnesses' accounts from the authorities were all highly partisan, and the doctor's evidence was nothing short of bizarre. After Fleming's death he had carried out the post-mortem, which revealed a heart condition that would have at some undefined time in the future proved fatal. As the fever had spread through his body, this condition had predictably worsened. Dr Christian, a man who himself was a wealthy resident of Dungarvan, revealed his loyalties when he provided his view on how Michael Fleming died. He absolved the military by claiming that, given the heart condition had existed prior to the gunshot wound, this was the cause of death. The military were, in light of this, absolved of responsibility.[19]

In the intervening month between the protests and Fleming's death, the wider social crisis deepened. As exports of Irish food continued unabated, the poor desperately struggled to afford to eat. The cheapest of food, Indian meal, would double in price by November.*

When Michael Fleming had been brought to Dungarvan Workhouse, an institution designed to provide food and

* Prices for Indian meal in Waterford rose from just over one shilling in September to two shillings in November when it was predicted to rise to three shillings. *Waterford Chronicle*, 12 Sept.1846.

board for the destitute, there had been 299 inmates. By the time he died on 23 October it had increased to 314. This was not abnormal – the institution had been built to cater for 600 in particularly bad years. But by February 1847 there were around 750 people in the same workhouse. On one day alone in March of that year, 2,000 starving people arrived looking for aid, according to Stuart de Decies.[20] Ireland by this point was firmly in the grip of a full-blown famine. The events that would play out over the following years were not only an appalling humanitarian crisis: the Famine also became a defining moment in the history of the island, a stage on which subsequent history played out, not least because of the reactions in London.

As the government insisted there would be no port closures, Dungarvan's docks remained busy as exports continued, but in early 1847 The Great Hunger began to morph into a slightly different crisis. The export of food would no longer be the heart of the Famine.

In late 1846 the government and private merchants had ordered large quantities of maize from the US, which began to arrive into Irish ports in early 1847 in large quantities. But economic orthodoxies demanded food should not be given out for free – a move which would undermine the market. In a report, the *Chronicle*, a local newspaper in Waterford city, another major port, pointed out the absurdity of the situation: 'Cork and this port are stuffed with breadstuffs. What we wonder is, where does the money come from to buy it all. Ireland has no manufacturers to produce cash – how will she continue to supply money?' There was only one solution in their eyes: 'It is plain England must supply the cash. Of course it is only giving back a portion of Ireland's money but England does not acknowledge this.'[21]

In February 1847 Daniel O'Connell had already made this case in the British parliament when he described the fate of Ireland in stark terms: 'She is in your hands – in your power. If you do not save her, she cannot save herself. One-fourth of her population will perish unless parliament comes to their relief.'[22]

But most in the House of Commons were unmoved: attitudes towards famine relief were hardening as the country faced several more years of starvation. It was clear the Great Hunger would not end in 1847 but would require ongoing intervention to address the problem. Many in London wanted nothing but to wash their hands of responsibility.

There can be little doubt O'Connell was correct. The commitment to laissez-faire economics in London unquestionably made the situation worse. Furthermore, key decision-makers in London began to view the Famine as an historic opportunity whereby they could carry out major reforms of the Irish economy.

At the mercy of Westminster parliament beholden to such views, Ireland not only continued to starve but the poor also faced large-scale evictions and clearances as part of these economic reforms. In the midst of the turmoil that followed, Michael Fleming would be forgotten in the tide of death washing over the island.

CHAPTER 4

Eviction

1847

For what is a man profited, if he shall gain the whole world, and lose his own soul?

(Matthew 16:26)

In the 1840s much of the Irish landscape bore a record of the island's history, or rather, a history of its people. Many Dublin street names catalogued the various aristocratic families that had dominated Irish life in the preceding century. Meanwhile, placenames in the rural landscape frequently told an older story, of the long-dead individuals who had shaped Irish history in times past.

By the nineteenth century, these names in the landscape began to adopt a somewhat cosmopolitan feel. After the ban on Catholics joining the armed forces was lifted in the 1790s, recruiters found that the poverty and lack of opportunity endemic in rural Ireland had created a large reservoir of ready recruits. Indeed, such was their success that Irishmen quickly accounted for 30 per cent of British Army manpower.

Their experiences in far-flung corners of the world were soon recorded in place names back home. Dublin streets led the way, with Blenheim Street, Fontenoy Street and Waterloo Road all recalling European battlefields where Irish soldiers had fought in the eighteenth and early nineteenth centuries. By the 1840s the new place names evoked even more distant battlefields. In 1842 the Khyber Pass, a narrow defile between Pakistan and Afghanistan, captured the popular imagination after a retreating British force was routed in the valley. Evocative accounts had been published in the press, and numerous locations across Ireland were named after the iconic pass in the Hindu Kush, including a hotel in the seaside resort of Dalkey in 1847 and the Vee Valley in South Tipperary, with its dramatic landscape and steep hills on either side.[1]

Then, for very different reasons, the townland of Dooherty, in County Roscommon, was also dubbed the Khyber Pass. The area lacked the mountainous terrain of South Tipperary or the rocky escarpments surrounding Dalkey; it was in fact unremarkable and relatively flat. The *Cork Examiner* noted that: 'It is called the Khyber Pass as a police station had been lately placed in the vicinity owing to the many outrages previously perpetrated there.'[2]

While it had earned a lawless reputation, the main thoroughfare through Dooherty still saw considerable traffic. It was the fastest route between the county town of Roscommon and Strokestown, the most important settlement in the north-east of the county; the alternative route was twice as long. For those seeking the fastest route between Roscommon town and Strokestown, the pass was their only option.

This might serve to explain the somewhat ill-conceived decision that saw two men board a horse and carriage in Roscommon town and set off down the Khyber Pass for Strokestown on 3 November 1847. That late in the year, darkness had already descended as their driver urged the horses on, his passengers – Denis Mahon, a local landlord, and Dr Terence Shanley, the local physician – securely shielded from the cold night air by the state-of-the-art Britzka carriage.[3] Their conspicuous vehicle, though, offered little anonymity for the wealthy passengers.

As the solitary carriage passed through darkness of the countryside, its size alone marked it out. In Roscommon in 1847, a county devastated by famine, few other than the local landlord, Mahon, could afford such transport. As it approached the Khyber Pass around six o'clock, those lying in wait along the road easily recognized who they were looking for.

Unbeknownst to its occupants, crouched in a low position along the grassy verge was a man waiting silently for the carriage. As it passed along an isolated stretch, the darkness was momentarily broken by the flash and piercing echo of two gunshots. The bullets ripped through the wooden frame of the carriage and, as the timber splintered, Denis Mahon cried out and slumped in his seat. The landlord had been shot in the chest, and though Dr Shanley tried desperately to help, there was nothing to be done. Mahon died on the roadside in the darkness of the Khyber Pass.

In the following hours, as his body was brought back to Strokestown, news of his murder spread throughout the countryside. A predictable reaction saw bonfires start to appear across the landscape, illuminating the night sky for miles around. In what was a macabre celebration, the people of North Roscommon were welcoming the news that the widely reviled Mahon was dead. The Famine conditions that had ravaged Ireland since 1845 had affected Strokestown in particular. Many held Mahon personally responsible given he had evicted starving, impoverished tenants.

Such were the levels of animosity that strength of feeling did not abate in the following days. As Denis Mahon's widow and daughter planned his funeral, they were offered no succour by the people of North Roscommon. When he was laid to rest, fears that his funeral might be targeted saw large numbers of police line the roads surrounding Strokestown. Details of the service were not shared with the public in advance, and once he had been interred in the family crypt behind the walls of his family estate, the mourners rapidly departed Strokestown. None were willing to risk travelling through the surrounding area after dark.[4]

The affair engendered a bitter enmity in the Mahon family towards the people of Roscommon. Within six days of the murder they had taken out advertisements in national newspapers announcing the sale of all stock, crops and equipment; pretty much everything, bar the family home and the land itself, was being put up for sale.[5] Mahon's only child, his recently married daughter Grace, left Strokestown vowing never to return, a pledge she maintained until she drew her final breath in 1914.

While his family fled, Denis Mahon's murder sparked fears among similar landed families in the region. Soon local rumours claimed that a list of twelve other targets, all landlords in Roscommon like Denis Mahon, had been drawn up.[6] Others hinted that all landlords and their agents in North Roscommon were going to be murdered and the hysteria spread far beyond Connacht. When a large house near the Khyber Pass was put up for auction at a sale in Dublin, bidding collapsed once it emerged that it was located close to where Denis Mahon had infamously been shot. Few were willing to live in the county.

Such hysteria was not surprising given that, in some quarters at least, reports surrounding the killing had been stripped of all context. Queen Victoria herself, for example, voiced the racial stereotypes many would fall back on to explain the murder when she confided in her diary that, 'A shocking murder has again taken place in Ireland. Major Mahon, who had entirely devoted himself to being of use to the distressed Irish was shot when driving home in his carriage. Really they are a terrible people.'[7]

The reality of the situation was somewhat more complex. Denis Mahon was far from the idealized, benign, patriarchal landlord the Queen considered him to be. Mahon himself had known his decisions in the months leading up to his murder may have put his life at risk, and had even taken to carrying a gun with him wherever he went.[8]

Born in 1787, Denis Mahon was something of an unlikely landlord. His grandfather, Baron Hartland, had owned the vast Strokestown estate, which stretched over ten thousand acres centred around a mansion – Strokestown Park House.

On his death, the house and lands had passed to his eldest son, Denis Mahon's uncle, a move which appeared to eliminate Denis from the line of succession. Assuming he would never inherit, Denis Mahon had instead pursued a career in the military, rising to the rank of major.

Back in Roscommon events took a somewhat unexpected course in his absence. In 1835 his uncle died, leaving the entire estate to his only child, Maurice Mahon. But within twelve months Maurice was declared insane, and the issue of inheritance was complicated by the fact that he had no heirs. This would see Denis Mahon and his first cousin contest the matter before the courts while the running of the estate was overseen by the Court of Chancery. Eventually the courts found in Denis Mahon's favour, and he finally inherited the family estate in late 1845.

While the estate was theoretically worth a considerable amount of money, like many similar estates in Ireland it had suffered from decades of mismanagement and was in a perilous state on the eve of the Great Hunger. The decades of war that had followed the French Revolution of 1789 had created something of a bubble in the rental market. High prices for agricultural goods and soaring rents had incentivized sub-division. This had seen farms broken into smaller and smaller plots to maximize rental income. But when peace finally returned to Europe in 1815, the wartime economic bubble burst. Irish agriculture, having reorientated itself to suit the needs of a Britain at war, needed major restructuring.

While astute landlords began amalgamating smallholdings into larger farm units that were more productive, profitable and economically sustainable, the Mahon estate had been one of many that suffered from chronic mismanagement.

While Maurice Mahon had never been in a position to manage the estate due to his poor mental health, his father before him, Baron Hartland, had been a reckless spendthrift. He had borrowed considerable sums of money to carry out extensive renovations to the family home. This financial profligacy encumbered the Strokestown estate with debts of £30,000, a sum that was nearly three times the total annual rental income it generated from the tenantry.[9] Meanwhile, the management of the estate's land had been disastrous. When it had been taken over by the Court of Chancery in 1836, the officials appointed had little appetite to carry out the reforms needed.

Because of this, the situation facing Denis Mahon in 1845 was considerable. As court administrators had taken little interest in the estate, the subdivision of lands had continued relentlessly. Theoretically there were 745 tenants on the estate, but this masked the large number of subtenants; there were nearly 12,000 people living on the land.[10] In many cases these people sublet land, which was in turn sublet from the legal tenants. Furthermore, as was common in such cases, many tenants had stopped paying rent when the estate was taken over by the courts in 1836, and arrears to the tune of £13,000 had accumulated.[11]

Though the problems Denis Mahon faced were acute, they were not unique – it has been estimated that one estate in twelve was insolvent and facing bankruptcy on the eve of the Great Hunger.[12] Indeed, the landlord class across the United Kingdom was deeply indebted. In England in the mid-nineteenth century, 50 per cent of all rental income was being used to service debts.[13]

By 1845 the Devon Commission, an investigative commission of the British government, had carried out years of research into Irish agriculture, and its recommendations pointed to several potential solutions. While farms would need to be amalgamated, the authors of the report warned that those who would need to be evicted in order to make this happen couldn't simply be cast aside. They advocated a range of options, from widespread public works to alleviate distress, to reclamation of wasteland for new farms, and emigration schemes for those wishing to leave Ireland.[14]

Less than twelve months after these recommendations from the commission, Denis Mahon finally inherited the Strokestown estate and, although he planned to tackle the problems facing it, his ambitions were overtaken by broader social crises. By 1846 starvation and disease ravaged the estate. The same year, a petition from the people of Cloonahee, three kilometres north of Strokestown, illustrated the growing desperation of the populace: 'Our families are really and truly suffering, we cannot withstand their cries for food. We have no food for them because our potatoes are rotten. We fear the peace of the countryside will be much disturbed if relief be not more extensively afforded to the suffering peasantry.' This, however, ended with an implicit threat that the people were on the brink of violence: 'We are not joining anything illegal or contrary to the laws of God or the land unless pressed by hunger.'[15]

Denis Mahon's own cousin in Roscommon wrote to him in August 1846, informing him of developments in the region: 'Matters look very threatening in Roscommon, last week a large assemblage paraded near Castlerea with a loaf on a pole and a placard "Food or Blood".'[16] Nevertheless, Denis Mahon remained determined to restructure the estate, which was haemorrhaging money. Recognizing that the scale of the problems needed outside expertise, he hired professional land agents from Dublin. They appointed his own cousin, John Ross Mahon, as agent.

Arriving in Strokestown, Ross Mahon took a new approach, and his first act was to survey the entire estate before identifying its problems and advocating solutions. His conclusion was alarming. The estate, he said, was in such bad shape that it would better to let it lie idle than allow the vast majority of the tenants who were paupers to continue living on the land.[17] This meant one thing – eviction. While his claim was certainly dramatic, it was rooted in a logic that was prevalent at the time. Many tenants were in no position to afford food, let alone pay rents, and by 1847 the trajectory and pace of events in London were incentivizing eviction.

In early 1847 the British government's intervention in the Famine in Ireland was at its most effective. They had ditched the disastrous public works programme, which had in some areas aggravated the situation further by demanding the starving population carry out laborious tasks such as road-building for wages too low to buy food. In its place they introduced the Temporary Relief Act. This oversaw the opening of thousands of soup kitchens across the island, and by the summer of 1847, the number of deaths was in sharp decline.

But this was only, as the name of the act under which it was introduced implied, temporary. It was designed simply to pave the way for what the government saw as the long-term solution. The British government increasingly wanted to absolve itself of financial responsibility for Irish famine relief. To this end, they decided that from the autumn of 1847, all famine relief was to be administered through Ireland's 130 Poor Law Unions. The plan was a disaster from the outset. The Poor Law Unions, which each administered one workhouse, had been designed to provide for around 100,000 people. But in 1847, three million or so Irish people were being fed by soup kitchens.

Critically, they were funded by local taxation and in the case of those too poor to pay, landlords were liable to pay the tax for their poorer tenants. In short, from the autumn of 1847 Irish landlords would face enormous tax bills, which were relative to the number of their tenants who were unable to pay taxes.

This decision by the government had catastrophic consequences. It had long been recognized that many estates needed to reduce the numbers of their tenants, but landlords were now being incentivized to do this as rapidly as possible. If they evicted their poorest tenants, their tax bill would drop rapidly.

This had not been lost on the architects of the plan in London. Those with their hands on the levers of power were coming to the conclusion that the Famine was a unique historic opportunity to reorganize the entire agricultural economy. The influential Treasury civil servant Charles Edward Trevelyan outlined this view in late 1847: 'Posterity will trace up to that famine the commencement of a salutary revolution in the habits of a nation long singularly unfortunate.'[18]

The Devon Commission, which reported its findings in 1845, had warned about the difficulties in reorganizing Irish agriculture, acknowledging it would be a long and complex affair. Throwing this caution to the wind, the British government now saw in the Famine a mechanism for rapid transformation. Such was the fervour of some of those in power in London that they believed the hand of God was at work. Trevelyan again explained: 'God grant that the generation to which this great opportunity has been offered, may rightly perform its part, and that we may not relax our efforts until Ireland fully participates in the social health and physical prosperity of Great Britain'[19]

To assist the likes of Denis Mahon, legislation to aid with evictions was passed. The Gregory (or Quarter Acre) Clause stipulated that in order to receive aid from a Poor Law Union, a person could not be in possession of a farm larger than a quarter of an acre of land. As most holdings were larger, the clear intention was to force the poor to choose between their farms on the one hand and receiving famine relief on the other; maintain their farm and starve, or relinquish it and receive famine relief. For most, this choice was no choice at all.

That this would incur a huge human toll was not lost on those in power either – they saw it as inevitable. The Master of Balliol College Oxford, Benjamin Jowett, later recalled a conversation with the influential economist Nassau William Sr: 'I have always felt a certain horror of political economists since I heard one of them say that the Famine in Ireland would not kill more than a million people, and that would scarcely be enough to do much good.'[20] The economists and politicians of Westminster didn't foresee that Denis Mahon or his ilk would rank among the casualties.

While these plans were passed in the British Parliament during the summer of 1847, in Strokestown Denis Mahon and John Ross Mahon were preparing to reduce the number of poor tenants, and with it the tax bill the estate would be liable for. But the local population were not passive bystanders in this process. Strokestown was no different to other parts of Ireland, and secret societies had long been active on the estate. Denis Mahon, initially at least, tread carefully.

Rather than launch major evictions straight away, he developed a scheme to ship thousands of his tenants to North America, a plan which was popular among those who wanted to leave but hadn't been able to afford the passage. Denis Mahon showed a degree of magnanimity by waiving the debts of tenants who owed arrears. This allowed them to sell their possessions, providing them with some money to start afresh in North America. But the landlord was not acting with humanitarian motivations. While the emigration scheme cost £5,860, it had already been estimated that it would save the estate over £11,000 annually on Poor Law taxes, which would have had to be paid if those who left had ended up in the workhouse.[21]

To implement the plan, Denis Mahon chartered four ships to North America, offering free passage – but in the weeks before the tenants departed, stark warnings reached Ireland of what lay ahead for these emigrants in Canada, where death rates were soaring in quarantine stations. This came in the form of a widely published letter from the Archbishop of Quebec, Joseph Signay, who pleaded with Irish archbishops and bishops to 'dissuade your diocesans from emigrating in such numbers to Canada, where they will but too often meet with either a premature death, or a fate as deplorable as the heartrending condition under which they groan in their unhappy country'.[22]

Denis Mahon's tenants were precisely the people Signay was referring to. Weakened by nearly two years of food shortages, they were in no position to undertake the rigours of a transatlantic voyage. The humanitarian warnings went unheeded in Roscommon.

Travelling first to Liverpool, 1,490 emigrants from Strokestown boarded four ships in that port: the *Virginus*, the *Erin's Queen*, the *Naomi* and the *John Munn*. The conditions on board these ships were appalling, and the predictions of Archbishop Signay materialized. Nearly half of those who had left Strokestown would never reach their destination alive, dying en route or in the quarantine stations on the St Lawrence River in Canada.

Meanwhile, back in Ireland, Denis Mahon continued with his drive to restructure the estate. His approach was the one advocated by Charles Trevelyan, who had suggested that a 'sharp but effective remedy' was best for Ireland. While news of the terrible fate of those who had emigrated would not reach Ireland until the early autumn of 1847, Denis Mahon had been busy serving eviction notices that would see another thousand people evicted.[23] The situation facing these people was desperate. Eviction was not just the loss of a home. In most cases the house was attached to a small plot of land where the family grew the potatoes and crops that sustained them through the year. Some also reared a few animals that could produce cash when sold. In one fell swoop, eviction amounted to the loss of a home, a job and one's ability to feed oneself.

In this eventuality many were left with no alternative but the workhouse. While this was a humiliating experience at the best of times, by 1847 it was also extremely dangerous, with diseases running rampant in the overcrowded, unsanitary conditions inside the institutions. There was also a deep emotional loss for those being driven from their homes. It ran far deeper than Denis Mahon's understanding of the situation – an economic equation to balance his accounts. An anonymous account from a tenant evicted from their home on an estate at Carrigallen in County Leitrim captured the deep-seated, generational sense of loss: 'We all lived in peace in this village, we were never at law with each other. Our forefathers lived here for generations past. You would say, if you saw it before this ruin came, that "it was a nice little village".'[24] Such concerns mattered little to Denis Mahon, and his bailiffs set about carrying out evictions and then wrecking the homes of tenants so they could not be reoccupied.

By late October tensions were reaching boiling point in Strokestown. Although Denis Mahon had cleared nearly a quarter of his tenants, he was still planning further evictions. As opposition mounted from the remaining tenants, the landlord was unmoved. Writing to his agent John Ross Mahon on 2 November he declared, 'I shall evict the whole [sic] and not one of them shall get land again.'[25] Less than twenty-four hours later, Denis Mahon left Roscommon town after attending a local relief committee meeting, where he had somewhat ironically argued for increased aid for his tenants. He never reached Strokestown alive, meeting his bloody end at the Khyber Pass.

Initially at least, the authorities received little or no help from the local people. Nevertheless, the hunt to find the culprits was relentless, with constables travelling to North America and England in their search for suspects. Despite a substantial reward of £800, little information was forthcoming.

But where money failed, even more morally dubious incentives succeeded. Those willing to give information were offered immunity from eviction or passage to America. Unsurprisingly, in the midst of the devastating famine, this coercion proved effective, and in total over thirty people testified for the Crown. Food was also used as a means to elicit confessions. The family of one of those accused, Michael Gardiner, was removed from relief lists, a move which led his mother to plead with him to reveal what he knew of the murder. Although Andrew Connor – the man considered by most to have been the key figure behind the assassination – escaped punishment, two others were successfully prosecuted and hanged on 8 August 1848. Whether he was actually responsible is another matter entirely – evidence was extracted from a starving population by offers of food and promises of protection from eviction.

Ultimately, the murder of Denis Mahon did little to affect the clearances from the estate. Thousands more were evicted from their homes in the final years of the Great Hunger, their houses demolished, their meagre possessions scattered. Mahon's was the most high-profile murder during the Famine. While Queen Victoria reached for racial stereotypes, some were willing to attempt a more nuanced understanding of these events. The *Cork Examiner* reflected on his death:

> We have to record another bloody deed, the result of the agrarian war which is still being waged in all its horrors between Irish men for the soil of Ireland. The murderous clearances, the desolation, the levelling and the burning of villages wrought by landlords – the still more bloody clearances of landlords wrought by peasants alike, proclaimed the necessity of legislative interference to put an end to such criminal mutual extermination.[26]

The *Examiner*'s sentiments gave voice to the new phase of the Famine, which had begun in earnest in late 1847 – one shaped in part at least by a vision of restructuring the Irish economy through evictions and clearances rather than famine relief.

While Denis Mahon was murdered for his role in these events, he was facilitated and indeed encouraged by the British government. Racism had nurtured an indifferent attitude towards suffering in Ireland. Sectarianism fed a providential belief in some quarters that the Famine was a punishment for Catholics.

However, the overriding policy that shaped reactions and decisions in London was the laissez-faire economic worldview which absolved politicians and law-makers of their responsibility. Denis Mahon had at times acted according to the mantra of James Wilson, the influential founder of *The Economist*, who had infamously stated in the 1840s that 'it is no man's business to provide for another'. The attempts to overhaul the Irish economy in the midst of the worst famine in living memory not only prolonged it, but proved a point of no return in modern Anglo-Irish relations.

On a local level, the events of the late 1840s permanently soured relations between the Mahon family and the community who lived on their estate. Patrick Mullooly, who grew up two miles from Strokestown and went on to serve as Quartermaster of the North Roscommon Brigade of the IRA in the revolutionary era, would invoke the memory of Denis Mahon and his 'cruel actions' when contextualizing the War of Independence.[27]

Meanwhile, the Mahon family clung to the idea that Denis Mahon had acted with benign intentions. His great-granddaughter Olive Packenham-Mahon, the last of the family to reside in Strokestown, continued to argue this position into the late twentieth century. In her final interview, days before she left Strokestown for the last time in March 1981, she defended Denis Mahon, claiming his actions had been misinterpreted.[28]

By the end of the Great Hunger, the lonely mausoleum where Denis Mahon was interred stood isolated, close to the entrance of an empty Strokestown Park House: his family had moved to England.

The 1851 census captured the devastation his plans and actions had wrought on the wider community. There had been 8,800 houses in the Strokestown region in 1841, and ten years later this had been reduced to 5,180. More startling still was the loss of people. In 1841 the region had been home to 25,413 souls. A decade later, only 15,050 people lived in a landscape blighted by the ruins of houses, homes, communities and graves.

CHAPTER 5

The Workhouse

1862

> And because of all this, we make a sure covenant, and write it; and our princes, Levites, and priests, seal unto it.
>
> (Nehemiah 9:38)

In the six years after moving to the Tipperary town of Clogheen, Richard Burke had established himself as one of the most recognizable men in the town. Although an outsider, he had enjoyed a meteoric rise through the ranks in the local workhouse. By 1848 the short and stocky Burke could look long-established and wealthy residents of the town eye to eye.

Burke may not have been as rich as the Grubb family who owned the local mills or Joseph NicCraith who owned numerous houses in the town, but as clerk of the workhouse he was an important and influential man in Clogheen. At one time this would have been a minor position but since the onset of the Great Hunger he was on the front line of the Famine.

Events in Clogheen had followed a similar trajectory to other towns across the country after the onset of famine. 1846 had seen major unrest: riots – similar to those that rocked Dungarvan and other the southern ports – erupted as the starving in Clogheen targeted the many flour mills in the town. By the late summer it had become almost impossible to move food of any kind through the surrounding countryside.

The British government established order by transporting the food in bulk. In some instances, convoys of flour and other food for export could be half a mile long, and the presence of a military guard ensured they would reach the southern ports safely. By 1847 the determination that the poor had demonstrated the previous summer had dissipated in the face of starvation. Hunger had reduced many to apathy and listlessness. Richard Davis, a traveller in South Tipperary, found the region, which had been rocked by riots only a few months earlier, eerily peaceful: 'Strange to say, I saw the flour and meal being conveyed along the road without any escort save that of the car driver . . . the people in these localities do conduct themselves peaceably and refrain from outrage in a remarkable manner.' [1]

The reality was that the will of the poor had been crushed by soldiers and starvation. On a daily basis Richard Burke, clerk of Clogheen workhouse, faced a relentless tide of desperation, destitution and misery. A letter by David Keane, a literate and well educated man desperate to leave Ireland, captured the situation facing many of Burke's neighbours. Writing to Michael Neile, who had already emigrated, Keane pleaded for help. His words spoke for an entire generation in Ireland. Keane opened his letter by explaining just how bad life had become in Ireland: 'Attempting to give you the least idea of the extent to which wretchedness prevails in this unfortunate country would be in vain, Ever since you left, famine stalked the land . . . mowing down all before it alas!'

After a few paragraphs sharing news of deceased acquaintances, he turned to the substance of the letter. Keane, like so many in Clogheen, was desperate to leave Ireland and he asked his friend to provide financial assistance to him and his sister Alice so they could emigrate. In describing his sister's plight, David Keane illustrated how, for many, there was no future in Ireland. Alice Keane, her brother wrote, was not even contemplating marriage: 'No inducement would make her marry here, of course it would be folly to think of it.'[2] Alice Keane's reluctance to marry had become the norm by 1847. Back in the early 1840s, there had been around forty marriages celebrated by the local clergy in Clogheen each year. By 1847, this had fallen to thirteen. In some areas, the Famine-induced decline was even more dramatic. In Bantry in West Cork, for example, the number of marriages fell by 75 per cent.

While Alice Keane's refusal of marriage echoed the plight of many, there was one Clogheen woman, Johanna Nic Craith, who had very different experiences and expectations about what the coming years had in store for her. The daughter of Joseph Nic Craith, a small landlord in the town, she was the only woman married in Clogheen, in January 1847, a month that traditionally would have seen half a dozen unions solemnized. Her husband was Richard Burke, a rising star and one of the most eligible bachelors in the town.

While David Keane would leave Clogheen, disappearing from the historical record, Richard Burke and Johanna Nic Craith looked forward to a bright future in Ireland. Although surrounded by misery in 1847, Richard Burke at the age of twenty-five was and one of the few people who could claim that their prospects had actually improved since the onset of the Great Hunger. A native of nearby Cahir, a town fourteen kilometres to the north of Clogheen, Burke had grown up in the 1820s and 30s. While the newspaper headlines of those decades were dominated by extreme violence, this had masked the profound and far-reaching changes that were taking root in Irish life. In the early nineteenth century literacy in Irish society was concentrated in towns and cities. In 1841 only 28 per cent of the population could read and write, although 53 per cent over the age of fifteen had some level of literacy.[3] Nevertheless, these statistics compared favourably with other countries in Europe and Richard Burke's generation grew up in a society where attitudes towards literacy were changing for the better.

In 1831 the British government passed legislation to establish free primary schooling up to the age of twelve, which would be standardized and open to all. This replaced the private system, which had been uneven at best. Although the first of the new schools opened in Cahir in 1834, Richard Burke had probably attended a school run by a local charity, which had opened in 1818. Either way, he was educated, and ideally placed to take advantage of the revolution of sorts underway in Irish society.

His literacy skills saw his career take off just as Irish society was imploding during the Famine. The drive to educate all in society was, in part at least, a recognition that the nature of the economy was changing. Literate clerks were increasingly in demand in the world of business, but also in the rapidly growing realm of public institutions. In the early decades of the nineteenth century, the idea that institutions of one kind or another could solve societal problems had gained widespread support. This saw a wave of them built across the country, as new prisons were built to tackle crime, asylums to address mental health problems, hospitals to cure the sick and workhouses to tackle poverty. They all operated along similar lines, with a seemingly insatiable appetite for record-keeping. Every last detail about those admitted to them was documented, while the central authorities demanded regular communication to keep them abreast of how the institutions functioned.

It was this world of institutions that first drew Richard Burke from his native Cahir to Clogheen in the early 1840s. The town had been selected as a site for one of Ireland's initial 130 workhouses. Opened in 1842, the Clogheen Workhouse was designed to provide for the destitute in society, offering food and a bed in spartan surroundings.

During its early weeks, on 8 August 1842, Richard Burke secured a position as the first schoolmaster for the boys of the institution, while a schoolmistress, Mary Nowlan, was appointed on the same day. The position demanded further education and, prior to taking up his position, Richard had to attend the Central Model School in Dublin for training. Only after producing his certificate of qualification did he start.[4]

Despite this rigorous training, the pay was modest. The annual salary of £15 was not dramatically more than he could have earned toiling in a field, like his family had done before him. However, his position offered regular and easier employment, in what was a rapidly expanding industry. These opportunities would present themselves faster than even Richard Burke himself could have hoped, when a series of unforeseeable opportunities opened a path for promotion.

Less than a year after he joined Clogheen Workhouse as schoolmaster, the institution was rocked by scandal when the clerk, Jeffrey Keating, had to resign.[5] Accused of 'immoral conduct' in the workhouse boardroom with a woman called Ellen Cahile, a major investigation was conducted. The accusations were never explicit, but as Cahile testified against him, it would appear they were abusive in nature. Another staff member, the porter James Cleary, was accused of facilitating Keating's actions and trying to intimidate Ellen Cahile into silence.[6]

In the new institutionalized understanding of the world, this complaint was taken down in minute detail, and records were despatched to the Poor Law Commission in Dublin, who oversaw the running of workhouses. Ultimately Ellen Cahile's testimony was disregarded as coming from a woman of 'bad character'. She had taken a considerable risk in coming forward – the tendency to disbelieve women claiming sexual assault has a long history. While Ellen was subjected to demeaning language in a subsequent meeting attended by an official from Dublin, Keating was nevertheless dismissed. The porter was found innocent.[7]

Jeffrey Keating was replaced by a new clerk, Henry Langley; but it quickly became apparent that he was also unsuitable for the position. By August 1845 Langley's ineptitude was revealed through irregular accounting, and the Poor Law Commissioners demanded his resignation.[8] An election was held, and Richard Burke put himself forward. The Board of Guardians deemed him the best candidate and, although only twenty-three years old, he was appointed clerk of Clogheen Workhouse.[9]

As clerk, Richard Burke's role changed dramatically from that of schoolmaster. He was now arguably the single most influential official in the institution. He not only took the minutes of the weekly meeting of the Board of Guardians, but it frequently fell to him to implement their decisions on a day-to-day basis. He also had to communicate regularly with the Poor Law Commission in Dublin. This new position also saw a substantial increase in his wages, from £15 to £52 per annum.[10]

But Richard Burke had secured his promotion at the worst time imaginable in the workhouse. The first failure of the potato crop, which would trigger the Great Hunger, took place only a few weeks later. Over the following year, Burke would be staring down a social catastrophe on a scale not seen since the seventeenth century. As mass starvation set in, the numbers of those in need of help in the workhouse rose dramatically. When Burke had been appointed clerk in August 1845, there had been 242 people in the workhouse. By Christmas 1846 it exceeded its capacity of 500 people for the first time.[11]

By 9 January 1847, the 556 people now in the workhouse faced severe overcrowding as famine-related diseases began spreading rapidly through an increasingly malnourished population. Richard Burke's life, however, was taking a very different trajectory. Over the previous years he had started a relationship with Johanna Nic Craith, daughter of prominent businessman Joseph McCraith, the owner of a local hotel and numerous rental properties in the town.[12] The McCraith family were inoculated from the direct impact of famine by their wealth – Johanna Nic Craith herself had been afforded an education and she was in the minority of literate women in rural Ireland. Harrowing though the workhouse could often be, Richard Burke thrived there. By the end of the year, the Board of Guardians acknowledged his work by increasing his annual pay to £65.[13]

The aptitude he displayed for his work had also come to the attention of the Poor Law Commission, who oversaw the running of the entire workhouse system. So impressed were they by Richard Burke that in 1848, when the Board of Guardians of Ennistymon Workhouse in County Clare were dismissed and the commissioners decided to take the running of the institution in hand, it was to him they turned.

He arrived in Ennistymon at a terrible time. The situation was far more serious than it had been in Clogheen. By November thirty people were dying each week. By January 1849 eighty-nine people perished in one week alone. Somewhat inevitably, Richard Burke contracted cholera during an epidemic that accompanied the later years of the Famine. Well paid and well fed, he managed to pull through.

During these dark days at the opening of their marriage, Johanna Burke remained in Clogheen and the two maintained what was effectively a long-distance relationship through letters. By 1850 Richard Burke had not only survived the Famine but – though still two years shy of his thirtieth birthday – was one of the most experienced workhouse officials in Ireland. In the eyes of many, the time had come for him to return to Clogheen, where he and Johanna could still start a family. But Burke himself had other ideas. He left Ennistymon that year but, rather than return to Tipperary, instead took a position as clerk of the workhouse in Waterford city. This saw his wages increase still further, to £250.

In a move that raised eyebrows at the time, Johanna did not join Richard in the city. While the decision for Johanna to remain in Clogheen while he moved to Ennistymon was understandable, given the death rate in the town, the continued separation was considered unusual for the time. The fact that Richard Burke did not buy a house but instead quartered himself in various hotels in the city suggested the move was never considered permanent. Separated by seventy kilometres, the two continued what appears to have been an increasingly strained relationship, communicating by letter alone. Though his relationship was in difficulty, his career went from strength to strength.

While the Famine eased in the early 1850s, extreme destitution and poverty remained a feature of Irish life. In January 1852 the Waterford workhouse, which had been expanded over the course of the Famine, still had over 2,300 inmates, and in that week alone nine people died. Four years later, in January 1856, there were 1,561 still institutionalized there. It was only by the end of the decade that some sense of normality had returned. At the opening of 1859 there were only 840 people in the institution, with a single death recorded.

By this point the Irish economy was beginning to emerge from the degradation of the Great Hunger. The island had been immeasurably transformed. The British government had passed the Encumbered Estates Act in 1849, which facilitated the sale of major estates that had gone bankrupt. This created new owners, many of whom oversaw major changes in rural Ireland. While farming remained central to the Irish economy, the nature of agriculture had changed. A trend toward ranching gained pace, as the cattle herd almost doubled from 2 million to 3.5 million by 1860. In this new economy, where work on the land was becoming increasingly scarce, Richard Burke had chosen his career wisely: in fact, the fastest-growing sector of the post-famine economy was services. Many aspects of this sector, such as shopkeeping, demanded high levels of literacy. Richard Burke remained with what he knew best – Poor Law administration.

As the twentieth anniversary of his service in workhouses approached, Waterford Workhouse was gripped by a sensational scandal in the summer of 1861, when accusations of serious misconduct were levelled at Burke by none other than the Catholic chaplain of the institution, Fr David McKeon.

Fr McKeon, a contentious man, learned that three women in the workhouse had accused Burke of sexual assault. Somewhat surprisingly, in an age where such crimes were routinely dismissed out of hand, the priest took them seriously. He helped the three illiterate women navigate what was the increasingly literate and procedural world of the workhouse. The precise dates of the incidents were never given, but the most serious charge against Burke was from a woman called Anne Cullen, who stated he had raped her. Following the assault, he had then admitted her to the workhouse on the promise that he would secure her passage to Australia. Nance Ryan, who had entered the workhouse a few years previously, stated that Burke had given her money in the workhouse and promised her shoes when she left. A third woman, Johanna Kenny, described how Burke seduced her and was, in her words, 'the ruin of her degradation', promising her she would never have to go into the workhouse. Burke countered by claiming that it was the women who had tried to seduce him but he could not deny that he had said to Mary O'Connell, another female staff member in the workhouse, that he was 'fond' of the ladies.

A report was conducted and submitted to the Poor Law Commissioners in Dublin. On 25 June 1861 they responded with their verdict. They dismissed the charges out of hand, based purely on their view that the three women were 'witnesses of the worst character', a similar dismissal to that of the charges levelled at Jeffrey Keating in Clogheen Workhouse eighteen years earlier. The commissioners did, however, take a separate accusation that he had had an affair with the workhouse schoolteacher, Miss Ryan, more seriously. While they stated that there was no evidence of an actual affair, they did say that there had been a 'great want of discretion'.[14]

Although Burke kept his position, the increasingly literate nineteenth-century Irish society took great interest in the case. Among the numerous publications to carry detailed accounts was South Tipperary's *Clonmel Chronicle*, and while its reporting largely vindicated her husband of abuse, Johanna Burke can only have been concerned that even in the best reading of the events, there had been a lack of discretion between him and the schoolteacher.

Furthermore, his admission to Mary O'Connell that his only fault was that he was 'fond' of the ladies was not encouraging. Richard and Johanna Burke had lived separate lives for nearly all of the fifteen years of their marriage, and these events now placed the relationship under increased strain. In the following weeks, when she wrote to her husband asking for an explanation, he rebuked her, saying it was none of her business.

While his infidelity was clearly the source of tension, by the 1860s money was also emerging as a point of contention.[15] Johanna Burke was not entirely dependent on her husband's income although her own income, derived from rental properties in Clogheen, left her struggling. This contrasted with her husband's life in Waterford, where he resided in a hotel. In late 1861 or possibly early 1862 she travelled to Waterford and demanded he help her financially.[16]

The following months remained difficult and the relationship appeared to be in terminal decline. While divorce was not an option for the couple as they were Catholic, they could decide, as people sometimes did, to go their own separate ways and acknowledge that the relationship was at an end. Indeed, this seemed to be already happening, given that there was little or no contact over that winter of 1861–2. To make matters worse for Johanna Burke, who suffered from epilepsy and was prone to having fits, her health was declining.

Somewhat suddenly, there was a dramatic change in their relationship. The two resumed contact, and the letters from early 1862 hint at a warming of relations. In March, Johanna Burke wrote an affectionate letter to her husband after he had promised to visit: 'I will get the potatoes down today. I hope the weather will continue fine until they will be finished. I hope to have the garden and oats down before you will come and then you will say that I am very good. I would rather hear that much from you than all the world besides.'[17]

In the following weeks Richard Burke travelled to Clogheen and the relationship continued to improve – but when he left again for the workhouse in Waterford, Burke had seen his wife for the last time.

On 14 April 1862 Johanna Burke's health deteriorated dramatically. After taking medicine in the hopes of treating her epilepsy, she suddenly developed a bad reaction, crying out, 'Bad manners to the blackguard medicine I am killed!' While her sister was being called for, she started convulsing uncontrollably, although in a manner different to her epilepsy attacks. A priest was summoned but Johanna Burke expired before he made it to the house.

When word reached Richard Burke in Waterford, he was said to be depressed but not surprised. He had believed she was sick and ailing for months, according to colleagues. He attributed her death to a heart condition and cancer. That his response was muted surprised few – he had lived apart from his wife for over fifteen years, but back in

Clogheen suspicions as to the nature of Johanna Burke's death were growing.

An inquest had been started and postponed on two occasions. When it finally went ahead on 9 May, it stunned the national press.[18] An autopsy was carried out and the contents of Johanna Burke's stomach sent to University College Cork for analysis. This revealed that her claim on her deathbed, that the 'blackguard medicine' had killed her, had been correct: she had in fact consumed a large dose of the lethal poison strychnine. This was supported by evidence from witnesses. Johanna Burke had mentioned the foul taste of the medicine to her servant Ellen Pyne; strychnine is known to be extremely bitter.[19]

With this evidence the inquest jury predictably pronounced a verdict of murder. But their remit also granted them the power to apportion blame and given the weight of evidence presented, they pronounced Richard Burke responsible.

Richard Burke's life had been in many ways defined by his education and his literacy and it was somewhat fitting that it would be this that led to his downfall. Over the course of their fifteen-year marriage, he and Johanna had communicated by letter, and he had orchestrated her death in similar fashion. For a man whose life's work had been to document and record events, it was bizarre that he overlooked the risks in this course of action.

It appears that Richard Burke had put the plan in motion when he visited Clogheen in late March 1862. Johanna Burke's niece Hanna, who was living with her at the time, recalled Richard Burke saying, 'Oh Johanna I thought you would have died of your heart beating last night. Dr Harrington had a sister who had the same complaint. She got a recipe from London which cured her and I will send you some of the same'.[20] On his return to Waterford Richard Burke had duly despatched a parcel to Johanna containing coffee, along with the medicine and detailed instructions on how it should be taken. Richard Burke was arrested and brought to trial in Clonmel, where the jury heard damning evidence. The workhouse physician, Dr Harrington, refuted his claim that he had recommended the medicine, saying that Richard Burke had concocted this story to explain why he sent magnesium, a silvery powder, which masked the presence of strychnine to the naked eye.

One of the many witnesses was Margaret Bohan, a destitute woman who had spent years in the workhouse. She testified to the court that she held a position of responsibility in the workhouse and, while carrying out her duties, she had seen Burke enter the apothecary's office and collect something.[21] Although Bohan was illiterate and couldn't identify what the substance was, the fact that Richard Burke took something from the apothecary's office, where strychnine was stored, was nevertheless significant.

As the case against Burke mounted, a series of letters found in his wife's house were entered as evidence before the court – cast-iron evidence that Richard Burke had sent something to his wife, which he claimed Dr Harrington had recommended. He also suggested taking the 'medicine' with sugar: the prosecution argued that this was done to mask the bitter taste of the strychnine.[22] Another letter sent a few days later asked if she had taken the powder, claiming Dr Harrington wanted to know.

Burke's defence rebuttal was weak. While there were 'respectable' citizens of Waterford willing to testify to his good character, this could not explain away the damning evidence against him. The one aspect of the prosecution case that was weak was the motive. The evidence presented implied that money was the main issue, but this was never made entirely clear.

Even lacking a clear motive, the jury had few qualms. After seventy-five minutes they found Richard Burke guilty. Although they urged the judge to treat him leniently, this was rejected. Donning the black cap worn only for such decisions, the judge sentenced Richard Burke to death. In the literate world that had provided him with exalted status but ultimately led to his downfall, the final word on his life was fittingly entered into an institutional register. After his conviction at the summer assizes, the prison authorities had detailed the sentence in jail records. Richard Burke was to be hanged and then buried in the grounds of the prison. On 25 August this was amended with a final entry, which simply stated: 'Executed'.[23]

CHAPTER 6

Land

1881

> They were driven forth from among men; they cried after them as after a thief.
>
> (Job 30:5)

In the four decades following emancipation the Catholic Church took full advantage of its newfound liberties, dramatically increasing its influence over Irish society. This was not only evident in the religious beliefs of the people, but took physical form in the very landscape itself. The countryside was changing as hundreds of Catholic churches sprang up across the island. The largest buildings in many areas, these churches quickly became the focal point of community life for Catholics, inserting the Church at the heart of day-to-day life.

The community of Killeenadeema outside Loughrea in south-east County Galway was no different. St Dympna's parish church, a modest T-shaped structure, had been built in the years following emancipation in 1829 and over the following decades the Catholics in the community gathered there for the most important rituals. Life began with baptism and ended with funerals in St Dympna's. And for twenty-six-year-old Judith Kirwan the most significant of all was her marriage on 17 September 1870.

In the church, Judith (usually known as Julia) married James Connors in a ceremony laced with expectation and an undercurrent of anxiety. After the wedding she would accompany him to his native Killarrive, leaving her native Sonnagh behind. But life with James Connors would be complex. Julia Kirwan would have to bridge the considerable age gap of twenty years between the two. While such a difference in age was common practice, it could not be dismissed. James and Julia were not only at different points in their lives; they were from very different generations and the twenty years that separated them happened to be among the most consequential in Irish history.

Born in 1844, Julia Kirwan was too young to remember the horrors of the Great Hunger, and had no recollection of pre-famine Ireland whatsoever. James Connors, on the other hand, had been born in the 1820s and was already an adult by 1845, when the potato crop failed for the first time. He had not only lived through those terrible years as an adult, but could remember the very different Ireland he had been born in. Nearly every facet of life had changed.

Even as they stood before the priest in St Dympna's that Saturday morning, the ceremony had little in common with the services of previous decades. Prior to the Famine, marriages had generally taken place in the family home of the bride. This had changed in recent decades. Cardinal Paul Cullen had returned from Rome in 1849 to take up the position of Archbishop of Dublin. The dramatic restructuring of the Church he then undertook spread to every town and village in Ireland.

Cullen marshalled the clergy into more obedient servants of the Church hierarchy. Wayward or lax priests, such as those who had partners, were defrocked. To further extend the influence of the Church, rituals such as marriages and baptism now took place in the churches that had been built across the island rather than the home.

While interfering with age-old custom had provoked resistance from some, the decades following the Famine had been ones of rapid change in general. James Connors could recall an Ireland that to his new wife was distant, remote and even dangerous. When they travelled to James's home at Killarrive after the ceremony, the community looked like any other to Julia Connors. There were twenty-three houses dotted across the townland, home to ninety-seven people.

James Connors, though, could see the changes all too clearly, the differences from that old world before the Famine. In his teenage years the community had comprised 240 people in forty-three houses. The story of where they had gone was a painful one of death, evictions and emigration. He also had more vivid recollections of the immediate aftermath of the Famine, when East Galway had been desolate. The end result of countless famine evictions was a ruined landscape of levelled houses. In 1856 Frederick Engels wrote to Karl Marx during a visit through the west: 'The whole of the west, especially in the neighbourhood of Galway, is covered with ruined peasant houses, most of which have only been deserted since 1846. I never thought that famine could have such tangible reality.' Of Galway, Engels claimed: 'The land is an utter desert which nobody wants.' [1]

This was somewhat of an exaggeration, or at least Engels failed to fully grasp what was happening. Some 200,000 farms of fewer than five acres had been erased from the landscape. In many cases, these had been amalgamated into larger holdings. In some places this saw people enlarge smallholdings into more sustainable farms. In other communities it paved the way for large cattle ranchers and graziers, practising a form of agriculture that emphasized cattle-herding rather than labour-intensive tillage. In short, cattle were replacing people across the landscape. Unsettling and painful as this change had been, the ability of the Irish economy to rebound had surprised many.

Agricultural prices had risen throughout the 1850s, and the economy had improved to such an extent that it even weathered a minor downturn in the early 1860s. The rest of that decade saw a return to growth, facilitated by technological developments. The use of imported fertilizer increased productivity, while the growing network of train lines connected even remoter parts of the west with Dublin, reducing journeys that had taken days into hours. Relentless emigration, which continued in the decades after the Famine, reduced the population at home and eased extreme poverty.

All told, James and Julia's plans to raise a family in the 1870s coincided with a general level of optimism the island hadn't known in decades. While they did not have a vast farm, their twenty acres was large compared to the holdings of past generations. James Connors supplemented his income by burning limestone to produce quicklime, for use in construction and as fertilizer.

Over the following decade the Connors lived a relatively uneventful life in the grand scope of history. Julia Connors's pregnancies passed without any major difficulty and by 1879 she had given birth to four children. With each passing year, it was clear that these children would live in a world remote from the Famine. While the economy had recovered rapidly, the political landscape witnessed equally dramatic changes. The Famine had seen Daniel O'Connell's Repeal movement peter out, while attempts at an uprising in 1848 had failed abysmally. However, in the 1860s and 70s, Irish nationalism in particular emerged rejuvenated, as a more sophisticated political culture took root.

In 1858 a new political organization, the Irish Republican Brotherhood, was established. This movement, which committed itself to establishing an independent republic through armed insurrection, enjoyed considerable success. Its membership in Connacht alone was estimated at seven thousand by the end of the 1870s.[2] But this did not represent a complete break with the past and the secret societies of old remained active, including in the Connors' native Killarrive. Yet the politics of the 1870s demonstrated a new degree of national confidence, perhaps unexpected in a country still recovering from the Great Hunger.

Modern constitutional nationalism, in the form of the Home Rule League, also established itself on the political landscape. This organization had more modest demands than the Fenians, seeking to restore the Dublin parliament abolished by the Act of Union. Its energies were focused on parliamentary methods, where it enjoyed considerable success by the late 1870s – by then it had around sixty Irish Home Rule MPs sitting in the House of Commons and, although sectarianism remained rife, violent conflict appeared to finally be in decline.

In 1874 there were 100 cases of murders and manslaughter, a considerable decline from forty years earlier, when there had been an estimated 240 murders.[3] Blunt as this metric is, it indicated that the Connors' children might just grow up in a more peaceful Ireland. But while James and Julia Connors raised their young family in what seemed to be a rapidly modernizing Irish society, these changes had not altered the deep-rooted inequality that remained at its heart. While farm sizes had increased, through the consolidations of holdings that followed evictions, society remained controlled by a tiny minority of landlords. Although a considerable number had gone bankrupt, most stayed solvent. By the 1880s only a quarter of Irish land had changed hands.[4] In many instances land remained in families who had owned it for generations. The Connors' farm was on the Dunsandle estate, which stretched over 33,000 acres. The neighbouring estate of the Earl of Clanricarde was 52,000 acres. Further east in Meath, the Earl of Conyngham's estate encompassed an incredible 150,000 acres of land. Indeed, only 6,500 families with farms in excess of 500 acres owned most of the land on the island. With such inequality at the heart of the system, the course of events was predictable.

When the economic recovery faltered in the late 1870s, the frailties of Irish society were revealed once more. Living standards and expectations plummeted and, in many places, cases of destitution and the spectre of starvation returned, revealing the shallow roots of the recovery. The technological changes that had facilitated development in Irish agriculture were inevitably a doubled-edged sword. While the new rail lines accelerated travel times within Ireland, steam-powered ships slashed the length and cost of transatlantic journeys in a similar fashion. This saw imports of cheap agricultural goods from the United States arrive in Europe in increasing volumes by the late 1870s. In the face of this new competition and falling prices, rural Ireland was inevitably facing a harsh adjustment.

A series of dire harvests in the last years of the decade plunged the island into a crisis, the likes of which had not been seen since the Great Famine. Poor harvests in 1875 and 1876 set the stage for more serious developments to come. The onset of unusually cold weather from October 1878 was followed by below-average temperatures for twelve consecutive months.[5] The reappearance of blight in 1879 added to the escalating situation. The memory of the Great Hunger only three decades earlier was to the forefront of many minds, including James Connors's. The situation facing some in the Killarrive area was once again dire. A report described how the poor, for want of fuel, were living off uncooked Indian meal.[6]

As farm incomes fell, the nature of land ownership set the stage once more for a major conflict between tenants and landlords. On the one hand, landlords had come to expect a level of rental income that had risen steadily over the previous two decades but tended not to change dramatically from year to year. Meanwhile their tenants, large and small, were vulnerable to the vagaries of agricultural prices and harvest yields, both of which fell in the late

1870s. As tenants watched their incomes fall steeply in the 1870s, landlords refused to reduce rents accordingly; arrears began to build, accentuated by very real fears of starvation in late 1879.

While the situation in many ways conjured up memories of the 1840s, the response of Irish tenants, both large and small, was very different. While the Great Hunger served as a stark reminder of what was at stake, the general population was better educated, more politically sophisticated and better organized than previous generations.

As early as April 1879 tenants had started to organize major protest meetings demanding rent reductions. Several Fenian organizers with political experience recognized the potential of the new Land League and provided leadership. The movement spread rapidly across the country, and one of its key successes was its ability to unify seemingly disparate forces.

Large farmers, small farmers (like James Connors), and labourers alike could all support the demands of the League. Furthermore, moderate Home Rule movement leaders such as Charles Stewart Parnell could work alongside the convicted Fenian gunrunner Michael Davitt. In 1880 the Catholic Church, unquestionably the most influential organization on the island – and which had initially been hesitant – lent its support to the movement. Viewing the Fenians as 'Godless nobodies' for espousing secularism, the Church feared their rising power, and sought to moderate their influence in the Land League. While alleviating the threat of famine in 1879 preoccupied the League's members, they found some landlords amenable to rent reductions at first; the Connors' landlord Lord

Dunsandle cut rents by 15 per cent on holdings less than £100, a measure for which James and Julia qualified.[7] But other landlords could be unyielding:[8] the Connors' neighbours on the Clanricarde estate had seen their request for rent reductions greeted with threats to evict anyone who did not pay.[9]

As the threat of famine eased in 1880, a major struggle between landlord and tenant began. While this ebbed and flowed in the following years, the key question at stake was who controlled the land, whether tenants would remain vulnerable to the whims of their landlords, or whether these would be bound by legal protections for tenants. It was a zero-sum game in the long term, as most tenants believed that they were the rightful owners of the land. Throughout 1880 the League spread across the country; by the latter half of the year, tensions in Killarrive were on the rise.

In August this resulted in a major meeting of tenants held on the Dunsandle estate. Drawing an estimated ten thousand people, the gathering demanded an end to evictions, and eventually landlordism as a whole. It also issued a stark warning that any who bought cattle seized in lieu of rent, or rented the lands of an evicted tenant, would be considered as traitors.[10] Lord Dunsandle himself was unmoved, and the very next day his bailiffs evicted a tenant who owed £99.[11] That evening the tenant was restored by a large group of men. However, this was only a temporary measure, and when the land was put up for auction, a farmer called Murty Hynes rented it.[12]

The League's response was swift. Organising a demonstration, they knocked the walls around Hynes's lands and destroyed his crops. The fact that the League could mobilize large numbers illustrated the cohesion it enjoyed in the south and west. In previous generations different groups in rural society had been divided, but the Land League did manage to bring together a broad alliance, from farmers down to landless labourers.

While the League officially rejected violence, the threat that individuals would carry out attacks was always implicit and at times explicit. In late 1880 another local landlord in East Galway, John Lambert, woke up to find a grave dug before his house, warning him to stop persecuting tenants.

Throughout 1880 the League also developed what was one of its most effective tactics – social ostracism or boycotting. This tactic was summarized by Charles Stewart Parnell, the president of the League, when he asked a crowd what should be done with a tenant who took the land of another who had been evicted. Some in the crowd replied 'kill him', but Parnell advocated a different strategy, one that would allow a chance for redemption – and until such a moment, he said:

> When a man takes a farm from which another had been evicted you must shun him on the roadside when you meet him, you must shun him in the streets of the town, you must shun him in the shop, you must shun him in the fairgreen and in the marketplace and even in the place of worship, by leaving him alone, by putting him in a moral Coventry, by isolating him from the rest of his country as if he were the leper of old, you must show your detestation of the crime he has committed.[13]

Life for those who were targeted by a boycott often became impossible. Shops and pubs refused service and they were hissed at every turn. This form of social ostracism was not only used on landlords, but also on those who worked for them, and in particular on the 'landgrabber', the person who would take the farm of an evicted tenant.

A few weeks later the tactic of shunning was first tested on Lord Erne's agent Charles Boycott, whose name would forever become synonymous with it. As this method spread, it became highly effective. It not only broke the resolve of those willing to defy the League, but it also polarized the country. It was almost impossible not to take a side if a boycott was called.

What the Connors thought of these developments through 1879 and 1880 is unclear. We can only assume that James and Julia tacitly supported the League, or at least had not openly expressed any opposition to it – they remained on good terms with their neighbours throughout 1880 as the political tension in their community continued to escalate.

In late 1880 the family dynamic changed when Julia Connors became pregnant again, expecting what would be their fifth child. This presumably put considerable financial strain on the family, given the wider economic situation. Whether it was the prospect of another child to feed or simply greed, in the spring James Connors set out on a precarious course of action when he decided to try and take advantage of the growing conflict in his community to his family's advantage.

James Keogh, a neighbour of the Connors family for decades, had come under increasing pressure to support the boycott of their landlord, Lord Dunsandle. To do this had major consequences for him and his family, as he was employed as a bog ranger and bailiff. Yet in fear that he too would be ostracized, and perhaps as a gesture of support for his neighbours, James Keogh resigned his position. For the local tenants, this helped to further isolate the landlord.

But the tenants' celebration was short-lived, as James Connors stepped into the breach and took up the position a few weeks later.[14] That the job appears to have been paid in land only increased the animosity. James Connors had not only broken the boycott, but he was also technically a 'land grabber', one who took the land of an evicted tenant.

As well as being a move against his neighbour, this action meant facing down the wider community. Furthermore, he did this as the situation across Ireland neared open rebellion. In April the British government had introduced a land reform bill in an effort to pacify the country, but this was rejected as too modest by the Land League leaders. A radicalization of the struggle resulted and, in East Galway, the reaction to James Connors' move was predictable.

The entire family was subjected to a boycott. Julia Connors would later recall how they were verbally abused no matter where they went: 'The people treated us badly. They shouted at us when we were coming out of the chapel.'[15] Local shops in Loughrea also refused to serve James or Julia. Not long afterwards, they became reliant on the police to provide them with food.[16] Even though this was done discreetly at night, it only served to distance the Connors from their neighbours. They had clearly chosen a side.

Animosity toward them had continued to mount through the spring of 1881, when they suffered further bad news after Julia's father Edward Kirwan died on 10 May. Having reached the age of seventy-five, Edward Kirwan's death presumably came as little surprise. While he had far exceeded the life expectancy for the time, in his last few years he had been battling with senility.

On Thursday 12 May James Connors hitched horse to cart and the couple set out for her native Sonnagh to bury her father. Given that the Land League was extremely active in that part of the county as well, they may have expected a frosty reception at the wake. This could explain why they did not delay long after the burial, but set out for home almost immediately. On the way they broke their journey at the house of one of the few people who were still talking to them. By midday they had reached Forgehill, only a mile from their own home when suddenly two shots rang out, shattering the silence of the day.

Julia, heavily pregnant and lying in the back of the cart for comfort, watched as four men appeared, one armed with a gun. The gunman took aim at her husband at the head of the cart and, as she heard the shots, James Connors was struck once in the shoulder while a second bullet entered his body through his right arm, lodging close to his spine. The impact of the shots knocked James Connors from the horse and cart. Julia Connors climbed out of the cart and made her way to her husband, who was writhing in agony as blood seeped from his wounds into the dirt of the road.

Lying on the rain-soaked road, Connors is said to have uttered the words, 'I am murdered' through gritted teeth. Julia Connors, kneeling on the roadside, knew all she could do was ease his inevitable passing. Making her way to the local parish priest's house, she returned with Fr Pelly to find her husband still alive. The priest had to kneel in James Connors's blood, which had pooled around his body, to administer the last rites. While the priest prepared him for death, James Connors desperately clung to life, undoubtedly aware of the fate that awaited his pregnant wife when he died. Funerals were never pleasant but his would be a lonely ordeal for his family.

Despite his injuries, James Connors was successfully moved to the family home. There he lingered between life and death while the doctor was sent for but as word spread throughout the surrounding community, it was a journalist from the area who reached the Connors' house first. As he entered what he would later call the 'miserable' dwelling, it was immediately clear that the wounded man would not survive.[17] James Connors could no longer speak. The scene in the house was heart-rending, with Julia Connors surrounded by four children; the youngest, Edmund, only seventeen months old.

The doctor finally arrived not long after the journalist, but all he could do was predict that James Connors would die soon, a prediction that was borne out at half past three that afternoon. The doctor later confirmed that the second bullet had penetrated the lung. The police immediately started an investigation. Three local men were arrested and taken to Bookeen police station that night, but the evidence against them was circumstantial at best.

The key piece of evidence the police had found was a hat band at the scene, but this item was hardly unusual in a society where all men wore hats.

Patrick Keogh, whose father had been evicted, was arrested because footprints from the scene of the shooting led close to his house and his clothes were wet, indicating he had been outside. Similar evidence saw another local man, Edward Fahy, arrested. The final accused was Timothy Dolan. He was secretary of the local branch of the Land League and it was claimed that the hat band fitted his hat.

Meanwhile, a distraught Julia Connors began to turn her thoughts to her husband's funeral. After a decade of marriage, she knew it would be a truly harrowing experience. Funerals had also changed since the end of the Great Hunger. Some old traditions were dying out. Keening, the custom of paying a woman to mourn the deceased in dramatic fashion, was increasingly rare by the 1880s.[18] Nevertheless, the fundamentals of the Irish funerary rites had endured. The wake served as a final celebration of the life of the deceased, but it also allowed friends, family and neighbours to rally around and support the bereaved family.

Yet even still, the boycott endured, and though Julia Connors had been violently widowed while six months pregnant, few would show her sympathy. James Connors had not shown solidarity to his community in life, so they would deny it to him in death – such was the situation that the police felt the need to place a guard around the Connors' house. In a display of intentional disrespect, the Connors' neighbours continued to go about their business, disregarding the grieving family. Very few bothered to visit the house.

James's funeral was also boycotted and in the following weeks, Julia herself continued to be ostracized. At the inquest, she had claimed she could not identify those responsible, but the police had nevertheless continued to hold the three men who had been arrested in custody without trial.

While the acts of the community seemed heartless, even cruel, many of Julia Connors's neighbours had suffered considerably during the Land War. In some instances, those who had refused to pay rent had lost their homes. James Connors had taken advantage of their solidarity for his own ends. In the eyes of many, he had no one to blame but himself.

Three months after James's murder, on 10 August, Julia gave birth to a son, named James after his late father. Even this did not move the community to end the campaign against her. The boycott continued. No one would help her bring in the harvest, and eventually she had to hire labourers from outside the area.[19] Meanwhile, her children had to leave the local school after they were bullied.[20]

This was not merely a petty local squabble. While the fact that they were neighbours may have infused the issue with bitterness, it was also influenced by wider events. Throughout that summer, as the Land War raged on, the surrounding region of East Galway became extremely violent. Sixteen days after James Connors was killed, Peter Dempsey was shot on his way to mass with his children. He had 'grabbed' a farm whose tenant had been evicted.

Five weeks later, on 20 June, local landlord John Lambert narrowly escaped with his life after being shot. By the end of the year another two men had also been shot dead; local constable James Linton, and a man subject to a boycott, Peter Doherty.[21]

All of this took place in the space of six months, within fifteen kilometres of James Connors's house. This level of violence was actually very unusual during the Land War. Despite its name, violence that resulted in fatalities was comparatively rare. Tensions in East Galway were undoubtedly heightened by the reactions of local landlords, particularly the Earl of Clanricarde, who had been unmoved by the suffering of his tenants. Who precisely had been responsible for each of the murders is unclear. Two convictions in the case of Peter Doherty were based on the testimony of informers, but the rest remained unsolved. This was in part a testament to the support the Land League commanded, as people refused to provide testimony even years later.

While many felt to one degree or another that the victims had been the architects of their own demise, the wall of silence was cemented by fear of retribution from the killers. The use of bullets from a Snider rifle in two of the killings indicates that local Fenians were involved. Through the 1870s they had started importing this make of rifle in preparation for an armed insurrection. Local tradition suggests secret societies were also involved.[22]

While the Land War exacted a terrible toll on individuals like Julia Connors, not to mention James himself, it had far-reaching implications for Irish society as a whole. At the height of the conflict, the British government had introduced the 1881 Land Act. Its provisions were extremely limited and it was rejected by the Land League leaders. The following year the government expanded the Act, paying the rent arrears of over 100,000 tenants. While this eased tensions, it was increasingly clear that land ownership as it had existed in Ireland for centuries was no longer sustainable. Landlords were facing increasing constraints, while tenants were realizing their power and influence. Conflict over land would remain the dominant feature of Irish life for decades to come. The Land War had also deepened bitterness and resentment towards the British authorities in many communities. Crown Forces – the police and military – had been used in the eviction of tenants and in the suppression of protests. Meanwhile, thousands had been imprisoned (over a hundred from the Loughrea region alone). Perhaps most damaging was the continued British policy of collective punishment.

In the early 1880s the costs of policing East Galway were not paid by the government, but by local taxes levied on the entire population. This came to the considerable sum of £11,000.[23] Given that all, regardless of their support for the Land League, they still had to pay this tax, it only fostered a sense of injustice even among those ambivalent to or not directly involved in the Land War.

In Killarrive, the legacy of the murder of James Connors lingered for years to come. In 1883 Julia Connors claimed that she could identify three of the four men involved in the killing of her husband as Patrick Keogh, John Ryan and Edward Fahy. The defence claimed that she only did this to aid a claim for compensation, which she had lodged with the government. While Edward Fahy fled, the case against Patrick Keogh and John Ryan collapsed. Meanwhile, the courts cast doubt on Julia Connors's claim that she recognized the men, because she had said many times over the course of 1881 that she had not.[24]

The following year Julia Connors did eventually receive compensation of £800. While this was a considerable sum, she refused to leave Killarrive. She lived side by side with people she suspected as having had a hand in the murder of her husband, and people the courts deemed she had wrongly accused of his murder. One of those men, Patrick Keogh, had spent several years in prison while his elderly parents struggled without his support. It's unclear how she was treated by her neighbours down the years, but given that struggles over land remained a feature of life, it's unlikely that her actions or those of her husband were forgotten.

Nevertheless, Julia remained in Killarive for forty years after James's murder, and died in her home in 1919, at the age of seventy-five. While the specifics of the incident that had claimed her husband's life were by then remote, the wider issues remained. In 1904 Michael Davitt, a leading figure in the Land League, wrote that the struggle had overthrown 'the system of land tenure in Ireland upheld for over two centuries by English rule'.[25] This was in many ways more a prediction than a reflection of things as they then stood. The struggle for land would continue for decades, with more deaths left in its wake by the end.

CHAPTER 7

Emigration

1894

Thou shalt not kill.
(Exodus 20:13)

The US Civil War remains one the most important conflicts in Irish history. While the causes and legacy primarily affected the United States, a staggering 170,000 Irish-born men and women served the Union and Confederate causes.[1] Thousands perished on battlefields from Gettysburg to Bull Run. That Irish-born emigrants would play a decisive role in a war, thousands of miles from Ireland, that had no direct effect on Irish society, was a testimony to the scale of emigration across the Atlantic. While it had reached unprecedented levels during and immediately after the Great Hunger, emigration had continued relentlessly through the nineteenth century. It ebbed and flowed, but it never ceased.

Indeed when twenty-one-year-old Mollie Gilmartin left Ireland in 1890s, the six days she spent in the North Atlantic was one of the few experiences that unified millions of Irish people. Born on 16 June 1873 and raised in rural Sligo in the north-west, the very concept of Irishness was divisive for her generation. There was no consensus on what it meant, who was included or, perhaps more to the point, who was excluded from the Irish nation. For many in her community, Catholicism and a belief in Irish nationalism were considered central to Irish identity. Yet in the north-east in particular, many Irish Protestants considered loyalty to Britain and the British monarchy as intrinsic aspects of their Irish identity.

As children of the Land War, many in Mollie Gilmartin's generation considered landlords and landlordism as anathema to Irishness. Yet there were many landlords who saw no contradiction between their extensive landholdings, their often-British ancestry and their Irish identity. Between these poles of identity there were Protestants who were not landlords, Catholics who were and republicans who believed that religion was a private matter. In short, few – if any – could agree on what it meant to be Irish.

Yet in October of 1893, when Mollie Gilmartin boarded the *Teutonic* ocean liner in the port of Cobh (still named Queenstown at this time) outside Cork city, these differences temporarily melted away. For six days she engaged in what most considered a quintessentially Irish experience – emigration. On board the *Teutonic* she shared with the other passengers her hopes and anxieties about what lay ahead as she faced the uncertainty of starting a new life in North America, tempered by a sadness about the life she was leaving behind.

Although not all Irish people emigrated, the sheer numbers who left the island in the latter half of the nineteenth century ensured virtually no one remained untouched by its effects. Like so many others of her generation, emigration had moulded Mollie Gilmartin's life long before she ever decided to leave her home. Rituals and customs surrounding emigration were central to Irish life at the time. Mollie had seen all too many American wakes – the farewell parties thrown for the departing emigrant. Her older brother Michael was a priest in Chicago, while another brother, John, was training to be a doctor in Baltimore, Maryland.[2] The trauma of these painful farewells was even etched into the landscape. The Bridge of Tears outside Dunfanaghy in County Donegal marked one particularly poignant point of separation, where the community bid farewell to their departing sons and daughters. Every town and village had a point that encapsulated this loss, albeit usually a less poignant local train station or the road to Dublin.

While emigration had become a way of life by the nineteenth century, it was not a recent development. Even by 1845, before the Famine, around one in seven Irish people were already living overseas – yet in the aftermath of those defining years of hunger and misery in the mid-nineteenth century, the numbers leaving Ireland every year had soared. In the four decades between 1851 and 1891 the population of Ireland dropped by 28 per cent due to emigration. By the end of the century the proportion of Irish people living overseas had risen to two in five.[3]

For those who remained at home, the emigrants' memory and absence cast a long shadow. The millions of letters sent back by emigrants informed communities at home of their new lives in Britain or the United States, while remittances sent back to Ireland continued to play a key role in the Irish economy. An estimated ten million dollars was being sent back annually by the end of the century.[4]

While Mollie Gilmartin was raised in what might be called an emigrant society, she was something of an unlikely migrant. She had left in a hasty, poorly planned and secretive manner. She had even lied to her father, Dominick, telling him she was planning to join a convent – news that was greeted with relief by her family. The four years prior to her departure had been difficult, to say the least, in the Gilmartin household. Mollie had endured traumatic teenage years in her native Carrowreilly, in the rural centre of County Sligo, near the town of Ballymote. At the age of fifteen she had been harassed by a local priest, Fr Thomas Doyle. Eventually the bishop of the diocese had to intervene, and Fr Doyle was removed from the parish (though in what was a well-established custom, he was sent to a new one in Australia).

As Mollie tried to move on with her life, the family suffered further setbacks. In August 1892 her mother contracted a fatal kidney infection. Even though her daughter was nineteen, Bridget Gilmartin had remained concerned about Mollie's future until her final breath. She had even gone as far as to ask the new Catholic curate in the parish, Fr Dominick O'Grady, to take care of her daughter. This well-meaning act would ultimately prove fatal.

As the priest took an interest in Mollie Gilmartin's life, the nature of their relationship became the source of gossip in the community. Initially it had appeared harmless, as the priest, a man of about thirty, spent increasing amounts of time with the twenty-year-old Mollie. Their behaviour throughout the summer of 1893 increasingly became the subject of local rumours. In the conservative Irish society of the time, the fact that the two had travelled alone to Belfast was enough to arouse suspicion. When they returned by night train, with Fr O'Grady only reaching the local church at Mullinabreena the following morning, scarcely in time to say morning mass, idle gossip began to harden into concrete fact. It was increasingly clear that the two were having an affair.[5]

Although even speculation about a relationship of this nature was enough to provoke major scandal, Fr O'Grady displayed a remarkable lack of discretion. When a local man, Bill Crosbie, displayed an interest in Mollie Gilmartin, the priest warned him away in no uncertain terms.

After this conversation, Crosbie wrote to her in what appears to have been a guarded threat, revealing that he was fully aware of the relationship. He referred to the priest as her 'loving friend and gallant admirer' and asked her not to tell 'the reverend gentleman' he had written to her.[6] In the context of these alarming rumours, Mollie Gilmartin's announcement that she wanted to leave Carrowreilly and enter a convent can have been nothing short of a relief to her family. Not only would she be under the supervision of a Mother Superior and beyond Fr O'Grady's reach, but it was a career that would enhance the Gilmartin family's reputation.

By the 1890s the Catholic Church had cemented itself as one of the most powerful organizations in Irish society. It increasingly dominated life outside the north-east, not least through its control of healthcare and education. Two of the Gilmartin siblings were already well-respected clerics, and the prospect of Dominick Gilmartin's wayward daughter taking Holy Orders would only strengthen his connections to the Church. He supported his daughter's decision and gave her two hundred pounds. This was presumably her dowry for the convent, which would guarantee her position as a choir nun. Without a dowry, she would have had to spend her life in the convent serving the choir nuns.

Mollie, though, had different plans. She had no interest in a celibate life in a convent, no matter what the status. When she left Carrowreilly in October 1893, instead of making for the convent, she travelled in secret to Dublin, where she met with her lover, Fr O'Grady. While the two appeared to have had plans to elope, Fr O'Grady postponed his departure and returned to Sligo, leaving her to travel on to the US alone, promising he would follow.

From Dublin Mollie Gilmartin continued on her journey, travelling south to the port of Cobh. Situated outside Cork city, this regular port of call for outbound transatlantic liners was a popular point of departure for Irish emigrants. It was there that she finally left Ireland on 18 October 1893 aboard the *Teutonic*, bound for New York.

Even in the 1890s the transatlantic crossing was one of the most daunting aspects of emigration. The ordeal of famine migrants in the mid-nineteenth century had left a strong impression on the Irish psyche – even in the best conditions, a death rate of 1–2 per cent among passengers had been common. This was hardly a surprise, as voyages lasted at least six weeks, the food was dire, and the conditions cramped. But by the 1890s the age of sail had given way to the age of steam and Mollie Gilmartin faced a safer, shorter journey.

Seasickness, which could be severe in the North Atlantic swells, replaced the genuine fears of death. The six-week journey was now a five- or six-day voyage. This, along with falling costs, removed the finality of the migration that earlier emigrants had faced. Steam power made the prospect of returning home a very real possibility for the first time in history. But as the *Teutonic* sailed across the Atlantic, Mollie Gilmartin was fearful that this could still be a one-way trip for her. Although she displayed remarkable naivety at times, she had no illusions about how her actions would be received at home. She knew that once it emerged that she had run away, and even more importantly, why she had left, she would never be able to return home. It's difficult to imagine a more controversial and scandalous course of action in late-nineteenth-century Ireland. She had voiced her fears in a letter to O'Grady, penned as she waited to board the ship in Cobh: 'I am beginning to think I will never see anyone from home ever again.'[7]

On 24 October 1893 the *Teutonic* steamed into New York harbour. Stepping ashore, Mollie Gilmartin began her life as an immigrant in the newly constructed immigration processing station on Ellis Island. Once declared fit, healthy and sane, she continued on to Manhattan. Like many Irish emigrants, she found the city bewildering.

For a woman who had spent her life in rural Sligo, the contrast between her home and her new surroundings was staggering. She had visited Belfast and Dublin, but those cities were dwarfed by the scale of New York and she found the world of colossal industrial US cities alienating and frightening. The city was a metropolis in every sense of the word. In the early nineteenth century – in anticipation of rapid growth – the city fathers had laid out a grid system stretching north across Manhattan at a time when the city could only populate a few blocks of its southern end.

In the following decades the city had grown at an extraordinary rate. In 1800 it had been home to 60,000; by the time of Mollie's arrival in 1894, 2.5 million people were living in New York. To accommodate this population boom, New York had not only spread north across Manhattan but had begun reaching upwards into the skies. The city already had numerous skyscrapers, awe-inspiring structures with no parallel in Ireland.

But the city was nothing if not unequal and alongside the immense wealth that funded these structures was grinding poverty. The tenements where the poor lived – one family to a room in some instances – was the reality most of the newly arrived emigrants endured.

Mollie Gilmartin was largely unimpressed by the city. A few days later she wrote to Fr O'Grady, who was still in Sligo: 'I believe it is a very wicked place. I really never thought that there could be so much badness in the world.'[8]

Although alone in the city, Mollie Gilmartin knew that she would be able to find familiar faces easily. Chain migration, common in nineteenth-century Ireland, had seen whole communities relocate. This was presumably what motivated her to travel to Springfield, Massachusetts, where she found several people she knew, possibly prearranged with Fr O'Grady. Either way, within days of reaching the city she was already able to trade what was essentially local Sligo gossip with her lover: 'Agnes Quinn has been flirting with some of the boys. I intend to be a good girl now. I should be flirting with fellows but indeed I never did it. I know very well you won't believe it.'[9]

But the close-knit nature of these Irish communities would prove a double-edged sword. As she found comfort in the familiar faces, the speed at which her older brother Michael was able to track her down was astonishing. Mollie had reached New York on 24 October, by which time it had become clear to all that she had not entered a convent.

Within weeks of her arrival, Michael had not only learned details of this from home, but had identified her whereabouts in Massachusetts and written to her. Mollie wrote to Fr O'Grady in Sligo, telling him of the letter from her brother: 'I had a letter from Fr. Mick today and he gave me a great scolding. He wants to know what I have done with that £200; who left me in Dublin and who planned my leaving and that I brought disgrace on the family.'[10] Perhaps fearing that Mollie's brother Michael would reach her first, Fr O'Grady decided to follow her to the US almost immediately after receiving this letter. Executing a similar exit to Mollie, he simply upped and left, informing no one, not even his bishop. He boarded a US-bound ship in Cobh on 9 November, reaching the US six days later.*

Two days after arriving in New York, the priest had travelled north to Springfield, where he was reunited with Mollie, but given that he had left his parish in Sligo without

* The timeline of the letters and O'Grady's departure are difficult to pin down: the letters are not dated. He may have received her letters after he returned to Ireland in December. However, her brother Michael appears to have tracked her down less than two weeks after she arrived in Springfield.

notice, and services had to be cancelled that Sunday and the following,[11] news of his departure spread like wildfire. It would take only days, perhaps just hours, before he was tracked to Springfield. Evading what seemed would be an inevitable interrogation from Mollie's relatives in the US, the pair fled Springfield the day after Fr O'Grady's arrival. On 18 November they travelled to Albany, with the priest recording their progress in his diary: 'Left Springfield with MC Gilmartin. Arrived in Albany, Spent first night together. Both resolved to quench it forever. We are so happy.'[12]

Over the following two weeks the couple travelled around the north-east, visiting Niagara Falls, Buffalo, Detroit and Toledo, pretending they were siblings to avoid unwanted attention. When they reached Toledo, Ohio, the two faced a crossroads. Mollie Gilmartin wanted to travel into the mid-west towards St Louis. This would take them further from the major Irish centres of the north-eastern US – New York, Boston and Chicago. Such a move would offer them a better chance of a fresh start, as they would never escape their past in the east, surrounded by Irish communities in constant communication with home. Fr O'Grady, however, was opposed to this idea. He noted in his diary that he thought 'it would end bad'. Instead, they decided to travel to Chicago to meet her brother.

What their precise hopes and intentions were for this meeting were never recorded, but the outcome was predictable. They reached Chicago on 1 December and shortly afterwards they met with Fr Michael Gilmartin, six weeks after Mollie had left home and a month after Fr O'Grady had departed unannounced. Expecting their claim – that they were merely friends – to be believed was naive in the extreme.

Fr Gilmartin instructed Fr O'Grady to return home to Sligo, while Mollie was to remain with him in Chicago. It was hoped that thousands of miles of ocean between them would be enough to break whatever connection the pair had developed. But they remained committed to each other, initially at least. Fr O'Grady did not leave, and the couple tried to keep in clandestine contact. Mollie had taken up lodgings in the parish house of the Church of the Holy Angels, on Oakwood Boulevard in central Chicago. While she received support, she also experienced what could be the oppressive, controlling aspect of Irish emigrant communities, particularly for women. Her movements were monitored and controlled by her brother and the other priests in the house. In the following weeks, her brother and his colleagues maintained an extremely close guard, taking her money and censoring any letters she received. But she found a woman, only referred to as B. Ward, to act as a conduit, through whom she maintained some contact with Fr O'Grady.

By now Fr O'Grady had resolved to return home, temporarily at least. After visiting Philadelphia, he continued on to New York and then across the Atlantic to Sligo. His diary entries on the ship back to Ireland reveal that the priest was increasingly conflicted. His dreams were filled with Mollie trapped in a convent and his mother crying. He reflected that, 'I feel inclined to change my life altogether.'[13]

While he didn't record specific intentions, his actions

in Sligo indicated the priest was beginning to plan a future in which he could remain in the Church, but he also harboured illusions of maintaining the relationship. Arriving back in Ireland on 22 December he was summoned before the Bishop of Achonry, John Lister, to explain his actions. He admitted he had been in the US and requested an exeat – essentially a leave of absence from his post, but not from the priesthood.

In order to find a new parish in the US, the priest needed a reference from Bishop Lister. Although Lister was fully aware of the relationship and had made reference to it in a letter on 19 March 1894, he did not mention Mollie Gilmartin in his reference, although he did allude to Fr O'Grady's departure for the US without permission. Far from a ringing endorsement, the reference at the very least implied Fr O'Grady was unreliable, and included a suggestion of improper behaviour. Lister also inferred that he was happy to be rid of Fr O'Grady, by stating that his erratic behaviour was the reason he was being granted the exeat. This created substantial obstacles for Fr O'Grady's plans to find a new position as a priest in the US.

Meanwhile, in Chicago Mollie Gilmartin was still being watched by her brother, and maintaining contact with Fr O'Grady was increasingly difficult. She was uncertain where he was, and sent letters for collection to the General Post Office in New York. Her last letter of 1893 informed Fr O'Grady that she was being sent from Chicago to Cincinnati.

As she prepared to relocate, she was also increasingly aware of the scandal developing back in Ireland. In that oppressively patriarchal society, she was being blamed for the affair. Furthermore, in a country riven with religious tensions, the case had developed a sectarian dimension as the Protestant community in Carrowreilly found it particularly newsworthy. Mollie Gilmartin informed Fr O'Grady: 'I had a letter that said poor father was dying and that he was not able to walk to the door and that he was praying every other day to die. They have no girl. I believe the people are talking very much about us, especially the Protestants.'[14] Whether she fully realized it or not, she could never return home.

In early January of 1894 she travelled from Chicago to Cincinnati, where she moved in with relatives. The Tibbles were a German-Irish couple living on Chestnut Avenue in the northern suburbs of the city, and here she began to develop medium-term plans. With no possibility of returning home, she needed an income.

In 1890 Cincinnati was somewhat provincial by American standards. Only the ninth-largest city in the US at the time, its population of 296,000 still eclipsed that of Dublin or Belfast. It had a more industrial, perhaps grittier feel than New York but this major industrial centre on the Ohio river offered emigrants who ventured there a wealth of opportunities. Labelled 'Porkopolis' due to extensive meat-production facilities, a deathly stench from the slaughterhouses palled over the city. By the late nineteenth century the Irish were well established, making up 20 per cent of the population. Mollie was able to secure a job working in the Pulvermacher Galvanic Company.

This was a dramatic shift in her life. In Sligo, her year had been structured around the natural cycles of the farming calendar. In Cincinnati she had to rise at six each morning and take a tram into work no matter what the season or weather. Difficult as this adjustment was, it had the potential to offer a young woman like her a level of freedom unattainable in Ireland. US wages were several times higher than those in Ireland,[15] while cosmopolitan city life in Cincinnati offered endless distractions. But distractions or no, in Cincinnati she remained under the strict control of relatives.

Even so, she had little interest in forging a new life there – she clung to hopes of a future with Fr O'Grady. She had been able to inform him of her whereabouts, and he prepared to cross the Atlantic for the third time in as many months, leaving Ireland in mid-January. By the 22nd, the priest had reached the US once again. He had hatched a plan that would see the pair move to California, putting them beyond the reach of her relatives for good. When he communicated this idea, Mollie flatly refused. She wanted to resolve matters with her family before she embarked on such a drastic course of action: 'I shall not go to California for years to come or at least til I know that I can go without being afraid of anyone.'[16] This infuriated the priest and he replied in the following weeks with claims that she had misled him, blaming her for his wider predicament. Mollie Gilmartin stood her ground and issued him with an ultimatum. Feeling aggrieved that he had essentially left her with her brother in Chicago, she stated clearly that she would not leave Cincinnati with him unless he left the priesthood.[17]

While the relationship was clearly under enormous strain, the entire situation became extremely serious for

Mollie when she started to realize something was wrong with her. While she never explicitly stated it, her letters inferred that something had changed – she was pregnant. She talked about being sick, her condition, and her desires to end her problems.[18] Fr O'Grady's reaction was not recorded, but the news doesn't appear to have had much of an impact on him. It certainly did not deter him from the course of action he had set out on back in Sligo. Displaying the characteristics of a man divorced from reality, he remained determined to resume his career in the Church while maintaining a relationship of some kind with his lover.

Dealing with their escalating problems was complicated further by the fact that Mollie did not want to risk meeting him in person. There were numerous other Irish priests and common acquaintances from Sligo in Cincinnati, and she was fearful that he would be recognized on the street. She was also afraid that if her family knew the pair were in contact, she would be moved again.

As references to what had been referred to as her 'condition' ceased, the priest became convinced she was being unfaithful. She repeatedly tried to assuage him, while remaining adamant that she would not leave Cincinnati with him and that he should not visit her. Eventually the priest ignored her and arrived in Cincinnati. By March, Fr O'Grady had become increasingly erratic and aggressive. On one occasion he arrived at the front door of the Tibbles' house, demanding a letter of exoneration, which he wanted for his bishop back in Ireland. Mollie refused to meet him, but wrote a letter O'Grady demanded denying the two had been in a relationship.

Addressing the bishop of Achonry, John Lister, she said,'My lord, I can state Fr O'Grady is not the cause of my leaving home. He had not anything to do with it. I left Ireland because I did not want to stay there.' This however would not satisfy the priest. [19]

Fr O'Grady became obsessive. As she did not want to meet, he rented a room across the street from the Tibbles' house and began to stalk her. He was also seen walking up and down Chestnut Avenue in a way that made people suspicious, and was described as 'acting like a crazy man'. Unsurprisingly, Mollie Gilmartin had become increasingly fearful of his intentions and began to ask Mrs Tibbles to walk her to the tram each morning before work – but on 25 April, not long after she boarded the tram, Fr O'Grady appeared and hailed the driver, who stopped. The priest demanded Mollie talk to him. Relenting, she alighted and the two were seen walking away together.

While it was unclear what precisely they were discussing, their conversation became increasingly heated. Then Fr O'Grady snapped, shouting, 'You do as I tell you and you listen to me!'[20] before grabbing her by the hair and throwing her to the ground. She started to run away, but he drew a gun and shot Mollie several times as she tried to flee, killing her on the spot. Then he discharged two more bullets into her lifeless corpse before kicking her body, shouting 'Now will you marry me?'[21] Walking out into the road, as if he was going to take his own life, he pointed the gun towards his chest and fired, but somehow missed.[22] He then turned and threw the gun back at Mollie Gilmartin's corpse.[23]

Fr O'Grady fled on foot, with a crowd of men giving

chase, but only reached the end of the street before running directly into a policeman, Jinks Kelly. As Mollie Gilmartin's lifeless body was carried into the Tibbles' house, Fr O'Grady was arrested. Evidence that he had been planning a murder-suicide for a considerable amount of time was soon discovered. Among his possessions, the police found a vial of arsenic, which had been bought in Philadelphia. Placed on a table in front of the prisoner, Fr O'Grady snatched the vial, but his second attempt at suicide failed when a policeman grabbed the poison.[24]

As the story broke, the case proved sensational in Cincinnati. Within twenty-four hours of Mollie Gilmartin's murder, *The Cincinnati Enquirer* had obtained possession of Fr O'Grady's diary and his letters from her. These were printed in full and prurient detail. In the increasingly globalized world of the time, initial summaries of the story spread across the US in a matter of hours and reached Ireland via transatlantic telegram cables in time for the following day's newspapers. The Gilmartin family may well have learned of her death when a brief story including her and Fr O'Grady's names appeared in the *Cork Constitution* newspaper on 26 April 1894.[25] Despite the sensational nature of the story, it did not receive the attention one might expect. Irish nationalist publications, whose readership was by and large Catholic, chose not to cover the story in any great detail, presumably because of Fr O'Grady's clerical background. Overseas, there was no such self-censorship. The story was reported far and wide, although in some accounts Fr O'Grady was portrayed as 'another priestly victim of Mollie Gilmartin's charms'.[26] The coverage was largely unforgiving to her.

In Cincinnati, a strange yet constant theme in the reporting was speculation as to whether she had been a virgin when she died. Her letters and the priest's diary, which had been printed extensively in *The Cincinnati Enquirer*, in several places inferred an active sex life. Furthermore, Mary Tibbles, her relative, testified at the inquest that Mollie Gilmartin herself had told her that she had been sleeping with the priest.[27] This became a more prominent issue when Mollie's brother Michael went to considerable lengths to present her as a virgin, and insisted that some of her letters were forgeries. Meanwhile the coroner, who initially claimed that he was unable to shed light on the matter, reversed this position after a private meeting with Fr Gilmartin. [28]

Over the following year the Ohio legal system struggled with how best to proceed with the prosecution of Fr O'Grady. While he was charged with first-degree murder, there was doubt about whether he was mentally capable of standing trial. Already in May 1894, the priest had started to refuse food in what seems to have been another attempt to take his own life, but after he was force-fed he began to voluntarily eat once more.[29] In October he was deemed fit to stand trial.[30]

Over the following months Fr O'Grady's mental health deteriorated, and he attempted suicide for a fourth time in April 1895. A prison orderly intervened and saved his life.[31] When the trial began on 26 November, Fr O'Grady was so ill, he had to be brought to and from the court on a bed.[32] He collapsed the following day and the trial was yet again postponed.[33] In March 1896 Fr Dominick

O'Grady was declared insane and moved to Long View Asylum, where his health slowly began to improve.

In June 1898 the priest managed to escape from the asylum, but then returned of his own volition.[34] Over a year later, on 21 November 1899,[35] he escaped again. This time he did not return.

Fr O'Grady never resurfaced after his second escape from Long View Asylum. Rumours at the time claimed he had been spirited across the US border to Canada, but these appear to have been rooted more in anti-Catholic conspiracy theory than fact. In more recent decades, it was claimed that he served as a priest after his escape,[36] but the assertion appears to be based on a case of mistaken identity. Fr Dominick F. O'Grady, who murdered Mollie Gilmartin in Cincinnati in April 1894, had been a priest in the parish of Mullinabreena. Meanwhile, his contemporary in the neighbouring parish of Kilshalvy was the slightly younger Fr Dominick J. O'Grady.

Yet amid the drama of the prosecution and O'Grady's escape, Mollie Gilmartin herself was largely forgotten. Given her affair was a source of shame for her family, they did little to draw attention to her case. She was buried in an unmarked grave and, with no direct relatives in the city, her story faded into obscurity. In 2011 relatives from Ireland erected a tombstone for Mollie in St Joseph's New Cemetery in the city.

CHAPTER 8

The Asylum

1890

> The spirit of a man will sustain his infirmity; but a wounded spirit who can bear?
>
> (Proverbs 18:14)

The Land League had illustrated the growing power of what had once been dismissed as the lower orders. Its drive for change in Ireland had tangible effects – self-confident tenants had won increased rights. Evictions could no longer take place at the whim of a landlord. In such cases they could expect co-ordinated and fierce resistance. There was also growing agreement that the only long-term solution to the land issue was the transfer of farms from landlords to tenants. This might still be years away for most but the fact it was being entertained illustrated a major shift in Irish society that would have been inconceivable in 1850.

Alongside these advances the increase in farm sizes resulting from emigration saw many live far less precarious existences than their ancestors. While there were still frequent food shortages in the west, larger farms had led to a considerable increase in living standards in Irish society across the board. Housing was also dramatically improved. In 1841 around one-third of Irish people were living in what was classified as fourth-class housing. These were little more than mud huts, scarcely fit for human habitation. By 1891, when the last census of the nineteenth century was conducted, fewer than one in twenty families inhabited such houses.

Despite these advances Mary Hart of Ballyneale in County Kilkenny remained deeply concerned for her only son Edmund's future through the 1880s[1] While the thirty-year-old's contemporaries enjoyed a considerably better living standards than their grandparents, Edmund was among a cohort trapped in poverty.

The rising tides of change did not raise all boats, or at least did not raise all boats equally. The city centre of Dublin had continued on a downward trajectory into a morass of poverty. While rural Ireland bid farewell to the mud hut, many who relocated to the city found the urban equivalent – the tenement – in abundance. The city's working class were mired in low wages, precarious employment and limited opportunities. There was also a rural equivalent to the city's poor – people like Edmund Hart, who were in no position to avail of the improvements in society.

While the Land League's successor, the National League, continued to deliver considerable improvements in rural Ireland, these had bypassed Hart. The major concessions extracted from successive British governments came in the form of loans for tenants to buy their farms, and increased legal protections against the harsher instincts of their landlords. Edmund Hart, however, like all landless labourers, got little if any benefit from these reforms. He had no land, so increased tenancy rights were meaningless, while the loans on offer were specifically for tenants to buy their farms, not for labourers to pull themselves out of poverty.

While he watched on as the lives of farmers around him improved due to land reforms, the contrast with the conditions of his own life must have been stark. He lived with his widowed mother Mary in what were abysmal conditions. Their house was not actually a house at all, but a disused office in what was known as the 'coal yard', situated outside Ballyneale in the south of the county, between the cities of Kilkenny and Waterford. The coal yard was a disused depot once used by boats on the River Nore. Designed to facilitate the transport of goods along the river, the three-sided enclosure had no protection from the Nore, rendering it damp year-round. Although technically not a fourth-class house because it had three rooms – a kitchen, a bedroom, and a loft – it was scarcely any better. Edmund Hart's future must have felt incredibly limited. Mary knew her son's chances of escaping this poverty were slim: there was every chance that if something didn't change, he would grow old poor and alone. Once he could no longer work, his only option would be the dreaded workhouse.

Edmund Hart's best hope in life, perhaps his only hope of having even a modicum of security, was getting a farm of his own – but given that access to land remained at a premium, particularly in the rich farmlands of South Kilkenny, and that he had only a meagre income as a fisherman, this was always a distant dream. If he was to marry a woman with land, or who was due to inherit it, then things would improve for him. But here too there were obvious problems.

While marrying a woman with land would allow him to escape a life of penury, there were few reasons to expect a woman with such prospects to marry a man with none – even finding a partner to share his poverty with was a challenge in the 1880s. Since the 1850s the demographics of Irish society had been changing. As women, and in particular young single women, emigrated in larger numbers than their male counterparts, the men who remained at home found it harder to marry.

In Edmund Hart's local area, the situation, while not as stark as in poorer counties like Mayo, was still concerning. By 1891 men outnumbered women, particularly in the age cohort eligible for marriage. The census calculated that there were 695 single or widowed men aged between fifteen and forty in Hart's area. This compared to just 591 widowed or single women.[2] Even if every one of those women married, 14 per cent of the men would remain single. By the late 1880s Mary Hart's hopes that her son would not be among their number were fading.

With all this in mind, it was somewhat against the odds when Edmund announced to his mother that he was not only marrying, but marrying a woman with land. Margaret Grace lived with her own widowed mother, who rented six acres of land in Russellstown on the opposite bank of the Nore. The farm was small, but it was better than nothing. Although there was no contract or written agreement, custom dictated that Edmund and Margaret would take on the lease once his mother-in-law passed away. Therefore, when the couple married on 17 February 1887, Edmund's life changed dramatically. He left the coal yard and moved into his mother-in-law's home with his new bride. While he continued working as a fisherman on the Nore, he now also worked his mother-in-law's land, improving the farm that would be his in time. However, the blissful domestic life he might have envisaged during the lonely nights in the coal yard never materialized, and the marriage rapidly fell apart.

While divorce was not an option for Catholics like Edmund and Margaret, separation was a course such couples often pursued when their marriages collapsed. By 1890, after only three years of marriage, Edmund Hart had moved out. What exactly had transpired between them was never clear, but it was suggested by some that Edmund's mother Mary had been the source of the disagreement.

After their separation Edmund returned to live with his widowed mother in the disused coal merchant's office on the western bank of the Nore, although he maintained hopes that he might be able to repair his relationship with Margaret. But he did not relinquish his hold on the land and each day he continued to cross the Nore and work the fields rented by his wife's mother.

Tend the land as he may, relations between Edmund Hart and the Graces failed to improve. In May 1890 Margaret and her mother took drastic action. They sold the lease back to the landlord, left their home in

Russellstown and moved to Killeen, several miles away. Relations with Edmund Hart had deteriorated to such an extent that they did not even inform him of their decision. Oblivious to his wife's departure, Hart continued to cross the river and work the land. Little did he know he now had no legal standing other than that of a squatter working someone else's land. Predictably, the landowner, John Howlett, despatched bailiffs along with the police to remove him. When they arrived, he was bewildered and shocked. Only at this point did he learn that the lease had been sold back and that he was powerless to prevent it. Despite having invested three years of work in the property, it would shortly be rented to another tenant, who would benefit from his labours. Furthermore, whatever hopes he may have harboured of rekindling his marriage, it was now clearly over. Margaret obviously wanted nothing to do with him.

Now aged thirty-five and separated, a long, lonely life stretched out before Edmund Hart. He could not remarry or divorce. Economically, his prospects were dire. The farm had represented the best chance – perhaps the only chance – of having land of his own, but it had been taken from him. There were few options left open to him. Some would have considered emigration, but this was a daunting prospect for Edmund. Although a later census would suggest he was literate, his experiences as a rural labourer offered little by way of skills that could be useful in the US cities to which most Irish emigrants were drawn. In 1907 the nationalist politician Laurence Ginnell had bluntly stated of the Irish population: 'While the physically and mentally healthy and energetic emigrate, the physically and mentally inefficient and dependent stay at home – some for want of courage, and some because they would not be admitted into a new country.'[3]

This state of affairs had been recognized as early as 1890,[4] and there was much to suggest that Edmund Hart fell into the latter category. In his dealing with his wife and her mother, he had displayed a degree of naivety that would have been ruthlessly exploited in a strange environment like New York, Liverpool, or even Dublin.

To add to his mounting plights, in the coming months, evidence that Edmund was suffering from severe mental health problems also emerged. While this would be a major challenge for anyone trying to enter the US, it was also a considerable problem in a place like Ballyneale. Hart began to threaten violence against those he perceived as responsible for his plight. He threatened to kill his mother-in-law, his wife, the landlord, even his own mother. This was not merely anger at feeling he had been hard done by. Neighbours commented that, although he had spells of lucidity, he regular engaged in 'romancing' or what one person referred to as acting foolishly.

For his mother Mary, this presented a major problem – what to do about her clearly unwell son. She could seek help from the authorities, but this was a path many people were reluctant to travel, for good reason.

The nineteenth century had seen dramatic changes in public healthcare in Ireland. The introduction of vaccines in the early 1800s had eradicated smallpox. Limited free public healthcare had also been introduced through a network of dispensaries. Major surgery was still highly risky and left a lot to be desired, but the foundations of a system which would lead to a dramatic rise in life expectancy in the twentieth century were being put in place.[5] But an outlier in this positive development was how those suffering from poor mental health were treated. While the changes that had taken place on this front were considerable, they could hardly be considered improvements. Mary Hart had good reason to be fearful about what would happen to her son if she informed the authorities that he was suffering from psychiatric problems.

In the early years of the century people suffering from poor mental health were frequently cared for in the community, or in more serious situations incarcerated in prisons. The care provided by communities varied widely. While in some places people were cast into a pit, the Census Commissioner William Wilde described how the poor in Irish-speaking communities had what he called a 'superstitious veneration'[6] of people with poor mental health, and did not stigmatize them. What Mary Hart feared was the growing intolerance that had accompanied government intervention.[7] The authorities had fallen back on what was the nineteenth-century solution to social problems, the institution; in this instance, the asylum. In 1830 there had only been four district asylums in Ireland, which housed 300 people. These were supported by a network of private asylums for those who could afford them. However, in 1838 the Dangerous Lunatic Act made provisions for dozens of county asylums to be erected, which were largely finished by the end of the Great Famine.

Having affected every aspect of society, the Great Hunger inevitably had a traumatic psychological toll on the population. In the later nineteenth century a physician commented: 'It seems probable that children born and partially reared amidst the horrors of the Famine and the epidemics of disease that followed it were so handicapped in their nervous equipment as to be weak-minded from the start or to fall victims to mental disease later'.[8] This mental toll seems to have contributed to a sharp increase in the numbers of people being incarcerated in asylums. Indeed, while the population as a whole was rapidly declining, the numbers of the institutionalized increased. By 1890 there were 16,026 people deemed to be of 'unsound mind' incarcerated in Irish institutions.[9]

While clearly a defining generational trauma, this sea-change in levels of incarceration could not solely be attributed to the Famine. A nearly 40 per cent increase in what were termed 'lunatics' throughout the 1880s was not necessarily a direct result of the Great Hunger, but to another related national phenomenon – emigration. In 1890 it was speculated that the sheer quantities of people leaving Ireland was revealing the true extent of mental health problems in the country, as those afflicted no longer had family members to take care of them.[10]

But the Great Hunger and emigration were not the only factors behind the dramatic rise in numbers incarcerated in institutions. The increase in diagnoses in part arose from the growing interest in mental health issues at this time, and the extremely broad criteria for diagnosis of it. Those confined included many who were not mentally unwell, such as people suffering from neurological conditions like epilepsy, or developmental conditions such as Down Syndrome. Incarcerating people who had no business being in asylums inevitably led to overcrowding. The conditions inside the asylums were often appalling. For those with mild conditions, or no conditions at all, the harrowing prison-like institutions had shocking impacts on their mental health. Regimes of silence matched with dire food was enough to strain the mind and body of even the healthiest of patients.[11]

The overriding idea was one of segregation – to protect the healthy from those suffering from poor mental health. On a local level, if Mary Hart raised her son's conditions with the authorities, she knew Edmund would be sent to the Kilkenny District Asylum, a large, imposing Gothic structure at the edge of the city, thirty-five kilometres away. It had garnered an awful reputation. Largely unchanged since its construction during the Great Famine, in 1890 the Inspector of Asylums, Edward Maziere Courtenay, found the institution overcrowded and run down. Describing the diet offered to patients there, he said: 'The diet does not in my opinion appear to be in accordance with the food in general use amongst the Irish peasantry, and is inferior to the diet given in many Irish asylums, but it is useless to go into the matter at present as no improvement can be attempted until a proper kitchen has been provided.'[12]

Mary Hart elected to try and care for her son, but his mental state continued to decline. The Harts' neighbours were also becoming increasingly aware of his condition. By Wednesday 9 July, Michael Finn and other neighbours in Ballyneale had become concerned about his welfare. Such was their concern, Edmund Hart's health was raised with a local physician by a member of the community during a chance encounter in the nearby town of New Ross. The physician, Dr Walsh, already acquainted with the Harts, agreed to visit Edmund on his way home.[13]

On arriving at Ballyneale the doctor made his way to the coal yard, where he found Edmund Hart in good health. He spent about forty minutes talking to him and, in his own words, found him to be 'clear and recollected' on every topic they discussed. While Dr Walsh did not doubt the testimonies of neighbours – that Edmund Hart was acting strangely and threatening to drown himself – there was nothing he could do. He had not witnessed this behaviour and, as was common, no one in Ballyneale was willing to testify to an authority figure about it. But that night Edmund Hart began to display symptoms of ill-health once again. Michael Finn, who spent several hours at the Hart household with Edmund, recalled he was 'rambling out of his mind'.

The next morning a local policeman, Sgt Meehan, called to the house, but Mary Hart denied there was any problem at all. Mary claimed that reports of Edmund's ill-health were 'all lies and stories of the neighbours'. For this well-meaning gesture to protect her son, Mary Hart would pay the ultimate price.[14]

After the policeman departed, no one saw either Mary or Edmund for the rest of day. Later that evening Finn, who had been at the house the previous night, called to the coal yard at nine o'clock. Seeing no one around, he approached the door and called to the Harts, but no one answered. A further inquiry was greeted again with silence, and after receiving no reply the third time, Finn turned to leave. It was then that he heard noise from within the house, which caused him to call out a final time. At the fourth call, it was Edmund Hart who responded from the shadows. Finn asked how Mary was, and Edmund solemnly replied that his mother was dead. [15]

The harrowing scene that presented itself would burn itself into Finn's memory for the rest of his life. As he entered the Hart household he left the bright summer's evening and his eyes slowly adjusted to the darkness within. Seeing no one in the kitchen he moved towards the inner bedroom. It was there he found Edmund. It took Finn a few seconds to take in the awful scene before him. He first saw Edmund, covered in blood. As his eyes moved around the dark room, illuminated only by a small window, he saw the bed was also covered in blood. It was only when he saw Mary Hart that the horror of what had happened dawned on him.

Edmund was lying on top of his mother. The seventy-five-year-old had clearly been murdered by her son. Even though Finn feared for his own safety, he rushed over and pulled the man off his mother. Edmund Hart lashed out and struck him to the ground but Finn was able to overpower him and forcibly dragged him to a neighbour's house. The police were called from the nearby Cooleen station, just over a kilometre away.[16]

When they arrived, Finn gave them the details of the horrific scene he had witnessed on entering the bedroom – he had found Edmund Hart eating the flesh from his mother's face. The mutilation of Mary Hart's body was severe. Her face above the nose was almost unrecognizable. Her son had also removed part of her intestine, most of her other organs, as well as the flesh from her thighs.

Searching for weapons, the police found a shovel with blood and hair on the handle and an axe in the loft, also covered in blood. A sharp blade, which doctors believed was also used, was never located. This, it was assumed, had been thrown into the nearby river.

As an inquest was convened at the house, Edmund Hart was first taken to the police station in Rosbercon and from there across the river to New Ross. He had breathed free air for the last time in his life.

In his cell, his mood fluctuated dramatically, from relative calm to loud screaming. He was heard to weep aloud and cry out, 'I killed my mother and she was a good mother to me.' [17] Edmund appears to have been in the midst of a psychotic episode and had lost all sense of reality. When the police entered his cell they found him under the bed, chewing the mattress. He cried out that the devil was in the bed and the cell was full of demons. A doctor noted that while he was clearly having hallucinations, he did have moments of sanity, and Edmund Hart was declared fit to stand trial. The following day he was taken to court in Rosbercon, where the case was put back to a further hearing as the authorities tried to grapple with the case. While Edmund was held in the local bridewell, the community in Ballyneale reeled from what had happened in their midst. While they gathered to bury Mary Hart in the village graveyard, the police continued to search the Hart household in the coal yard trying to understand what had happened – they had still not found the weapon used.

Four days after killing Mary Hart, Edmund was brought before the courts for a second hearing in Rosbercon. While he was formally charged with murdering his mother, the police asked for more time. The search for the weapon used – a sharp blade of one kind or another – had continued but try as they may the police could not find it. After this hearing Burke was taken from Rosbercon and brought to the larger Kilkenny jail.

Although his full trial was due to take place at the winter assizes in Kilkenny, his state of mind disintegrated further in September 1890 – such was his condition that he was removed from prison to the district asylum. When his case came before the judiciary that winter, Edmund Hart did not appear. Instead Dr Myles, the physician in the asylum, provided testimony that he was insane and the jury came to the decision that he was not fit to stand trial by reason of insanity.

After this verdict Edmund Hart's journey deeper into the institutional labyrinth of late-nineteenth-century Ireland continued. Having been imprisoned in a police station in New Ross, then Kilkenny jail, and then Kilkenny District Asylum, he was transported to the Central Criminal Lunatic Asylum in Dundrum, County Dublin. Here Edmund Hart would spend the rest of his days, incarcerated with other mentally unwell patients who had committed violent offences. He would never be released.

His only interaction with the wider world was through the pages of the annual inspector's report. In 1890 he appeared in the report appendix, in an anonymized list of the cases admitted to the asylum. While some details are altered in the report, his initials, age and crime identify him. There was a brief synopsis of his health:

> Reported as depressed in spirits, sullen, and morose, and refusing his food, believing it to be poisoned. On admission his face had a very heavy, brutalised expression. He has, however, behaved quietly, and his mental condition is much improved since his admission.[18]

The asylum system, designed to segregate the mentally ill from society, was effective in that regard at least. Edmund Hart was quickly forgotten. Outside the walls of the asylum, a scandal surrounding Charles Stewart Parnell was growing. The man who had been the President of the Land League, and who had been known as the uncrowned king of Ireland, had committed what was a cardinal sin; he had been engaged in an affair with a married woman for years. While such dalliances were commonplace, Parnell's naming in a divorce case created moral outrage. Wider Irish society was divided into pro- and anti-Parnell camps. Although Parnell would die in 1891, the bitter division haunted Irish politics for a generation.

But sensational political stories such as Parnell's downfall, or even the horrific murder of Mary Hart, masked what was a growing problem in Irish society. Decades of stigmatization of people with mental health problems, combined with the often dire manner in which they were treated, created an atmosphere where few wanted to admit to mental problems they or loved ones endured. All the while, this was happening in an ageing society, as emigration syphoned away younger generations. People who struggled with mental health were thus increasingly likely to be looked after by their elderly parents, a situation complicated still further by poverty. These older carers were in some instances economically dependent on their unwell adult children. Edmund Hart, for example, provided for his mother with his income as a fisherman. At every turn there were reasons for her not to seek aid. This had predictable results.

Mary Hart was not the only older woman to suffer a violent attack of this nature during this period. In fact, three years after her murder, the village of Ballyneale – home to less than 100 people – witnessed a remarkably similar incident. On that occasion, another fisherman, thirty-four-year-old Richard Keeffe, attacked his mother in July 1893.

Keeffe, it was later stated, was suffering from delusions, or 'religious mania' as it was described at the time. He had become convinced that, while God had ordered him to perform a miracle, his mother was trying to stop him. On 8 July he attacked her with an axe. It was only the intervention of a neighbour that saved her life.[19]

Meanwhile, behind the walls of the Central Criminal Lunatic Asylum, Edmund Hart remained out of sight and out of mind. He lived on for several decades. He was registered in the 1901 census, then aged forty-six, and again recorded by his initials, E.H. His identity was discernible by his place of origin, Kilkenny, and the length of time he had been in the institution, ten years and three months. Thirteen years later, on 29 August 1914, now listed as Edward Hart, he died in the asylum in Dundrum. Aged sixty, his cause of death was septic pneumonia.

Irish independence eight years later offered little succour to those suffering from poor mental health. The rate of incarceration in asylums continued to increase. By the mid-twentieth century, the numbers in Irish asylums had grown from 17,350 in 1891 to 21,000 in 1961. When the smaller population of the country is allowed for – arising from partition of the island in the 1920s and ongoing emigration – this represents a sharp increase. In 1891 around one in every 300 Irish people was incarcerated in an asylum; by 1961 this had risen to one in 133. This did little to improve society's general understanding of mental health. If anything, segregation only increased stigmatization of the mentally unwell.

Although deinstitutionalization of mental health had begun in the late 1980s, tragedies resulting from poor understanding of it remained a feature of Irish life. In 2000 John Carthy, a man suffering from serious mental health problems, was shot and killed by Gardaí after a two-day armed standoff at his home. A subsequent public inquiry, the Barr Tribunal, would state in its findings that the widespread lack of understanding of mental illness and how to deal with it engendered by Irish society had led to Carthy's death. Similar sentiments could have been written about Mary Hart in 1890. Her desperate attempts to protect her son from a society that wilfully misunderstood and mistreated people like Edmund so poorly contributed to her tragic death.

CHAPTER 9

Divided Loyalties

1919

> The elders have ceased from the gate, the young men from their musick.
>
> (Lamentations 5:14)

In her later years, Bridget Wright carried the scars of grief that marked what had been a hard life. Although she was predeceased by several children, it was the murder of her brother Bill in Waterford back in 1919 that haunted her dreams. He was one of the thousands killed in the political violence sweeping Ireland in those years, but in terms of understanding the personal tragedy visited on her family, the major political motives for his death were cold, intangible and amorphous.

It was easier for Bridget to focus her grief on the multiple small decisions that led to Bill's death. What if he had never moved to Waterford? What if he had never gotten involved in local politics? Even though she had no hand or part in his death, Bridget may well have blamed herself.

Seven years before Bill's death, in 1912, she and her husband William had moved house, relocating their family to Harrington's Lane. At the time she could not have foreseen the political turmoil that would sweep through Waterford or that Bill would follow in her footsteps and meet his violent end outside the door of her new home – back in 1912 the move had been a positive development even if tinged with sadness. When Bridget had packed up the last of her family's belongings at their old house in Smith's Lane, it was an emotional farewell to a community where she had lived, loved, grieved and above all, endured the hardships that life had inflicted on her.

The lane, dirty, narrow and dark as it was, had been where she had met her husband, William – they had been neighbours before they were lovers. After their marriage in August 1888 the couple had gone on to start their own family in the narrow cul-de-sac. Smith's Lane had also seen some of the darkest days of the Wrights' marriage. In 1902 she had watched her daughter Kate succumb to whooping cough at the age of just eight months. Of the nine children Bridget had brought into the world, three had died by 1912.

Such hardship may have been common in working-class communities, but this did little to soften the blow of such a loss. But for Bridget Wright and thousands like her, there was a certain inevitability to tragedies like these. They were inflicted on the poor by the conditions they lived in. Overcrowding was a common problem for working-class communities throughout Ireland, from Belfast to Cork. On Smith's Lane, for example, 145 people lived in just twenty-one houses in 1911. Ventilation was a particular problem in the lanes of Waterford: the houses had been built down alleys and back streets where there was no adequate space, with little more than a few feet between them on either side of the street. In many cases there were no backyards, leaving the houses dark and lacking circulation of fresh air. The practice of keeping pigs, essential to the household economy, only added to the unhygienic environment.[1]

In 1912 the move from Smith's Lane to Harrington's Lane offered Bridget something of a step up in life. She could never have foreseen where it would lead, or the tragedy that would befall her brother Bill on the lane seven years later. He was twenty-five years younger than Bridget and had yet to move in with her family.

In 1912 Harrington's Lane was a step up for the family. Another cul-de-sac off Barrack Street, it was closer to where the city became open countryside. This lane was less crowded; the house, number 10, was similar in size to their old one, comprising just three rooms between the eight members of the family, but they shared the lane with far fewer people. The fourteen houses were home to just sixty-five residents. Though an improvement, Harrington's Lane was still far from ideal: the Wrights had no running water, and the nearest pump was on Barrack Street.[2] Nevertheless, the family quickly adapted to life in their new home, a transition eased by familiarity – their next-door neighbour at number 9 was another of Bridget's brothers, Thomas Grant.

Despite the less cramped surroundings, the Wrights could not escape the tragedy that had marked their marriage. In December 1913, not long after they had moved in,

Bridget's sixteen-year-old son James died in the house from tuberculosis. Then, in what was arguably an even greater blow, her youngest daughter Mary, just six years old, died from meningitis in March 1914. She was the fifth child to predecease Bridget, who had yet to turn fifty.

The tragedy that defined Bridget Wright's life at times seemed to be part of an unbroken link through previous generations, a lineage defined by grinding poverty, though there was no doubt that Irish life was changing for the better in many ways. While this change had not come fast enough to save her deceased children, those who did survive would have better opportunities in life than Bridget had been offered.

From its humble beginnings back in the 1830s, the public education system was beginning to have a dramatic impact. Bridget Wright had received the most basic of educations. She claimed that she could write, but never signed her own name – on official documents she marked her signature with an X. By contrast, her three oldest children, William, Nora, and James, were all literate.

In general, the decades following the Land War of the 1880s had seen continued change and rising expectations in Ireland, and the tangible if modest improvements on an individual level were mirrored by significant political changes. Demands for Home Rule, increased autonomy for Ireland within the United Kingdom, had grown with each passing decade. Liberal Party governments in Britain had even brought forward Home Rule legislation on two occasions, only to see it defeated in parliament's upper chamber, the House of Lords, which was dominated by the Conservatives. Realizing that ignoring the issue was not an effective strategy, staunch opponents of Home Rule in the Conservative Party resolved to take action. By introducing a raft of major reforms, they hoped that these would stem the rising discontent in Ireland. While largely aimed at the more well-off, these reforms would eventually even impact life at 10 Harrington's Lane.

Central to these reforms – designed to 'kill Home Rule with kindness' – was the 1898 Local Government Act. As its title suggested, this created local governments across the island of Ireland. Significantly, the bill enfranchised the heads of all households and did not exclude women. Therefore, working-class heads of households, including widows or single women, could vote in local elections even though they remained disenfranchised from national elections.

Were Bridget's husband William to die she would, for the first time in her life, be eligible to cast a vote, a measure once considered inconceivable for women. However, this extension of voting rights to a larger part of the population did not have the impact its conservative architects had envisaged. Rather than shore up support for the status quo, it had the opposite effect: if anything it served to raise expectations in Ireland, and the demands for change continued throughout the early years of the twentieth century.

Politics in the opening years of the century also made its presence felt in more subtle ways. The Gaelic League, which aimed to arrest the decline of the Irish language and revive Irish culture, spread across the country. Although the League proclaimed itself apolitical, its emphasis on the distinctiveness of Irish identity provided implicit support for the concept of Home Rule. Attracting tens of thousands of members, it organized Irish language, music and dance classes, and this may explain why Bridget's sons James and William could both speak Irish although neither of their parents could. And while these developments did not offer any opportunity for the Wrights to escape the grinding poverty of their daily lives, the opening decade of the twentieth century indicated that major changes were coming on this front as well.

If the 1880s had been the time when tenants found their voice during the Land War, the urbanized working class began to express its power in the years after the turn of the new century. In 1907 a major strike of workers on the Belfast docks began over the issue of union recognition, the first major labour dispute of the twentieth century.[3] Six years later it was eclipsed by an even larger conflict, when attempts by the Irish Transport and General Workers' Union (ITGWU) to organize workers in Dublin faced bitter resistance from employers. When the latter locked out unionized workers, this led to a prolonged, bitter and violent conflict that lasted into early 1914. Despite ending in a conclusive defeat, as poverty and hunger forced workers to leave their unions, it was clear that organized labour was emerging as a major force in Ireland.

Although sometimes slow, the pace of change in the early twentieth century appeared to have a sense of inevitability to it. However the seeming forward march of history was derailed dramatically in 1914. The outbreak of World War I proved a defining moment in Ireland for Bridget Wright's generation. This was particularly the case in Waterford where the war, if anything, initially eased tensions in the city. However, as Irish society took off down a new path, the consequences for the Wrights became more direct.

The outbreak of hostilities in August 1914 came at a critical juncture for wider Irish society. In the previous months it had seemed that, after three decades of hopes and vague promises, Home Rule would finally be enacted by the British parliament. After the 1910 general election, the Irish Parliamentary Party held the balance of power in the House of Commons. Their price for supporting the Liberal government of Herbert Asquith was Home Rule, the party's raison d'être.

But by 1914 the prospect of enacting the measure was leading to rising political tensions in Ireland. A considerable minority of the Irish population remained implacably opposed. Unionists in Ulster had formed the Ulster Volunteers, a paramilitary force that pledged to resist the measure by violence. In reaction, the supporters of Home Rule formed their own paramilitary force, the Irish Volunteers. When the Austro-Hungarian Archduke Franz Ferdinand was shot in Sarajevo, few in Waterford realized the significance of the assassination, which ultimately triggered World War I. In July 1914 a civil war in Ireland between the loyalist Ulster Volunteers and the nationalist Irish Volunteers seemed more likely than a European war between the great powers.

But when the United Kingdom entered World War I on 4 August, these tensions melted away with surprising speed. As expected, the Ulster Volunteers immediately supported the war effort, but in a move that surprised some, most Irish nationalist leaders then followed suit.

John Redmond, leader of the Irish Parliamentary Party,

declared at a meeting of the Irish Volunteers at Woodenbridge, County Wicklow, that:

> The duty of the manhood of Ireland is twofold. Its duty is at all costs to defend the shores of Ireland against foreign invasion; it is the duty more than that of taking care that Irish valour proves itself on the field of war as it has always proved itself in the past. The interests of Ireland, of the whole of Ireland, are at stake in this war.[4]

This stance provoked a split in the Irish Volunteers, but the overwhelming majority supported Redmond. A small minority who retained the name were vocal critics of the war, but in 1914 they had little traction in wider society.

John Redmond's words had a considerable impact – not least in Waterford, where he had been an MP since 1891. Indeed, enlistment rates in the city were remarkable, with around one in every three men of military age joining the armed forces. The split the war had caused in the Irish Volunteers although innocuous-sounding at the time, would be a defining moment for Bridget Wright and more poignantly for that of her brother Bill.

In those early days of World War I it became clear that the conflict was going to be good for business, and would even offer opportunities to Bridget Wright and her family. While the nearest battlefields may have been in Belgium and France, Waterford was quickly identified as a major port that would be used to ship men and war materials from Ireland. By 11 August the city was already flooded with horses, as the British Army bought as many as it could across Ireland for use in the military. People's Park, the major public amenity in the city centre, was transformed into a large paddock, where the animals were fitted with the necessary harnesses in advance of being shipped to England.[5]

Amidst the excitement, there were the inevitable rumours that German spies were active in the port and in mid-August, local newspapers reported that plans were afoot to poison the city water supply.[6]

In these opening months of the war, there were considerable advantages emerging for Waterford. The scale of enlistment opened up job opportunities at home. This may have been what finally brought Bridget's brother Bill Grant to Harrington's Lane. Bill was considerably younger than Bridget, having been born to their father's second wife. His arrival must have been akin to the arrival of a new child for Bridget – albeit an adult one given she was a generation older than him.

Bill, still in his mid-twenties, easily slotted into life at Harrington's Lane – and during the early stages of the war these were happy times for the family as the extended Wright-Grant clan continued to expand. In November 1914 Bridget's eldest daughter Nora married Thomas Cunningham. The marriage appears to have been prompted by a pregnancy – Nora gave birth to a boy, William, three months later in February 1915. The house at Harrington's Lane now had three generations of the family, as the young couple lived there too.

However the initial excitement and enthusiasm the war had elicited during the summer began to wane as the warmth of the autumn gave way to the colder, darker winter months. The failure of either side to land a decisive blow in the fast-moving operations of the opening weeks ensured that the conflict would not end by Christmas 1914, as many had predicted. Then in October Bridget Wright's old neighbour from Smith's Lane, fifty-year-old James Flynn, was killed at Le Pilly close to the French–Belgian border: Flynn's death underscored the very real toll the war would take.

In 1915 life on the Home Front became more and more difficult. The economic advantages that the war had created were increasingly being negated by inflation. By March 1915 Waterford City Council was reporting a 20 per cent increase in the cost of living in the city.[7] This may have been what provoked Thomas Ryan, a neighbour of Bridget Wright's on Harrington's Lane, to commit what was a risky act of forgery. In 1916 Ryan forged papers that allowed him to receive compensation due to the father of John Condon, a Waterford soldier who had been killed in the war.[8] Predictably, Condon Sr queried the matter and Ryan was arrested in what was a particularly tragic case: it later emerged that the deceased son was actually a fourteen-year-old child who had lied to army recruiters, and the youngest British Army casualty of the entire war.

That year of 1916 was decisive in terms of the Irish experience of the war. The Irish Volunteers who had rejected the calls of John Redmond to support the British Army in 1914 had remained consistent in their critique that the war was an imperialist venture. In April 1916, increasingly under the influence of the Irish Republican Brotherhood, they launched an uprising in Dublin.

The Volunteers occupied numerous strategic buildings in the city and declared themselves the provisional government of an independent Irish Republic. This went far beyond the traditional demands of the Home Rule movement that had dominated Irish nationalism for decades. The Rising, as it would become known, was brutally suppressed by the British Army, in a manner that had far-reaching consequences.

The leaders of the Home Rule movement initially rushed to condemn the revolt. Even after the British Army had executed three Volunteer commanders in Dublin, John Redmond stood before the House of Commons and offered his support to the military, proclaiming, 'This outbreak, happily, seems to be over. It has been dealt with with firmness, which was not only right, but it was the duty of the government to so deal with it.' [9]

After another of the Rising leaders, Joseph Plunkett, was shot the following day, these words seemed particularly callous. As the executions continued over the following weeks, it became increasingly clear that John Redmond's political judgement was out of step with wider opinion in Ireland. The chairman of the Skibbereen Board of Guardians in County Cork recognized that the repression in Dublin would have a very different impact than Redmond was assuming, when he stated 'the continuance of martial law, though obviously intended to strike terror into the people, will result in defeating its own object. It will simply foster and beget bitterness, intense bitterness, which it may take many years to soften and eradicate.'[10] This analysis would prove all too accurate in the years to follow.

In Waterford, however, the rebellion in Dublin had seemed far removed. The republican movement in the city was very small – as late as November 1915, its leaders claimed that they could only mobilize thirty men for an insurrection.

If anything, the city's loyalty to John Redmond, and his loyalty to the British government, appeared to be paying off. Waterford City Council had been lobbying for months for a munitions factory to be built in the city. In May 1916 this was approved,[11] and construction was soon underway with the first cartridge produced in March 1917.[12] This, and the employment it created, perhaps explains why Bridget's brother, Bill Grant, would not only support John Redmond, but even die in his name – Waterford was somewhat unique as Irish politics was transformed in the later stages of World War I.

On a broader level, the British reaction to the 1916 Rising, which had resulted in sixteen executions and thousands of arrests, was increasingly considered excessive and extreme, and the republican movement's consistent opposition to World War I resonated more and more with a war-weary population. The summer and autumn of 1916 witnessed the Battle of the Somme in France, with a level of death and violence unprecedented in human history to that point – after almost four months of battle with little or no territorial gains, there would be an unimaginable one million casualties. By the end of the year, the republican movement, now reorganized, was ready to flex its muscles again.

As four Irish Parliamentary Party MPs died throughout 1917 from natural causes, four by-elections were held, in Roscommon, Longford, Clare and Kilkenny. This provided the republicans with a chance to challenge the Home Rule leaders and their support for the war. In all four by-elections, candidates who supported the 1916 Rising were returned over the Home Rulers. And history would haunt John Redmond in the following years. He could not escape his enthusiastic support for the war and his words of encouragement for Irishmen to enlist. This became a major problem in the later stages of the war, when the British government planned to introduce conscription to Ireland because of its manpower crisis.

The republican movement, now organized through the previously marginal political party Sinn Féin and the reconstituted Irish Volunteers, played a leading role in the opposition to conscription. Along with the increasingly powerful trade union movement and the Catholic Church, it mobilized Irish society throughout the spring and summer of 1918. The Irish Parliamentary Party, chained to an increasingly unpopular war, could do little but watch its support ebb away.

Waterford remained one of the few places where John Redmond remained popular. His support in the city transcended class divisions, and some of the poorest of the city's poor remained loyal. Bridget Wright's brother Bill Grant had by this point become an activist and ardent supporter of Redmond in the city.

This drew him into an increasingly violent world, as John Redmond's followers were determined to resist the rise of Sinn Féin, who started to organize in the city in 1917. Starting from a modest beginning of just one branch with sixty members, by November of that year the party had twelve branches, with over seven hundred members.[13] Growing in strength as they were, they faced fierce opposition from the supporters of Home Rule.

When the newly-elected President of Sinn Féin, Éamon de Valera, visited Waterford in November 1917, a move designed to provoke a response, the police struggled to stop supporters of the two parties clashing in the city. While major violence was avoided on that occasion, political tensions in Waterford escalated further still when John Redmond died suddenly the following March in London. Although he had been the leading politician in the city for two and a half decades, the question of who would replace him was clearly going to be a bitter contest.

The Irish Parliamentary Party selected John Redmond's son William to contest his seat, while Sinn Féin put forward local physician Dr Vincent White. The campaign was one of the most violent Ireland had seen in decades. Sinn Féin rallies were frequently attacked. Éamon de Valera's insistence that he would be able to canvass in the city without a bodyguard was quickly revised after he was attacked in the streets. Violent rioting was a feature of the election, with the police only intervening if Sinn Féin supporters started to get the upper hand. The Sinn Féin candidate, Dr White, struggled to even cast a ballot. He only succeeded on his second attempt, having been assaulted during the first.[14]

When the votes were counted, William Redmond polled 1,242 compared to 764 for Dr White. The son of the dead Home Rule leader claimed that Sinn Féin were now on the run, but this was clearly an exaggeration. The fact that republicans had taken 38 per cent of the vote in an emotionally charged election following the death of John Redmond, in a stronghold of the Irish Parliamentary Party, was a straw in the wind. A definitive answer as to which was the most popular party was not long in coming. The end of World War I six months later in November 1918 provided the ultimate test in Irish politics: a general election, the first one called since 1910.

This contest would be dramatically different from previous polls. All men over the age of twenty-one, and most women over thirty, could now vote. This may have been the first general election that Bridget Wright was eligible to vote in. Nevertheless, even for people unable to express themselves at the ballot box, the bitter election of December 1918 provided multiple ways for the people of Waterford to register their views, as the contest was marred by serious rioting.

William Redmond retained his seat, but Sinn Féin now took 47 per cent of the vote. Although his supporters burnt an effigy of Dr White, again the Sinn Féin candidate, it was clear that they were a spent force. Across Ireland, Sinn Féin had taken 73 out of 105 seats; while the Irish Parliamentary Party lost 68 of the 74 seats they had won in the 1910 election leaving them with just six MPs. Unionist candidates of various stripes took the remaining twenty-six seats.

Nevertheless, the bitter feuding between supporters of Home Rule and republicans in Waterford continued. Violence flared up again around St Patrick's Day in 1919, when Irish Parliamentary Party supporters mobilized considerable numbers to attend a commemoration of John Redmond in Wexford on Sunday 16 March. When their train was attacked at Ferrybank as it returned that evening, major disturbances took place later that night as the two sides clashed in the city.[15]

Over the previous months Bill Grant, Bridget Wright's half-brother, had emerged as an increasingly well-known supporter of the Home Rule movement, or at least well-known enough to be recognized on sight by republicans in the city.

Three weeks after the March clashes, on 7 April, he was walking to Harrington's Lane around 11 p.m. After he had turned into the narrow cul-de-sac off Barrack Street, a group of young men appeared at the top of the lane and shouted, 'Up White,' a reference to the Sinn Féin candidate in the recent election. He responded with two words, 'Up Redmond.'[16]

One of the young men stepped into the lane. Bill Grant immediately took off his belt to use as a weapon. When Bridget Wright stepped out into the lane she heard the young man call to her brother, 'Come on now Billy, come up again,' to which he retorted, 'You will pay for that, boy.'[17]

Then Bridget and two of her daughters, Bridget Jr and Nora, saw the young man charge down Harrington's Lane at Bill. Seeing the risk to her uncle, Bridget Jr cried out, 'Don't kill him!' The man threw what they thought was a bottle as he made his way down the lane. The missile hit Bill Grant and he collapsed, while his assailant fled the scene. Bill was then carried indoors and put lying on the floor of the house.[18]

When a policeman arrived a few minutes later, he could see that the Home Ruler was gravely wounded, and he summoned a doctor and priest. Half an hour passed before a doctor arrived, and he saw that Bill Grant had three severe injuries. While Bridget Wright and her daughters had seen a bottle thrown, the words of his attacker, 'Come on now Billy, come up again,' indicated that he had been attacked before he reached the lane. Whatever the case, the doctors who assessed his wounds were adamant that something more serious than a bottle had been used – possibly a hammer.[19]

Both left and right temple bones were fractured, and he had a bad wound under his right eye. Dressing the wounds, the doctor moved Bill Grant to the workhouse hospital. On 8 April two doctors performed surgery to try and remove the bone fragments that had penetrated his brain. Thought Grant survived the procedure, he never recovered. Bridget Wright lost yet another family member from Harrington's Lane when Bill Grant died of his wounds on 29 April.

He was buried in early May 1919, having died in what was a postscript to one of the key political struggles in early-twentieth-century Irish history. Between 1916 and 1918 Sinn Féin and the Irish Parliamentary Party had struggled for dominance in Irish nationalist politics. While this had often taken place at the ballot box, it had also been fought out in countless street brawls and riots, which would continue in Waterford and parts of the north-east. Bill Grant was one of the surprisingly few fatalities Waterford saw in this conflict.

His death, however, was utterly pointless by the time it occurred. Grant died for a cause that was effectively dead on a national level, having been buried at the 1918 election. Sinn Féin and the Irish Volunteers, who would soon reorganize into the Irish Republican Army, were now the masters of nationalist Ireland.

CHAPTER 10

War & Revolution

1920

> But take heed lest by any means this liberty of yours become a stumbling block to them that are weak.
>
> (1 Corinthians 8:9)

June 1897 saw a truly global celebration as events took place across the British Empire to mark Queen Victoria's Diamond Jubilee, the sixtieth anniversary of the monarch's coronation. Having ascended the throne in 1837, Victoria not only embodied the Empire as its figurehead, but for many she had come to represent an entire set of values and an epoch of history – the Victorian Age.

In Britain the occasion was enthusiastically embraced by large public displays of adulation, but the response to the Jubilee was somewhat lacklustre elsewhere. In India the population was focused on more pressing matters.

The subcontinent was labouring under yet another famine aggravated by British policies, as food exports continued despite widespread starvation.[1] Meanwhile, it was the memory of another famine – that of the Great Hunger earlier in Victoria's reign – that overshadowed the Diamond Jubilee in many communities across Ireland.

There were numerous public expressions of support for Victoria across the north-east, where support for the union with Britain was strongest, although elsewhere in Ireland the reaction had been decidedly muted. In Dublin monarchists had been left to convene their own event to congratulate the Queen, after the nationalist-controlled city Corporation voted down a proposal to send official greetings on Dublin's behalf.[2]

While several protests took place across the island, the most poignant took place in the West Cork town of Skibbereen. A sombre event saw hundreds parade behind an empty coffin to the cemetery, where flowers were laid on graves to mark the Great Hunger that had devastated the town. A banner hoisted above the crowd proclaimed their attitude to the Diamond Jubilee: 'England rejoices, Ireland mourns today her martyred dead, her banished sons, her famine-stricken people, her reduced population, her poverty through overtaxation.'[3]

As emotive and poignant as the Skibbereen demonstration was, this would be one of the last times that survivors of the Great Hunger would protest against what happened to them. By the turn of the twentieth century it was becoming a remote and distant event in the memories of the people. Queen Victoria herself died in 1901, severing yet another link to the 1840s.

The Famine would undeniably continue to haunt Irish society in a myriad of ways, but for the young it was increasingly difficult to relate to an event that had taken place over five decades earlier. Eileen Gilligan was a case in point. Born in April 1895, she was raised in Raheen Kilkelly, outside the town of Gort in south County Galway.

Her grandfather, Martin Greene, who could remember the events of the 1840s, had been born in 1831, but by the early 1900s most of the people in her community only knew of the Famine through second-hand accounts. Even for her parents it was an event beyond their memory: Martin Gilligan had been born in 1856, and his wife Margaret in 1861.

For them, and perhaps even more so for Eileen Gilligan, it was not just a matter of time but a more fundamental one of lived experience that separated them from the Great Hunger. Eileen Gilligan grew up in comfortable surroundings. While food shortages still periodically affected the West, the Gilligans did not endure hardship like that of the previous generations. The family farm was considerable even back in 1855, stretching over sixty acres In 1890, when Eileen's other grandfather Denis Gilligan had died, he left an estate valued at £211 to her father Martin.[4]

Not a fortune by any means, it nevertheless provided a foundation for him to secure a comfortable life for his family. Eileen Gilligan had been afforded an education, which continued for two years after she turned fourteen – the mandatory age for school attendance. In those first years of the new century, families like the Gilligans were looking to the future with rising expectations and optimism. In 1903 it seemed that the issue of land ownership, which had dominated and divided rural Ireland for decades, would be resolved in their favour once and for all.

The Gilligans had rented a sizeable farm for decades, but the fear of eviction had been a feature of life. However, when Eileen Gilligan was just seven years of age, the British government announced a major package of reforms, which included provisions to allow families like her own to buy their farms from their landlords. Since the Land War of the 1880s, it had been clear that landlordism in Ireland was coming to an end, but precisely how this would happen had been a point of contention. While landlords were willing to sell, and tenants wanted to buy, a workable mechanism had proved elusive. Finally, the Land Purchase Act of 1903 provided a practical model. Under its terms the British government provided large sums of money, in long-term loans at favourable rates, for tenants to buy their land.

While this appeared to be a panacea for an issue that had led to repeated violence in rural Ireland, its implementation was difficult. Landlords began to drag the process out in an effort to extract what many considered to be exorbitant prices for the land. By 1904 it appeared that rural Ireland was regressing by three decades. The mood of optimism had changed to one of frustrated hopes, and another land war broke out in 1904, although Eileen Gilligan was spared the extreme violence that her parents had endured in the 1880s.

It began when tenants on the Dunsandle estate, where James Connors had been shot in 1881 (see Chapter 7) organized a rent strike aimed at forcing their landlord to sell. When this worked (Dunsandle sold his estate the following year)[5] the tactic inevitably spread. By January 1908 there were sixty-three strikes across ten counties[6] and increasing numbers of landlords began to sell their estates to their tenants. While there were threats of violence, and occasional physical attacks, they were relatively few when compared to the 1880s.

In the following decade, this delivered huge changes to Eileen Gilligan's native South Galway. The Earl of Clanricarde and Lady Augusta Gregory, two major landlords in the region, had both sold the bulk of their estates to their tenants by 1915. The scale of land transfers was enormous. Between 1904 and the outbreak of World War I more than five million acres of land was sold to tenants.[7] This was a phenomenal change to life in rural Ireland. These wealthy families, who had dominated the country in some cases since the Middle Ages, finally relinquished their hold on the land, giving many farmers a stake in society that had proved elusive for decades. For Eileen Gilligan, these changes took place just as she was reaching adulthood. Hers was the first generation of her family who would live in an Ireland where the fear of eviction would increasingly be a feature of the past.

A few years after she finished school, Eileen married Malachy Quinn, a neighbouring farmer, on 27 August 1917. She moved to his family home in the adjoining townland of Corker, where the couple farmed a substantial holding. By 1920 they had amassed one hundred and forty acres of land. While they owned seventy acres themselves, they rented another seventy acres from what was left of Lady Gregory's estate, based at nearby Coole Park.[8]

The couple began to raise a family. Their first child, Alphonsus, or Alfie, was born in 1918. Within months of giving birth, Eileen Quinn became pregnant again, but by the time her second child Eva was born, the situation in Ireland had changed dramatically. Political violence was on the increase and in South Galway, the issue of land was leading to rising tensions once more.

The general election of 1918 had seen seventy-three Sinn Féin candidates elected, presenting a considerable problem for the British authorities in London. These candidates, who represented 70 per cent of Irish constituencies, refused to take their seats in Westminster. Instead, they mounted a direct challenge to the legitimacy of British rule in Ireland by convening a parliament in Dublin, referred to as the Dáil or Dáil Eireann, and declaring itself the legitimate government of Ireland. This took place alongside rising tensions after the nationalist paramilitary force, the Irish Volunteers, now reorganized into the Irish Republican Army (IRA), began to mount attacks on the Royal Irish Constabulary.

These events, initially at least, remained distant from the Quinn household in Corker. In early 1919 the IRA campaign was limited to Munster, while the machinations of politicians in Dublin and London had a limited bearing on their lives. During this time Eileen Quinn had little time to think about matters like these. After giving birth to her second child, she became pregnant once more shortly afterwards.

Yet it became increasingly difficult to remain ignorant of wider events in the following months. The response of the British government forced the Quinns, and others like them across the country, to take notice. Initially distracted by the post World War I peace talks, the government elected to ignore events in Ireland, assuming the momentum of the republican cause would fizzle out if it was starved of attention. This proved a critical underestimation of Irish republicanism and the depth of discontent that had been building in wider Irish society since the 1916 Rising. As Sinn Féin established an alternative government, and even began operating its own legal system, the IRA campaign started to gain momentum.

In April 1919 the republican parliament in Dublin called for a boycott of the Royal Irish Constabulary by the general public. British power across the island began to disintegrate. Meanwhile, a resurgent trade union movement made its views clear. In March 1920 it organized a general strike to secure the release of IRA prisoners. That summer, transport workers began a munitions strike, refusing to operate trains that carried military equipment.

While Ireland slipped into a full-blown war of independence, aspects of the political situation were troubling to many. While Irish unionists were diametrically opposed to the aims of the republican movement, a substantial number of the more conservative-minded nationalists were also dubious about where the wider revolutionary situation would lead the island.

For larger farmers like the Quinns, the emerging war had been accompanied by alarming events, particularly in the west. While the IRA, particularly in Munster, was directly attacking Crown Forces, a wider sense that major change was possible swept across the country. Land, never far from the heart of Irish politics and an issue that seemed impossible to resolve, resurfaced again.

By the time the War of Independence broke out, tensions

over land had been increasing in the west for some time. The sale and redistribution of landlord estates had ground to a halt back in 1914 as the British government diverted its energy and resources into World War I. To add to the rising tensions, the war restrictions also led to a dramatic decline in emigration. Given that 25,000 people had left County Galway between 1901 and 1911[9], this created a large reservoir of disillusioned young people.

All of this fuelled resentments that had lingered over the way the landlords' estates had been broken up. While some farmers had been able to purchase their own land, for many others, these changes in the order of land ownership had not led to material changes in their lives. Landless labourers remained landless, while poor tenant farmers still frequently farmed tracts of land too small to sustain a family – an imperative, whether they owned the land or not.

Calls from the poor for the subdivision of large ranches of grazing land led to rising tensions with larger farmers, who rented or bought these lands to expand their farms. As the IRA eroded the British administration's ability to function, violence began to break out over the issue of land in Eileen Quinn's community. The poor, sensing they were living through what was an historic opportunity, did not want to wait. They wanted to stop larger farmers renting vast tracts of grazing land and initiate a more equitable redistribution of the old Landlords estates.

In the space of three months, between April and June 1919, four men were shot and wounded in three separate incidents within a few hundred metres of Eileen's front door. All four survived, although one man lost an eye. The reason for the first shooting, that of Florimund Quinn and his employee Thomas Diviney, was clear. Florimund Quinn, who was not from the immediate area and was already a substantial landowner, had rented a local farm.[10]

The other incidents were described by the *Connaught Tribune* in more vague terms as being related to 'agrarian disputes'. In the twelve months that followed, this bitter conflict spread throughout the west. In April 1920 the *Tuam Herald* proclaimed that the increasing numbers of threatening letters sent to large farmers were 'symptomatic of the land agitation sweeping the west like a prairie fire'.[11] The newspaper acknowledged that 'the rough and ready methods' of the landless labourers were delivering results. The growing radicalization of the rural poor had been on display when the red flag of socialism was paraded at the May Day march in Gort in 1919.[12] In this rapidly escalating situation, larger farmers were increasingly uneasy about where things would lead.

Despite the misgivings of some in Irish society over the unfolding revolution, the reactions of the British authorities in Dublin would only serve to alienate the majority, and lacked sophistication, nuance, or acknowledgement of local factors. Rather than seizing on the emerging divisions over land retribution, they provided ample distraction from it.

Led by the Lord Lieutenant, Lord John French – a man who believed his ancestral links to Ireland gave him a unique understanding of the island – incompetence marked the authorities' response. Government policies, such as declaring entire counties 'Special Military Areas', where civil liberties were severely curtailed, alienated many who, wary of radical change, might have supported a more intelligent strategy. Treating all expressions of Irish culture as suspicious, Irish music and dance events were classed as subversive gatherings. This only served to polarize Irish political opinion, legitimizing the republican movement even among those fearful of where the revolution would lead. Seamus Babbington, a member of the Third Tipperary Brigade of the IRA, later reflected that, 'With their intensive hostile action, their ruthless treatment of the civil population and their unbridled hatred of any suspected of genuine republicanism and nationalism, this open tyranny at the time was a godsend.'[13]

Sir Warren Fisher, the head of the British civil service, who arrived in Dublin in 1920 to review the situation, concurred. He described the British authorities in Ireland as 'obsolete' and 'woodenly stupid and quite devoid of imagination'.[14]

In a very different situation, a more efficient administration might have been able to take advantage of the brewing land war in the west between large farmers and the poor. This issue divided not only Irish public opinion, but Sinn Féin itself. The party and the wider republican movement had grown at an exponential rate throughout 1918 and 1919, and contained an extremely wide range of views and opinions. An issue as controversial as land distribution risked dividing it, something that could have been exploited by a more canny British administration. As the authorities launched waves of repression, Sinn Féin kicked the issue to touch, and in the spring of 1920 the republican parliament issued a ban on land-related protests, stating that, 'The present time, when the Irish people are locked in a life-and-death struggle with their traditional enemy, is ill-chosen for stirring up strife amongst our fellow-countrymen.'[15]

While this begged the question of what Sinn Féin's policy would be after the War of Independence, the tactics of the British authorities presented the likes of the Quinns in South Galway with far more immediate and pressing problems. Having largely lost Irish public opinion to Sinn Féin, the British administration set about enforcing subservience through a ruthless war that only served to make day-to-day life increasingly unbearable for the general population. Indeed, by the summer of 1920, the British civil servant John Anderson, who had recently arrived in Dublin, noted that, 'the population of the south and west, so far as it is not actually hostile, is out of sympathy with the government and cannot be relied upon to co-operate in the carrying out of even the most reasonable and moderate measures'. [16]

Even though military leaders in Ireland warned that increasing repression would not work, the British government ignored this advice.[17] Instead, it raised two new forces to support the Royal Irish Constabulary, culled from World War I veterans – the Black and Tans and the Auxiliaries. Both forces would soon earn a reputation for brutality and indiscipline. They began to carry out reprisals on the general population in the aftermath of IRA attacks. While this policy would be officially adopted by the government in December, it had already become a well-established practice several months earlier: an assault on Balbriggan, north of Dublin, after an IRA attack in the locality, was covered extensively in the local, national and international press.

A session of the Irish House of Commons, College Green, Dublin. The parliament was dissolved under the Acts of Union in 1800. Ireland was subsequently ruled directly from Westminster. (Everett Collection Inc / Alamy Stock Photo.)

A Food Riot in Dungarvan, October 1846. (Pictorial Press Ltd / Alamy Stock Photo.)

Strokestown Park House, the seat of the Mahon Family. The Strokestown Estate witnessed some of the most notorious evictions during the Great Hunger. (Eye Ubiquitous / Alamy Stock Photo.)

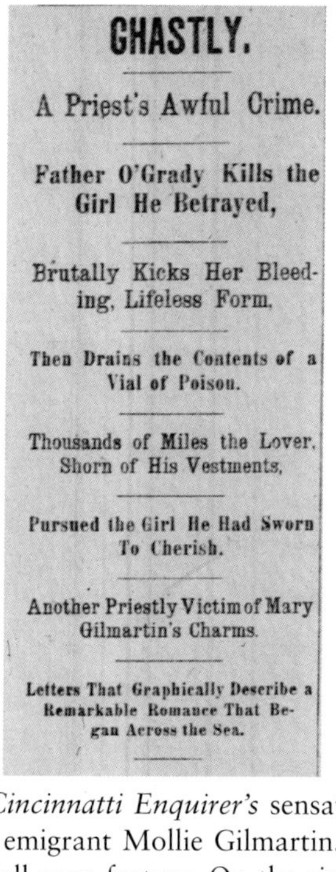

GHASTLY.

A Priest's Awful Crime.

Father O'Grady Kills the Girl He Betrayed,

Brutally Kicks Her Bleeding, Lifeless Form.

Then Drains the Contents of a Vial of Poison.

Thousands of Miles the Lover, Shorn of His Vestments,

Pursued the Girl He Had Sworn To Cherish.

Another Priestly Victim of Mary Gilmartin's Charms.

Letters That Graphically Describe a Remarkable Romance That Began Across the Sea.

THE VICTIM OF THE PRIEST'S BULLET.

The Cincinnatti Enquirer's sensational coverage following the murder of the Irish emigrant Mollie Gilmartin. On the left is the headline that ran above the full-page feature. On the right is an artist's interpretation of Gilmartin from the article. (© *The Cincinnati Enquirer* – USA Today Network.)

Kilkenny County Asylum, one of a network of similar institutions built across Ireland in the mid-nineteenth century. (Shim Harno / Alamy Stock Photo.)

Founded by the Vikings in the tenth century, Waterford remained one of Ireland's major ports into the early twentieth century. (Ilbusca / via Getty Images.)

A house destroyed in a British reprisal in Tuam, Co. Galway, during the War of Independence in 1921. (Chronicle / Alamy Stock Photo.)

Belfast's Royal Avenue, early 1900s. Belfast emerged as one of the fastest growing cities in the Northern Europe in the early twentieth century. (KGPA Ltd / Alamy Stock Photo.)

A sectarian riot in Belfast, 2 September 1920.
(Pictorial Press Ltd / Alamy Stock Photo.)

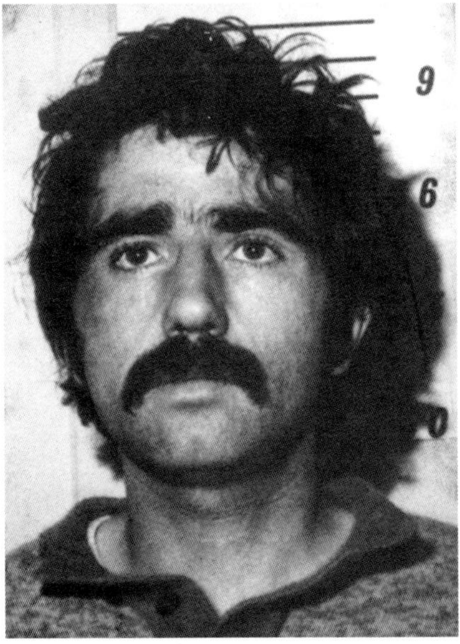

Brendan Hughes emerged as a key figure in the Provisional IRA in the 1970s. His great uncle Owen had been shot dead in a random sectarian killing in 1922. (© Viktor Patterson, Images4Media.)

British Crown Forces searching civilians in Dublin during the War of Independence. (Classic Image / Alamy Stock Photo.)

The Ardnacrusha Hydroelectric power station on the River Shannon. Sean Sexton / (Contributor via Getty Images.)

Richard Mulcahy, the former IRA Chief of Staff and later Minster for Defence in the Irish Free State Government, inspects National Army troops in 1922. (Walshe / Stringer via Getty Images.)

DUBLIN. FLATS COLLAPSE IN FENIAN STREET: THIS SCENE COULD HAVE BEEN TAKEN AFTER AN AIR RAID IN WORLD WAR II. FIREMEN AND RESCUE WORKERS RUSHED TO THE SCENE, WHERE TWO FOUR-STOREY TENEMENTS CAME APART ON JUNE 12. TWO CHILDREN WERE BURIED AND DIED IN THE RUBBLE. *(Radio photograph.)*

The Dublin slums were among the worst in Europe. Building collapses, similar to this one on Fenian Street, Dublin, in 1963 were a constant concern for tenants. (Chronicle / Alamy Stock Photo.)

A Traveller encampment in Belfast, 1969. The Travelling community was increasing marginalized by successive governments in the Republic and Northern Ireland during the twentieth century. (Homer Sykes / Alamy Stock Photo.)

BEAR BRAND PURE SILK STOCKINGS

Daily Express

Audience see revolver drama at London lecture

SIR M. O'DWYER SHOT DEAD AT CAXTON HALL

Lord Zetland and Lord Lamington wounded

HIT BY TWO SHOTS

SIR MICHAEL O'DWYER, Governor of the Punjab at the time of the Amritsar "massacre" in 1919, was shot dead in full view of 150 people in London yesterday afternoon.

Just as a lecture in Caxton Hall, S.W., held by the East India Association and the Royal Central Asian Society, was about to end, six reports startled the audience. Sir Michael fell dead, with two bullets through his heart.

BATTLE OF SHOTS

'BRING DOCTORS'

'I saw my dear friend shot'

—SAYS SIR PERCY SYKES

R.A.F. snap U-boat, then sink it

STOP PRESS

MANNERHEIM LAYS THE BLAME

Lightning just misses girl in bed

'HARD TO GIVE UP'

2oz. MORE BUTTER

But you may need coupons for restaurant meat meals

Lady Margaret Drummond-Hay acquitted

'Red Dean' cuts out Russia

Gracie and Monty in wedding 'fight'

Prisoner escapes

Belisha will blame the Government

'MEET' RATIONING with BOVRIL

BOVRIL PUTS BEEF INTO YOU

The Indian revolutionary Udham Singh being led during from Caxton Hall, London, after the murder of Sir Michael Dwyer. (John Frost Newspapers / Alamy Stock Photo.)

By September 1920 Crown Forces were also creating an intolerable situation in South Galway. Lady Gregory, the landowner and celebrated playwright, noted in her diary that Malachy Quinn, Eileen's husband, had come to her looking for materials to rebuild a neighbour's house which had been destroyed in the conflict.[18] Crown Forces had raided the home of the Burke family, looking for their son. When they couldn't find him, they burnt the house. Worse still, Gregory also recorded the sexual assaults of local women by the Black and Tans, although the women's families preferred to cover it up.[19]

When forty IRA volunteers ambushed a police patrol a few kilometres from the Quinns' house, killing a policeman, the community knew that reprisals, by this stage an established if still unofficial policy, would be exacted on the community. Nevertheless, in a society increasingly adapting to wartime, Malachy Quinn went to the local market in Gort the following day. Predictably the Black and Tans arrived in the town, eager to make a violent display of force. Although they fired randomly in the air to threaten the population, no one was killed. Leaving, they headed towards the townland of Corker, arriving there slightly after 2.30 p.m., firing wildly as they made their way along the road. Eileen Quinn came out her front door to see what the commotion was.

Heavily pregnant and carrying her youngest daughter Teresa, she rested on the wall as the lorries approached. As the first lorry passed, no more than a few feet away, a shot rang out, striking Eileen in the groin. Without stopping, the two lorries continued up the road, firing at the Quinns' neighbours, killing farm animals and breaking windows. Eileen Quinn had been gravely wounded. Managing to pass her infant to a servant, she collapsed, bleeding profusely.

The following eight hours proved agonizing. Word was sent to Gort to fetch Malachy Quinn, who fainted at the sight of his wife's grave condition. Although two doctors tended to her through the evening, they determined that there was little they could do to save her life. They turned their efforts towards inducing a birth to save her unborn child. This too failed, and Eileen Quinn passed away at 10.45 p.m., eight hours after being shot.

What precisely had happened to Eileen Quinn immediately became a topic of intense debate in County Galway and beyond. The shooting of a pregnant woman with no political affiliations, sitting outside her house, was another benchmark in the increasingly brutal war. In peacetime, her death would have been investigated by a coroner's court but these had been suspended by the British authorities a few months previously. The investigation was carried out instead by the British Military Courts of Inquiry. While this heard testimony from several key witnesses, its findings were never published. It was stated instead that Eileen Quinn had died by misadventure – that she had been shot accidentally. This assertion was based on the testimony of the police witnesses. One stated that, 'When travelling along a suspicious-looking place like a wood, we would fire our rifles in the air, but would not fire near a house nor near a decent-looking civilian.' [20] They also claimed that there had been a bend in the road, obscuring the view.

That this defence was not credible was self-evident to the local community. The nearest wooded area to the

Quinns was their landlord Lady Gregory's residence at Coole Park, which the Black and Tans had passed by the time they approached the Quinns' home at Corker.

A cursory glance at a map, or a visit to the Quinns' home, would reveal that the house was not obscured by any bend in the road. Lady Gregory, writing in her diary, was dubious that Eileen Quinn could have been hit by a bullet fired into the air. Examination of the wound, which had a low upwards trajectory, supported this.

Father Considine, the local priest who had administered the last rites to Eileen as she was dying, wrote a letter to several publications on 11 November with a damning testimony. Describing the inquiry as an attempt to 'cloak and extenuate', he outlined how he had personally called the police to the Quinn home. They had arrived at 3.20 p.m., seven hours before she died, but refused to take a statement from her. He described the surrounding countryside in detail, showing how the policemen in the lorries had a clear view.[21]

He also questioned how Eileen Quinn could have been shot by accident, as the gun was fired at close range and she had been fully in view. The priest summarized with his conclusion; dismissing the notion that the police had been firing wildly to pre-empt an ambush, he stated: 'There is one alternative. Either Mrs Quinn was deliberately killed by a bullet aimed directly at her, or she was killed by a bullet fired in her direction by a policeman who must have seen her and who did not care whether he hit her or not.'[22]

The British establishment would not countenance such a theory. When Eileen Quinn's case was debated in the House of Commons, Prime Minister David Lloyd George shut down debate by responding to a question thus: 'The honourable gentleman knows perfectly well that that was a most unfortunate accident, and no decent person would suggest that it was deliberate.'[23] Hamar Greenwood, the Chief Secretary for Ireland, repeated the line that the police had been pre-emptively firing in anticipation of an ambush.

While Eileen Quinn was laid to rest a few days after she was shot, her case symbolized the problems facing the British government in Ireland. Outside the north-east (which is explored in the next chapter), Anglo–Irish relations had reached a point of no return. Even those in rural Ireland who were wary about what change would bring had been alienated by the relentless government assault on communities. The authorities were, in effect, creating a truly national movement, their violence papering over the very real cracks in Irish nationalism.

Independence, whatever it might bring, increasingly seemed the best option. W.B. Yeats, a regular visitor to Coole Park, asked in the poem 'Reprisals':

> *Where may new-married women sit*
> *And suckle children now? Armed men*
> *May murder them in passing by . . .*

By 1920 the Crown Forces had been reduced to an army of occupation, with extremely limited support outside the north-east. Tragically, Eileen Quinn was by no means the last to die – indeed, she was one of the first victims in what was the extremely bloody new phase of the war that began in late 1920.

The day before she was shot the Lord Mayor of Cork, Terence MacSwiney, who had died on hunger strike in

Brixton Jail, was buried in his native Cork City. On the day she died, Kevin Barry, an eighteen-year-old IRA Volunteer, was executed in Mountjoy Jail in Dublin, despite widespread appeals for clemency. Two weeks after Eileen Quinn was murdered, a Catholic priest in Galway city, Father Michael Griffin, was killed by the Black and Tans. They buried his body in a bog, where it was discovered a few days later. On 21 November, Bloody Sunday in Dublin saw the IRA target British intelligence agents in the city. The Crown Forces responded in a particularly brutal manner when they opened fire on a crowd at a Gaelic football match at the city's Croke Park, killing fourteen people. A week later the IRA inflicted one of its most serious defeats on the Crown Forces, at Kilmichael in West Cork, when seventeen Auxiliaries were killed. While the war would grind on for another seven months, the British government continued to prove incapable of redeeming the situation.

By June 1921 Sir Nevil Macready, the commander-in-chief of British forces in Ireland, told Lloyd George he had two options: 'all out or get out'. Macready's assessment, that the British could escalate the war or withdraw, was a false choice. Escalation had been effective back in 1798, but this was not a viable strategy in 1921. Public opinion in the USA, which had been a key consideration and restraining influence on British military planning during 1920, would not stomach such a campaign. The other option was withdrawal.

By the end of July a truce had been agreed and the President of Sinn Fein, Éamon de Valera, was in London for preliminary peace talks. He was followed by a larger delegation in October, led by Michael Collins, which agreed a treaty in December. This was ratified in January, paving the way for twenty-six of Ireland's thirty-two counties to leave the United Kingdom and form what was called the Irish Free State. This entity, while not a republic, controlled most aspects of day-to-day life in these twenty-six counties.

Ultimately, the Union of Britain and Ireland had never functioned properly. Theoretically, Ireland had an equal position to any other part of the United Kingdom after the union in 1800, although this notion had never moved beyond rhetoric in Britain. Over time, this attitude was compounded by a complete failure and unwillingness to understand the Irish experience of the Union. Back in 1897, when the people of Skibbereen recalled the Famine that had devastated their community, their grievances were dismissed by one British newspaper as typical of the 'disloyal Irish'.

In their private communications, political leaders in Britain frequently voiced their honest views of Ireland. The last Commander-in-Chief of Ireland, Macready, had as recently as January 1919 revealed his views when he wrote of Ireland, 'I loathe the country and its people with a depth deeper than the sea and more violent than that I feel against the Boche [Germans].' The cabinet minister Winston Churchill, a year later in March 1920, wrote, 'I expect it is that treacherous, assassinating, conspiring trait which prevented the Irish from becoming a great responsible nation with stability and prosperity.'

The Union, dissolved formally in 1922, had never worked in any meaningful way. Over 2,300 people were killed in the Irish struggle for independence between 1916 and 1921. Eileen Quinn's murder symbolized the counter-productive British policy and general sense of injustice in the way the island was being governed.

And while the Anglo-Irish Treaty of 1922 brought the war to a conclusion, it was an unsatisfactory peace. Most republicans were dissatisfied with the concessions they were being asked to accept. The social and economic values of the new Free State would also be major points of contention; the republican movement was extremely divided on these matters as well. But in early 1922 the situation in the north-east in the emerging state of Northern Ireland was the most pressing. The levels of violence there had been increasing since the truce of 1921 and would soon come to a head.

CHAPTER 11

Partition

1922

Woe to him that buildeth a town with blood,
and stablisheth a city by iniquity.

(Habakkuk 2:12)

When Ann O'Neill married Thomas Hughes in Lisburn, County Antrim, in 1888, it was far from a fairy-tale wedding. Perhaps in different circumstances they would have returned to Ann's home parish to be surrounded by their kith and kin. However, that course of action would have invited criticism. They had both moved to Lisburn – Thomas from his native Derry and Ann from County Louth – in search of work. Having secured positions as servants, they had met, fallen in love and decided to marry at the comparatively young age of twenty.

While marrying at such a young age was not an unusual course of action at the time, Ann's parents may not have been happy with the match. Owen O'Neill was a farmer and may have been nonplussed by the news his daughter was marrying the son of a labourer. To avoid such unwanted interference and perhaps to save time (and, importantly, money) they married in October at St Peter's Church, in Ballymacward outside Lisburn, where they were both working.

Within a few weeks of the wedding they had conceived their first child. As Ann's waist began to grow, the pregnancy brought the need to make considerable changes for the couple. Once her pregnancy began to show, Ann would be dismissed if she did not leave her position in domestic service. This left the couple reliant on Thomas's income and may have spurred their decision to find a better position than a servant's, with its long hours and poor pay. With little to hold them in Lisburn, the young couple gravitated towards the bustling city of Belfast, ten miles to the north-east.

By the time Ann went into labour in August 1889 the couple were living in Englishtown, outside the southern suburbs of Belfast, where Thomas had secured work as a labourer. The child, a boy named Henry-Joseph, was born hale and hearty, but it was not long before the family were on the move again. They soon moved into Belfast itself, drawn by the city's insatiable demand for labour.

By 1891, when Ann gave birth to a second child, their only daughter Sarah Ann, they were living on Excise Street, off the Falls Road, the major thoroughfare into the city from the south-west. Four years later they had moved again, further down the Falls Road to Sultan Street. It was here that they would find a degree of stability, remaining on the street for over sixteen years. Thomas's mother Mary would join them there, and Ann would give birth between

1895 and 1904 to sons James, Thomas, Patrick, Charles, Owen and the youngest, John. For their rapidly expanding family, Belfast in those years had advantages over nearly every other town and city in Ireland – it was booming.

Around the Falls Road the Hugheses were surrounded by people with similar experiences to their own. Most of the 403 people in the community were not Belfast-born but had come to the city in search of work. Many had come from the surrounding counties of Antrim and Down, but others had been drawn from across Ireland and a handful had even migrated from Britain. This was a testament to Belfast's experience of the previous decades, which had defied the trend of economic instability and emigration that defined life across most of Ireland. By the turn of the twentieth century, Belfast was thriving.

It had been little more than a provincial town at the turn of the nineteenth century, but the following hundred years had seen the city grow at an almost exponential rate. The population had trebled in the decades before the Famine and then doubled again between 1861 and 1891.[1]

Belfast entered the new century as it had left the old, confident about its future and growing fast. In the first decade of the 1900s the population grew by an additional 10 per cent, standing at 385,000 in 1911. It was far and away the largest city in Ireland, and the fastest-growing in the UK. The key to Belfast's growth had been its economy. While the rest of the island had remained orientated around agriculture, Belfast and the surrounding region had become one of the most industrialized parts of the UK. The city had emerged as a major textile centre, the centre of what was called the Linen Triangle.

Over the nineteenth century, it had also become recognized as a centre of shipbuilding – the two major shipyards, Harland & Wolff, and Workman, Clark & Company, employed 20,000 workers by 1912.[2] In 1911 around 40 per cent of all workers in the city were employed in manufacturing, at a time when the Irish average languished around 10 per cent.[3]

The different experience Belfast offered in the late nineteenth century was not only attractive to the likes of Thomas and Ann Hughes, but it was immediately evident to visitors. The city looked and felt different to other Irish cities, its wealth apparent in the city streets. The 1912 *Black's Guide to Ireland*, marketed at visitors, described Belfast thus: 'Though not historically or socially the capital, Belfast is from a commercial and industrial standpoint the metropolis of Ireland.'[4] Describing the wide, well-lit streets, the guide marvelled at the Harland & Wolff shipyards, where the ill-fated *Titanic* had been built the previous year, proclaiming the Belfast yards as industry leaders on a global stage.[5]

People frequently compared and contrasted Belfast favourably with Irish cities. Dublin's poverty at the time was notorious. By 1912 *Black's Guide* had dropped its reference to the city's ubiquitous slums that had appeared in earlier editions, but this did not reflect any change in the reality of life in Dublin.

The experience of the Hughes family in Belfast was a testimony to how different life was there. Even though Thomas was the only member of the household working in 1901, his wage as a manual labourer still afforded his growing family a four-roomed house. Over the following decade, as the family continued to expand, they enjoyed a modest improvement in their lives.

As each of their children completed mandatory schooling, at the age of fourteen they entered the world of work and, by 1911, there were five salaries supporting the household. Thomas himself had now secured work in the linen industry, as had the couple's daughter, Sarah Ann, and their fourteen-year-old son, Patrick. Meanwhile, James was a farrier while fifteen-year-old Thomas was a labourer. Charles, Owen and John remained in education, but would also in time support themselves.

It may have been this increased income that facilitated the family's move closer to the shipyards and the industrial heartland north of the city centre. Leaving Sultan Street and the Falls Road, where they had lived for nearly two decades, they moved into a house on Skegoneill Street in North Belfast sometime after 1911.The annual rent at 16 Skegoneill Street in 1913 was £20 a year,[6] at a time when a government report estimated the 'rent-paying capacity' of a working-class household in Dublin to be less than £10.[7] Thomas and Ann had come a long way since their marriage back in 1888 – but the move from the Falls Road in West Belfast to Skegoneill Street in North Belfast also took the family across an invisible frontier into somewhat unfamiliar and potentially dangerous surroundings. While Belfast enjoyed great economic success and offered opportunities unavailable elsewhere in Ireland, the city had the most fractured religious and political landscape in the UK.

As Belfast had grown throughout the nineteenth century, it had not only absorbed migrants from the rural north-east but also the religious and political divides of the wider region. Rather than wither in the densely packed urban environment, these divisions intensified and crystallized in the city, where they became infused with tensions over work and opportunities.

To meet the insatiable demand for labour in the city factories and shipyards, large numbers of Catholics gravitated to Belfast, a city that had been almost exclusively Protestant and unionist in outlook. Over the course of the nineteenth century the Catholic population of Belfast had grown from less than 10 per cent to 25 per cent by the turn of the twentieth century. Although Belfast offered Catholics employment, they soon found that there were limits to the extent they could advance.

As Catholics, this was evident to Thomas and Ann Hughes. While Belfast had offered them work, housing and a degree of comfort they would have struggled to find elsewhere in Ireland, they had reached the limits of how far they could advance. The next step up would have been to secure work for their children in the highly skilled trades of the shipyards, but as Catholics this would be extremely difficult.

Despite the large influx of Catholics throughout the nineteenth century, Belfast remained firmly under the control of the city's Protestant community. Protestants not only dominated the world of politics and business, but Catholics also found themselves blocked from the best-paid skilled jobs in the city's industries.

This was the case for the children of Thomas and Ann Hughes. They had not secured skilled trades, but remained in manual jobs. The family's success was based around the fact that many of them were engaged in paid employment, rather than any of them having better-paid skilled work.

This sectarian divide in the world of work pervaded almost every aspect of life in Belfast. It unquestionably overshadowed the decision of the Hugheses to leave Sultan Street and move to Skegoneill Street. Belfast was not just a city divided in terms of work and opportunity; it was also divided geographically. Catholics tended to live in the south and west of the city, in the Falls Road area where the Hughes family had first settled when they arrived in the late 1880s. On Sultan Street in 1911, 400 of the 403 residents were Catholics.

The move to Skegoneill Street after 1911 took them to a very different community. The street, and the adjacent Skegoneill Avenue, were home to 260 people, only thirty of whom were Catholic. While living in the street suggested a growing level of financial stability, it also brought risk. Removed from the security of the large Catholic community around the Falls Road, they were more vulnerable in the event of an outbreak of sectarian violence, which flared regularly. The memory of the 1886 riots, when political and sectarian tensions had seen people turn on their neighbours, was engrained in the city's memory.

Back in the late 1880s Belfast had been rocked by the worst sectarian violence in living memory. The issue at stake was ostensibly a matter of politics – Home Rule. However, as was the case elsewhere, attitudes to this issue closely overlapped with religious affiliation. Belfast's Catholics supported Home Rule, while the city's Protestants opposed it.

In 1886 tensions over the issue came to the fore when

the British government of the day, reliant on the support of the Irish Parliamentary Party, introduced a Home Rule Bill. This alarmed unionists, who feared that they would lose their disproportionate power and influence. They dubbed the proposition 'Rome Rule', a reference to their concern over the influence the Catholic Church might exert over Irish society if Home Rule was enacted.

Even though there was little chance the Bill could pass in the Conservative-dominated House of Lords, the debate exacerbated tensions in Belfast, leading to major violence in the summer and autumn of 1886. It began in a petty dispute between two workers in the shipyards, but would spark months of rioting. The origin of the matter was never clear, but in the summer of 1886 two workers, named only as Murphy and Blake, the former a Catholic, the latter a Protestant, had a disagreement.

According to a subsequent government report, Blake had been struck by Murphy who allegedly said that when Home Rule was enacted, Blake 'nor any of his sort should get leave to work there, or earn a loaf there or any other place'.[8] The words 'any of his sort' was a clear reference to Blake's Protestant faith.

The veracity of the story is difficult to determine, but the interaction reflected why sectarian tensions over the issue of Home Rule in Belfast were so bitter. Protestants feared that they were facing a loss of power, influence and opportunity, and Catholics resented the fact that they struggled to find well-paid work.[9]

The comment, or the belief that the altercation had taken place, led to major violence in the shipyards. Protestant mobs forced Catholics from their workplaces and in the following days, violence spread into the surrounding communities.[10] As rioting continued throughout the summer, thirty-two people were killed and hundreds were injured.[11] One of the most concerning aspects of the violence was the attacks on homes, something that happened with alarming regularity when sectarian violence flared in Belfast.[12]

Internment sectarian violence became a feature of life. Another Home Rule Bill in 1893 provoked sectarian clashes in the city. Five years later in 1898, nationalist events to mark the centenary of the 1798 Rebellion somewhat inevitably sparked further violence in Belfast once more.

Amid this bitterly divided history of the city, Thomas and Ann Hughes decided to move their family to Skegoneill Street sometime after 1911. Whether violent clashes would erupt again in the city was never really in doubt – the question was when. Indeed, tensions had clearly been on the rise since 1910. The general election of that year had seen the Irish Parliamentary Party hold the balance of power in Westminster again. On that occasion, their conditions for supporting the Liberal government of Herbert Asquith included not only a Home Rule Bill, but guarantees that it would actually be enacted. In order to deliver this and other policies, Asquith's government set about removing what had been the major legislative obstacles to change in the past – the veto the Conservative dominated House of Lords had on Legislation. When this was done in 1911, Home Rule appeared inevitable.

Determined to resist the measure by all means, unionist leaders in the north-east demonstrated their opposition in an event called Ulster Day in September 1912. This would see nearly half a million unionists, men and women, pledge their opposition to Home Rule.

As women signed the Ulster Declaration, pledging their determination to support resistance, men signed what was called the Ulster Solemn League and Covenant, which pledged to use 'all means which may be found necessary to defeat the present conspiracy to set up a Home Rule parliament in Ireland'. Political leaders in London fuelled the violent atmosphere building in 1912. The Conservative opposition leader, Andrew Bonar Law, supported the threat to use violence when he said: *'I can imagine no length of resistance to which Ulster can go in which I should not be prepared to support them.'*

To make good on these threats of violence, politicians in the Ulster Unionist Council established a paramilitary force, the Ulster Volunteers. The situation escalated still further in 1913 when nationalist leaders formed the Irish Volunteers, a paramilitary formation supportive of Home Rule.

While the issue at the heart of what seemed like a looming Civil War was political, recent history indicated that this would inevitably take on a sectarian dimension in Belfast and the north-east in general. The Hughes family, members of a Catholic minority in North Belfast, were acutely aware of how vulnerable they were.

If the signatures on the Ulster Solemn League and Covenant were an indication of the political tensions, the community on Skegoneill Street was not as polarized as some. Of the Hugheses' neighbours, Sarah Dodds and June Douglas signed the Ulster Declaration, while only one man on the street, John Neill at Number 3, signed the covenant to resist Home Rule by all means necessary. The fact that most of their neighbours didn't sign was cold comfort – on the adjacent Skegoneill Avenue, dozens of men and women had signed the pledges.

The outbreak of World War I in 1914 calmed tensions in Belfast considerably. Both the Ulster Volunteers and the Irish Volunteers mobilized to support the war effort, draining the city of young men and political tension, and Belfast remained comparatively calm as hostilities rose rapidly elsewhere in Ireland in the final stages of the war. The seismic general election of 1918, which saw the republicans of Sinn Féin dominate polling outside Ulster, had little impact in the city.

Unionists' influence in Belfast saw electoral constituencies drawn in their favour. There were nine constituencies in Belfast and unionists took eight of them. In the only one guaranteed to return a nationalist, that of the Falls, Joseph Devlin, the Irish Parliamentary Party candidate, easily beat the Sinn Féin leader Éamon de Valera. (Belfast was never the focus of de Valera's energies. He also stood and won seats in the constituencies of Clare East and Mayo East in an electoral system that allowed candidates to stand for multiple seats.)

By that year in the Hughes home, Thomas and his sons Thomas Jr, Patrick and James, could all vote. Whether they bothered to do so was another matter entirely. The result in the Duncairn constituency where they lived was never in doubt. Two nationalist candidates, one from Sinn Féin and the other from the Irish Parliamentary Party, did stand, but neither had a chance. Edward Carson, the Ulster Unionist leader, took 80 per cent of the vote.

As the War of Independence began in Tipperary in 1919, Belfast remained quiet. Nevertheless, when the Orange Order (the sectarian, oath-bound society formed in 1795. See chapter 2.) parades took place the following July, Thomas and Ann Hughes, who had seen dozens of similar events, could detect the unmistakeable signs of rising sectarian tensions in the city. Observers that year noted the thousands of young men flocking to the ranks of the organization. Edward Carson, addressing the Orange Order parade in Belfast in 1919, reiterated the unionist commitment to resist Home Rule, or any other attempt to change the relationship between Britain and Ireland, with violence: 'If there is an attempt to take away one jot or title of your rights as British citizens, I tell them at all consequence once more I will call out the Ulster Volunteers.' [13]

There was little doubt that events elsewhere in Ireland were concerning unionist leaders. As the IRA campaign against Crown Forces gained momentum, they began to fear where it would lead.

That being said, even into the early months of 1920, as the war intensified in Cork and Dublin, the north-east around Belfast remained relatively calm. During that winter of 1919–20, Thomas and Ann Hughes had concerns far removed from the world of politics.

Their eldest son Henry was living something of a wayward life. At the age of thirty he was still living in the family home. In November 1919 he was arrested and charged for the robbery of several chests of tea. Awaiting trial, he was then stabbed in an unrelated incident in a pub. While the wounds were superficial, he was convicted of the theft of £220 worth of tea when his case came before the court in March 1920.[14] The family humiliation was complete when their address was published in local newspapers. However, this embarrassment would be quickly forgotten when Belfast was consumed by unprecedented levels of violence later that year. Few homes in the city were left untouched, not least 16 Skegoneill Street.

The comparative calm Belfast had enjoyed in the opening phase of the War of Independence arose from the city's unusual political landscape, which differed considerably from most of Ireland. As the 1918 election indicated, Sinn Féin and the IRA were weak in the city.

In Belfast, and across the north-east, sectarian organizations – such as the Catholic Ancient Order of Hibernians, aligned to the Home Rule movement, and the Protestant Orange Order, aligned to the unionist movement – dominated the political landscape, and republicans struggled to win influence. John McCoy, the adjutant of the Newry Brigade of the IRA, described how republicans criticized both sides of this sectarian divide:

> The Ancient Order of Hibernians was definitely sectarian and anti-Protestant in its policy and it has no doubt played a most sinister part in all the northern counties.
>
> Sectarianism could have only bad results. It caused Unionists who had Liberal or Nationalist tendencies to get suspicious or alarmed, and amongst the Orange Order it was a God-send as it enabled the 'Diehards' to come out with their war cries of 'No surrender', 'No Popery' [and] 'No Home Rule'.[15]

Even though the IRA did not have the support to mount a major campaign in the north-east, war would come to Belfast. But it would take a very different form to other parts of the country. Given Belfast's political and religious landscape, the conflict in the city would quickly descend into inter-communal and sectarian violence, developing its own momentum. While this may have been rooted in the city's fractured history, the violence that consumed the area after 1920 originated in the corridors of power in Westminster.

As the War of Independence intensified, the British government escalated its military operation in Ireland. This led to growing international pressure, particularly from the US, to introduce some political reforms to Ireland – a carrot to accompany the stick. In reaction to this the government resurrected the plans to introduce Home Rule. At the outset, this Home Rule Bill was little more than theatre. Home Rule was in many ways a relic of pre-World War I Ireland. As difficult as it would have been to implement in 1914, it was impossible in 1920. The Conservative Party was in power, and unionists in Ulster now had considerable influence over its backbenchers. They were adamant that they would resist any attempt to place the north-east under a government in Dublin, no matter how limited its powers were.

Meanwhile, the nationalist movement in Ireland, which had originally demanded the measure, was increasingly dominated by republicans who rejected Home Rule because it was not radical enough. Indeed, the politicians proposing the measure had few illusions it could work – their motivations lay elsewhere. The Cabinet minister

Lord Birkenhead described it as 'an ingenious strengthening of our tactical position before the world'. [16]

The Home Rule bill of 1920 delivered permanent partition of Ireland, thus guaranteeing Ulster Unionists complete and total dominance over life in the North East. As the leading unionist, H.L. Garrett, explained in 1920: 'The time has come when Belfast and the North of Ireland should not be associated with the rest of Ireland in any sort of way.'[17]

The concept of partitioning the island, temporarily at least, was not new, but the idea of the permanent partition of Ireland into two separate countries enraged most Irish people. Nationalists opposed partition, as did unionists living in the rest of Ireland, who considered it an act of betrayal. Nevertheless, using their influence in Westminster, the Ulster Unionists pressed ahead.

A government committee to formulate the details of the Bill was headed by former unionist MP Walter Long. By late 1919 his committee proposed that Ireland should be partitioned, with separate parliaments in Belfast and Dublin. But Long did not advocate absolute partition: the bill at this stage intended a common judiciary across the island and other measures that indicated a shared future between the two polities.

The Ulster Unionists threatened to 'wreck' any bill that did not deliver their ultimate vision of permanent partition. Throughout early 1920 they successfully lobbied for two separate judicial systems although the key issue came down to where the border between the emerging Irelands would be drawn.

Early discussion focused on the ancient border of Ulster

but the inclusion of Donegal, Cavan and Monaghan, with their large nationalist and Catholic populations, alarmed unionists, who envisaged a polity they could control effectively and permanently. It would be democratic in name only – Catholics were to be relegated from power and influence.

After consulting the leaders of Ulster unionism, Walter Long informed Prime Minister David Lloyd George that, 'the inclusion of Donegal, Cavan and Monaghan would provide such an access of strength to the Roman Catholic party, that the supremacy of the unionists would be seriously threatened'.[18]

Having eventually secured all their demands, the Government of Ireland Bill was passed with the assent of the Ulster Unionist Council in late 1920. While it created two parliaments, one in Dublin and one in Belfast, few believed the parliament in Dublin would ever meet. Sinn Féin would clearly dominate any election, and it already had its own parliament, the Dáil. Meanwhile, Unionists in Ulster were focused on establishing their own separate and distinct jurisdiction.

As these debates played out in the corridors of power, the war finally spread to the north-east, while unionists on the ground in Ulster began a parallel process to the one playing out in Westminster. This saw them physically exert their complete dominance over what was going to become the new jurisdiction of Northern Ireland.

In the summer of 1920 the unionist leader Edward Carson, when addressing some 25,000 people at an Orange Order parade at Finaghy in Belfast, told the crowd: 'We must proclaim today clearly that come what will and be the consequences what they may, we in Ulster will tolerate no Sinn Féin, no Sinn Féin organization, no Sinn Féin methods and these are not mere words. I hate words without action.'[19]

Sinn Féin had, by 1920, become a catch-all term for opposition to unionist dominance in the north-east. Carson's demand for action over words amounted to stochastic terrorism and had predictable consequences.

Violent attacks on Catholics, reminiscent of what had played out in the city in 1886, began a few days later in mid-July 1920. When the IRA shot a divisional commander of the RIC, Gerald Smyth, this triggered a wave of attacks on people assumed to have republican sympathies in his native Banbridge, a town twenty-five miles outside Belfast. Although the residents of Banbridge clearly had no involvement in an attack in Cork, some 200 miles away, this type of collective punishment would become an enduring hallmark of the war in the north-east.

By the time the violence spread to Belfast, workers were returning to the shipyards after the traditional summer break. Gangs of unionist workmen in the Harland & Wolff shipyard began attacking Catholic workers, as well as Protestant socialists and trade unionists dubbed 'rotten Prods'. From Harland & Wolff the sectarian violence spread to other major employers. Thousands were permanently forced out of their jobs.

Following a well-established trajectory, the violence spread from the workplace to the community. Catholic homes and business were attacked and burnt. Within days, over twenty people had been killed.

In the following weeks the violence in the north-east

ebbed and flowed. In August 1920 the IRA shot and killed Detective Inspector Oswald Swanzy in Lisburn. Swanzy had fled Cork city following his involvement in the murder of the city's republican Lord Mayor, Tomás Mac Curtain. Although support for the IRA was limited in the north-east, scores of houses in the town were burnt out and Catholics driven from their homes in retribution.

The IRA became increasingly active in Belfast later that year, attempting to wage war on the unionist authorities in the city, but struggled to have the impact it did elsewhere. It did not enjoy the support of the population: the majority in Belfast was unionist and most of the population with nationalist sympathies supported the Home Rule movement instead. IRA brigade staff in Belfast reported that, 'IRA forces were fighting among a hostile civil population and all through the struggle for independence these forces in Belfast were handicapped much more than any other unit in Ireland.' [20] In general, the conflict in the north-east differed considerably from the war in other parts of Ireland. While sectarian attacks did occur in the south and west, sectarianism was never the driving force it was in the north-east, where it soon became all-consuming. People were murdered purely on the basis of their religious background. In some instances, armed men fired into neighbourhoods knowing their random target would be a Catholic or a Protestant.

The British government stood firmly behind their allies in the unionist movement. Under pressure from unionist leaders, it formed the Ulster Special Constabulary. Theoretically raised to support the police, this was little more than a unionist militia. As attacks continued, Belfast became one of the most violent places in Ireland. What distinguished the violence there was the enormous number of civilian casualties. In Dublin, a comparable urban environment, civilians accounted for 45 per cent of deaths. In Belfast civilians constituted 85 per cent of fatalities.[21]

As Belfast descended into violence, the broader unionist plan to forge their own state of Northern Ireland, one of the underlying causes of the conflict, continued to progress. In the summer of 1921 the Government of Ireland Act took effect. King George V travelled to Belfast and opened the parliament there in June. As the British government transferred power to the unionist government of Northern Ireland over the following months, Ireland was in effect partitioned, and the War of Independence became two separate conflicts, one in the north-east, the other in the south and west. Mid-July 1921 displayed the diverging dynamics in a stark fashion.

On 9 July the IRA in Belfast, having received a tip-off, ambushed a police convoy attempting to arrest its volunteers, killing several constables. The following day, 10 July, dubbed 'Belfast's Bloody Sunday', saw the police, in concert with unionist civilians, attack nationalist communities, killing sixteen people. Meanwhile, the situation elsewhere was dramatically different. On 11 July a truce between the IRA and Crown Forces came into effect. While this theoretically covered the entire island, it had almost no impact in Belfast. The conflict raged on. Although a delegation of Irish republicans negotiated in London with the British government throughout the autumn and winter of 1921, the situation in the north-east was not discussed in any detail.

For the Hughes family, life was only getting worse as the war finally came to their door. In November 1921 their son Patrick was listed among the injured in the Mater Hospital in Belfast. Detail of what happened to Patrick Hughes were not included although he was lucky – the same report carried the names of six people killed, while a seventh, also in the Mater, had a bullet wound to the chest.[22] But there was still no end in sight.

That same month the British government passed control of security and policing to the unionist government, and what little restraint had previously existed now vanished. The Special Constabulary, demobilized under the terms of the truce, was brought back into service. It would become involved in brutal sectarian violence in early 1922: this included the murders of six Catholics at the McMahon family home in Belfast in March 1922 and the murder of a further six Catholics in Arnon Street in the city in April, which saw some of the victims bludgeoned to death in their beds.

By 1922 the conflict was effectively unlimited sectarian warfare. The IRA in Belfast, which had previously criticized the sectarianism of the Ancient Order of Hibernians, itself began to engage in sectarian attacks, throwing bombs at workers coming from the shipyards. As the Anglo-Irish Treaty was passed by the Dáil, establishing the Free State in the twenty-six southern and western counties of Ireland, the situation in the north-east grew intolerable. Relentless sectarian attacks continued, the most notorious of which saw a bomb thrown at Catholic schoolchildren, killing four.

On 4 March violence flared yet again in what was an

almost nightly occurrence in the city centre, on York Street. Owen Hughes, the second-youngest son of Thomas and Ann, was returning home late that evening as the sound of gunfire echoed around the city. After nearly two years of violence, this was par for the course for life in Belfast.

On that evening, the tram on which Owen Hughes was travelling came to an abrupt stop, at the junction of Henry Street and York Street, a mile south of Skegoneill Street. As the passengers looked out, they saw that a large crowd of men had blocked the road.

Three of their number then entered the tram and questioned a passenger, demanding to know their religion. When they responded that they were Protestant, the men moved on, making their way upstairs to where Owen Hughes was seated beside one of his brothers. The men stopped at Owen Hughes and asked him his religion. He responded 'Catholic'. It was the last thing he said.

The man who had asked the question drew a gun. Pointing it directly at Owen Hughes, he shot him in the head, killing him instantly. The killer then left, saying to the others who had entered the tram with him, 'That's one of them.'[23] The tram then continued up York Street towards Skegoneill Street, Owen's lifeless body slumped against his brother.

In the following days his case was mentioned in the press, but given that a pregnant woman had been shot at her doorstep in Belfast that evening, that story dominated the headlines instead. The Hughes family were gripped with fear in the aftermath of the murder. When the inquest took place (at a hearing during which the coroner investigated nineteen murders simultaneously) Owen's brother, never identified by name, took the stand. He obscured the truth of what had happened.

He described the general situation that night and said that there had been gunfire in the surrounding streets, suggesting a stray bullet may have killed his brother.[24] This was directly contradicted by numerous witnesses on the night and at the inquest. Henry Kielty, who had also been on the tram, stated that none of the windows were broken – a fact that belied the notion that a stray bullet had killed Owen Hughes. The Protestant passenger who had been interrogated first also provided clear testimony that Owen had been shot in the head after being asked his religion.

It appears that the Hughes family knew the identity of the killer, but for understandable reasons feared retribution. Decades later, another member of the family would state it was an individual named Alexander 'Buck Alec' Robinson.[25] A police file in 1922 shows that they were also aware of this, as it noted that Robinson had shot 'a young fellow named Hughes on the top of a tram car'.[26] But it came as little surprise that Robinson was never prosecuted for the murder.

The murder and its aftermath encapsulated the situation in Belfast and the emerging state of Northern Ireland. Robinson, twenty-one years of age at the time, had a string of convictions for various crimes ranging from theft to assault.

Despite or perhaps because of his past, he had been enlisted in the Ulster Special Constabulary. Robinson was also a member of the shadowy Ulster Protestant Association, which had become a death squad in the early 1920s, bent on killing Catholics. Yet he did not fear prosecution, or at least in early 1922 he didn't – he was known to brag about the murders he committed. In Belfast at this time, religious background and political allegiance (in Robinson's case Protestantism and unionism) were all that mattered, as the unionist leaders forged what would later be called a 'Protestant state'. Robinson's past was not only overlooked, but in the bitter violence consuming the city he was a useful figure for the authorities as they established unionist control and dominance.

The first priority of the new government of the North was bringing about the supremacy of unionists. A few weeks after Owen's death in March 1922, the Northern Ireland government passed what would become the cornerstone of its security policy – the Special Powers Act. This included provisions for the Minister for Home Affairs to 'take all such steps and issue all such orders as may be necessary for preserving the peace and maintaining order'. This sweeping legislation severely curtailed civil liberties and would be disproportionately used against Catholics.

A month later the IRA launched what was known as the Northern Offensive. This saw internal divisions over the Treaty set aside in an attempt to destabilize the state of Northern Ireland. It proved an abysmal failure. By the end of the summer of 1922, the unionist government had achieved total dominance. Through a range of measures, Catholics, some 33 per cent of the population, were being edged out of the world of work and increasingly public life, and formally treated as second-class citizens.

As the State moved from war to peace of a kind, the

unionist government acted to rein in the likes of Buck Alec Robinson. He was interned in 1922 and again in 1923, but never prosecuted for the murder of Owen Hughes, or the numerous other killings he had perpetrated. While he left Belfast for a time, he had returned by 1927, when he moved into Skegoneill Street. Whether the Hughes family were still living at Number 16 is unclear.[27]

The murder would have a lasting legacy. While Belfast had offered Thomas and Ann a future in the 1880s, the situation for their children and grandchildren in the twentieth century would be drastically different. The unionist state would discriminate against them at every turn. Although this alienated them from the city they lived in, the memory of Owen's murder and the official unwillingness to prosecute his murderer may explain the family's increasing involvement in the republican movement in the years that followed.

The most prominent of the family was Owen's great-nephew Brendan Hughes, who became a central figure in the Provisional IRA in the 1970s and early 1980s. In an interview in the early 2000s, he would recall the story of his great-uncle's murder when contextualizing his republican activism.[28]

Buck Alec Robinson lived in Belfast until 1995 where he died at the age of ninety-three.

CHAPTER 12

A Free State?

1923

> And I will make your cities waste, and bring your sanctuaries unto desolation.
>
> (Leviticus 26:31)

In the early twentieth century there were few institutions that enjoyed closer links with the British establishment than Oxford University. One of the oldest centres of learning in Western Europe, it also fulfilled a key political function – providing the British Empire with civil servants, diplomats and prime ministers. Even future monarch Edward VIII was a student before World War I.

Oxford's connections to the British establishment left the Irish students, who had been attending the university for centuries, in a difficult position during the Irish Revolution and War of Independence. Although drawn from the wealthiest in society, they held a range of views on the war and the subsequent establishment of the Free State. Unsurprisingly the Irish Society in Oxford, which organized talks on matters relating to Ireland, in an effort to maintain cohesion among this variety of opinion, declared itself neutral on the war, stating Irish people of all religious backgrounds and political viewpoints were welcome.

This attempt to straddle both sides of opinion would see a wide and varied list of speakers address the society meetings before and after independence. In the autumn of 1924 their programme of events was finely balanced. Sir Michael O'Dwyer (see Chapter 13) a controversial Tipperary man and former governor of the Punjab, began the season with reminiscences of his service to the Empire. He was followed by William Hickie, commander of the Irish Division in World War I, who reflected on the conflict. Oliver St John Gogarty, a Free State senator, provided balance with a talk on patriotism.

But without doubt the most controversial speaker was the Irish cabinet minister Kevin O'Higgins. He arrived in Oxford in October 1924 and made what proved to be one of the most famous speeches of his career. O'Higgins's agreement to address the society had been something of coup for the organizers. Although he served as Minister for Defence, many considered him the most influential member of the Free State Cabinet. The timing, meanwhile, could not have been more opportune, as O'Higgins was in many respects the man of the hour.

In late 1924 he was in a position to reflect on the tumultuous early years of the Irish Free State, which had been indelibly marked by a brutal civil war. Taking office after the ratification of the Anglo-Irish Treaty in January 1922, the following months revealed major opposition in the IRA to the Treaty and the Free State government.

While the political leadership of Sinn Féin – men like O'Higgins supported by a minority of IRA volunteers – had argued that the Treaty was the best offer available, the majority of IRA volunteers opposed its terms.

Meanwhile Liam Lynch, a leading opponent of the Treaty, reflected the views of many IRA volunteers when he said, 'We have declared for an Irish Republic, and will not live under any other law.'[1] Although originally written in 1917, these words embodied the attitudes of the Anti-Treaty side for many.

These irreconcilable tensions finally erupted into bitter violence in June 1922. By the time O'Higgins arrived in Oxford his Free State forces had crushed their opponents but the wounds of war were still fresh. The fighting had claimed some 2,000 lives, including O'Higgins's own father who had been killed in a raid on his house.

When he rose to speak to the Irish Society in Magdalen College Oxford, O'Higgins did not disappoint. His address, later published in pamphlet form under the title 'Three Years Hard Labour', saw O'Higgins launch into a stinging rebuke of critics of the Irish Free State at home and abroad. When he turned to the subject of the defeated forces in the IRA, he was uncompromising and dismissive. Recalling the aftermath of August 1922 when the Free State lost its two leading figures, Arthur Griffith and Michael Collins, he conjured up the scene he and his Cabinet colleagues faced in oft-quoted lines, 'the provisional government was simply eight young men in the City Hall standing amid the ruins of one administration, with the foundations of another not yet laid, and with wild men screaming through the keyhole'.[2]

O'Higgins had chosen his words carefully. His dismissal of his opponents as 'wild men' did not solely stem from the grief of a son who had lost his father in the recent civil war. He had an eye on history, well aware that some of his actions in the war could be judged harshly. In the months following August 1922, some of the most controversial events in the Irish Civil War had taken place. O'Higgins was aware if there had been wild men screaming through the keyhole at him, he and the other Free State leaders had their own wild men screaming back.

In the six months after August 1922, the moment O'Higgins cast himself as a young man trying to rebuild Irish society, the war had been marked by barbarism and brutality. Much of what followed could not be blamed on the IRA. His own cabinet colleagues had sanctioned the execution of dozens of prisoners in jails across Ireland. This paled in comparison to the atrocities committed by the Free State Army Forces, which had to one degree or another become a law unto itself. While they had massacred prisoners on several occasions, reports of atrocities against the civilian population also emerged.

That very night he rose to address the Irish Society in Oxford, 31 October, marked the anniversary of the first of two brutal anti-Semitic murders in the aftermath of the Civil War. While O'Higgins was at pains to portray his opponents as wild men, police in Dublin were closing on sensational suspects; men with connections to senior figures in the Free State Army and even the late Michael Collins himself.

Few in his Oxford audience had ever heard of the victims, Bernard Goldberg and Ernest Kahn, but the fate of these two Jewish men symbolized the somewhat chaotic nature of life in the opening years of the Free State, better than any flourishes of rhetoric from O'Higgins did.

Ireland's Jewish community had emerged in the late nineteenth century when hundreds of Jewish families fleeing persecution in the Russian Empire began to arrive in Ireland. Violent anti-Semitic pogroms in 1881, 1883 and 1903, involving thousands of murders, saw Jews flee westwards in droves. Among those to move to Ireland was the Kahn family, who arrived around 1899 when Lena Kahn gave birth to the family's youngest son, Ernest, in Dublin. The Jewish community they found in Ireland was small but well-established. From humble beginnings in 1881, when there had been only 198 Jews on the entire island, this had grown to over 3,000 by the turn of the twentieth century and stood just short of 5,000 a decade later.

Much like Irish emigrants in the US, Ireland's Jewish immigrants gravitated toward the large urban centres. Many came to Belfast, Cork and Limerick,[3] but the Kahns settled in the largest community, which became known as Little Jerusalem, in Dublin. While never exclusively Jewish, this area of south inner-city Dublin had a higher proportion of Jews than any other part of the city, or the island for that matter. Here they enjoyed modest success. By 1911 only four of Dublin's 329 Jewish families were living in the city's tenements, the appalling subdivided houses in which families shared a single room.[4] Ernest Kahn was raised in a five-roomed house on Lennox Street, which he shared with his grandmother Fanny, his mother Lena and his three siblings. His father was an infrequent presence at home, possibly due to his work as a travelling salesman.

Nevertheless, by the early twentieth century the Kahns were well adapted to life in Ireland. They began to change their names to sound similar to those of their neighbours, while still retaining their Jewish identity. Therefore Ernest's mother Lena, herself born in the Russian Empire, changed her name to Lea. His grandmother Fanny changed her surname from Abrahamovitz to the more English-sounding Abrahamson. Ernest himself was originally named Emmanuel.[5]

Their quality of life in Ireland before the outbreak of World War I had shaped the opinions of many Dublin Jews towards the British Empire, and subsequently their attitudes to the revolutionary era. From the perspective of most Irish Jews, the United Kingdom had not only provided them with a safe haven but had also allowed them to practise their religion free from state repression. Indeed, it was a state where they could even aspire to high office – the nineteenth-century British Prime Minister Benjamin Disraeli had been Jewish before converting to Anglicanism. Bethel Solomons, a Jewish student in Dublin in the early twentieth century, explained their general experience of the United Kingdom: 'Great Britain tries to be a just and tolerant nation and is the safest place in the world for those who are likely to be victims of intolerance . . . especially people of my own Jewish race.'[6]

This experience led many Irish Jews, particularly in Dublin, to espouse unionist beliefs in their politics. While generally the case, this was not universal and as the community settled in, the Judaeo-Irish Home Rule Association was formed in Dublin in 1908.[7] In the main, though, Dublin's Jews had little reason to support political change in the early years of the twentieth century. At the outbreak of World War I they were vocal in their support for the British war effort. The rabbi at the Adelaide Road Synagogue in Dublin informed worshippers in late August 1914 that, 'Jews are anxious, as ever, to show their fidelity to their native adopted land. They respond to the call of the country, joining many regiments of his Majesty's Army, as well as the Navy.'[8]

While this was an expression of deeply held patriotism for their new home, it was also motivated by fear. The early weeks of the war had seen violent protests target Germans living in Dublin, which led to Jews being assaulted in cases of mistaken identity. This prompted the Jewish community in the city to publicly point out its Russian, not German, origins.[9] The following day the leaders of Derry's Jewish community followed suit and also proclaimed their loyalty to the King and the United Kingdom.[10]

Ernest Kahn, aged only fifteen in 1914, was not old enough to enlist in the British Army at the outbreak of the war. The following year he started on an alternative career in the British civil service in Dublin. Taking his clerkship exams in Skerry's College on St Stephen's Green, he received the twenty-third-highest mark in Ireland.[11] This secured him a position in the Department of Agriculture, which was becoming increasingly important as Ireland was integrated into the war economy of the wider UK. As international trade plummeted and food shortages loomed, the government introduced tillage orders that demanded 10 per cent of all land be devoted to grain production in 1917, a figure increased to 15 per cent the following year.[12]

The outbreak of the 1916 Rising had little direct effect on the Jewish community of the city, at least initially. Somewhat inevitably, as clashes spread through the city, several of the Kahns' neighbours were caught up in the fighting. Abraham Harris, from nearby Portobello, was shot and killed by the British Army at a checkpoint on 24 April.[13] The following day a Catholic neighbour of the Kahns from Lennox Street disappeared, and was assumed to be among the unidentified civilian casualties.[14]

With the violence and upheaval that it brought about, the radicalization of Irish society in the following years was not welcomed by many Irish Jews. The onset of the War of Independence in 1919, and the intensification of revolutionary violence, was deeply disquieting. In 1920 a major riot between soldiers and the public on Portobello Bridge – no far from the quietude of Little Jerusalem – saw shots fired.[15] And yet, for all the drama and bloodshed of those years, the wars remained somewhat distant from day-to-day life in the inner-city Jewish community.

The only casualty from Lennox Street during the War of Independence was twenty-six-year-old Catholic Jane Boyle, who was killed in November 1920. She was one of the fourteen people who were shot dead on Bloody Sunday when Crown Forces opened fire on the crowd attending a Gaelic football match in Croke Park (see Chapter 10).[16]

The final year of the War of Independence saw a complete breakdown in law and order and ushered in a period of profound uncertainty and anxiety for all in

Irish society, not least the Jewish community, which had its own particular fears and concerns. While its experience in Ireland had been largely positive, casual anti-Semitism was by no means uncommon. Ernest Kahn himself had suffered anti-Semitic taunts at his workplace in the Department of Agriculture.[17] His father, a travelling salesman, would undoubtedly have encountered similar anti-Semitism in rural Ireland. In 1906 a twenty-six-year-old Jewish man from Sligo, Bernard Epstein, was convicted of selling pirated music. Sentenced to fourteen days in prison, his jailers made pains to underline the fact that Epstein was Jewish.[18]

That same bigotry had found an organized and collective expression in 1904, in what was called the Limerick Pogrom, an event which darkened the Jewish experience in Ireland. Even though the Jewish community in Limerick city was minuscule, numbering 150 in a total population of around 40,000, it had come under sustained attack from a local Catholic priest, Fr John Creagh. The cleric preached age-old anti-Semitic diatribes, blaming Jews for killing Jesus Christ and accusing them of being duplicitous in their business dealings.[19] Creagh's tirades from the pulpit led to attacks on Jewish property and a boycott of their businesses in the city.

Revolutionary situations, notably in Russia, had seen violent anti-Semitism erupt before, but there was no repeat of the events of 1904 during the revolutionary era in Ireland. Nevertheless, the agreement of the Treaty between republican negotiators and their British counterparts in December 1921, bringing the possibility of a return to peace and stability, was more than welcome.

But this brought its own problems, for Ernest Kahn in particular. Having joined what was the British civil service in 1915, it was unclear what would happen when the Irish Free State was established and the British began to withdraw. While provision had been made to retain the vast majority of civil servants, there were concerns over whether their work conditions would remain the same.[20]

On 16 January 1922 the new Provisional Government of the Irish Free State informed the civil service that it was now the effective government, but the ambiguity around Ernest Kahn's future wages, pension and working conditions remained. The following months, far from bringing the stability hoped for, were marked by continued upheaval right across Irish society. As the British administration and garrison began to withdraw from the twenty-six counties of the Irish Free State, the new government, led by Arthur Griffith and Michael Collins, began to set out an economic programme and vision for Ireland. It quickly emerged that there were major disagreements over most issues. The Treaty itself, the foundation document of the State, was rejected by considerable numbers of IRA volunteers. In March of that year they held a convention, stating that they no longer considered themselves answerable to the Dáil.

Meanwhile, as the new government began to reveal its deeply conservative economic views, this led to tensions with the 250,000-strong trade union movement, which had grown rapidly during the War of Independence. During that conflict it had largely supported the IRA, but as tensions grew between the opposing wings of the republican movement, the trade unions became increasingly determined to set their own agenda.

In the spring of 1922 they organized a general strike in an effort to stop a civil war, with one official giving their view: 'The strike showed the power of free labour to do anything it wished. Labour is opposed to Free Staters, Republicans, and Unionists alike. We are out for a Workers' Commonwealth.'[21]

However, this could not stop the rising tensions within the Republican movement over the Treaty, which erupted into all-out war in June 1922 when the Free State began to assert its authority. That month it issued an ultimatum to an IRA garrison opposed to the Treaty, which had occupied the Four Courts in Dublin city centre, to surrender. When this was rejected, government forces shelled the court buildings, starting what would be eleven months of warfare.

But in terms of the general population, the Civil War was somewhat removed in comparison to the experience of the War of Independence. There was little mobilization of the general public in favour of either side. After government forces defeated the IRA in Dublin in a matter of weeks, they then went on to seize most major towns over the summer of 1922.

Their opponents in the IRA fell back on guerrilla tactics, and a low-intensity conflict, which was nonetheless extremely bitter, ensued. Largely limited to Munster, it was marked by tragedy and atrocity. Leading republican Michael Collins, the commander-in-chief of the National Army, was killed in a skirmish at Béal na Bláth in West Cork on 22 August while the government, in an effort to break resistance, began executing prisoners in larger numbers throughout the latter part of 1922. The IRA responded with a campaign targeting property and infrastructure. The final months of the war were particularly bitter, marked by escalating levels of brutality.

The actions of government forces in County Kerry became notorious. In separate incidents in March 1923, prisoners were killed in the most brutal fashion – tied to landmines, which were then detonated.[22] The IRA meanwhile attempted to respond by targeting prominent figures in the Free State. The government TD Sean Hales was shot dead in December 1922. Three months later, a raid on Kevin O'Higgins family home in Laois resulted in his father being killed when he tried to resist.

These events, shocking as they were, were to a certain extent remote for people such as the Kahn family in Dublin, where major fighting had ended nine months earlier. After the IRA chief of staff Liam Lynch was shot and killed in the Knockmealdown Mountains in April 1923, his successor ordered the IRA to 'dump arms' the following month.

Yet while the government exerted increasing dominance over Irish society, violence did not end. Government forces continued to conduct what was in effect a secret campaign, as the intelligence division of the National Army, the Criminal Investigation Department (CID), persisted in the hunt for its opponents.

In August 1923 a neighbour of the Kahns, Henry McEntee, a carpenter who lived at 22 Lennox Street,[23] was found dead near Finglas, a village north of Dublin. He had been shot several times. The inquest revealed that McEntee was a member of the anti-Treaty IRA, the losing side of the Civil War. Even though the conflict had technically ended, McEntee's wife testified that detectives had told her that she would find her husband dead in a ditch. It was widely suspected that he had been killed by the CID. The family's legal representative at the inquest pointed out that several opponents of the government had by then been found shot dead in fields and quarries around Dublin.[24]

As similar executions continued, it was increasingly clear that the army was becoming something of a law unto itself. A litany of abuses, particularly in Kerry, where some of the worst fighting had taken place, emerged, most notably the so-called Kenmare incident.

In June 1923 the house of Dr Randall McCarthy near Kenmare, County Kerry, was raided, and his two daughters, Flossie and Jessie, were subjected to a horrific ordeal. Their hair was covered in motor oil, which had the effect of making it fall out. The sisters were whipped with Sam Browne belts and then raped.[25]

There was no question of a political motive – the McCarthy family were supporters of the government. The motivation seems to have been jealousy: according to one account,[26] the women had rejected advances from the soldiers. Further still, the attack was not simply the action of junior recruits: senior army figures, including Paddy Daly, the commanding officer in Kerry, were directly involved in the attack.

Despite the gravity of the incident, attempts to prosecute the guilty men were undermined by Richard Mulcahy, the commander-in-chief of the National Army and Minister for Defence.[27] While there was growing unhappiness among some in the government, notably Kevin O'Higgins himself, about control over the army, the incident went unpunished.

It was in this context that rumours began to circulate around Dublin that government soldiers were implicated in attacks on Jews, which was alarming in the extreme. The first incident was very unusual and at first appeared to be motiveless. The targets of the attack were Samuel Goldberg and his brother Bernard, who was visiting from England. As the brothers walked through the city centre at midnight on 31 October 1923, they were accosted by three men. They demanded that the Goldbergs stop, and began to question them. After asking their names, the soldiers insisted that the brothers accompany them. After just a few steps, they started to beat Samuel Goldberg with something heavy and, as he fled, he heard two gunshots. His brother Bernard had been fatally wounded.[28]

The police were able to ascertain from witnesses that a car had been seen leaving the scene. An initial police report written that night was later amended with further details; that men dressed as military despatch riders had been seen in the area.[29]

The inquest determined Bernard Goldberg's death to be one of wilful murder. No motive was stated, but the fact that the soldiers knew little more about the murdered man than his name, clearly Jewish in origin, strongly suggested anti-Semitism.

Just two weeks later, on 14 November 1923, Ernest Kahn was on his way home, having spent the evening in the company of friends at the Jewish Literary and Social Club on Harrington Street. In the company of another Jewish man, David Miller, they set out for nearby

Lennox Street. However, during the short journey, events alarmingly similar to what had happened to the Goldbergs two weeks earlier unfolded. Two men approached Kahn and Miller and stopped them. They started to question them about their names, what they were doing, and their religion. At the end of an interrogation, which lasted five minutes, after the friends had identified themselves as Jews, one of the men stated 'You'd better run for it.'[30]

As Miller and Kahn ran, their interrogators drew weapons and opened fire. Miller was struck by a bullet in the shoulder, but Ernest Kahn sustained five gunshot wounds to the neck and shoulders. As Kahn lay bleeding in the street, the two assailants jumped into a car and sped from the scene. Miller immediately summoned help, and both men were taken to the nearby Meath Street Hospital. While Miller's injuries proved non-life-threatening, Kahn had been fatally wounded. He was already dead by the time they made it to the hospital.[31]

On this occasion, the Dublin City Coroner was unequivocal about the motive behind the attack, stating that the men had been targeted because they were Jews, and that this was an attack on Dublin's Jewish community.[32]

Fears began to spread in the febrile atmosphere of Dublin in 1923, especially among the Jewish community. When a photographer turned up to Ernest Kahn's funeral, the mourners covered their faces to protect their identities before one individual took the camera and threw it into the street.[33] When asked for comment, the Chief Rabbi of Ireland, Isaac Herzog, declined to make a statement on the murders, except to state that Ernest Kahn had received no threat, and he was not aware that any member of his community had done so.

Casual anti-Semitism saw journalists and editors frame the killing in stereotypical ways. Reports claimed that Ernest Kahn had been mistaken for a moneylender, and that he had been seen in the company of Christian women. The inquiries of the Dublin Metropolitan Police, who investigated the case, had different and troubling findings. They recognized that anti-Semitism was the motive, given that Bernard Goldberg had been shot in remarkably similar circumstances, and that the only thing that linked the cases was the fact that both victims were Jewish. Their inquiries also led detectives to believe that army personnel were involved in both attacks.

However, the investigation was immediately blocked by the army. Within weeks of the murder, detectives contacted the nearby Beggars Bush Barracks and asked to see the logbooks for all cars leaving the barracks on the nights Ernest Kahn and Bernard Goldberg had been shot. When these were handed over, the entries recording movement on the nights of 13–16 November, which included the night Ernest Kahn was murdered, had been torn out.

The logs for 31 October, the night Bernard Goldberg was murdered, revealed that one car had in fact entered the barracks around 2.30 a.m., shortly after the attack. A subsequent army investigation would state that the car, somewhat conveniently, belonged to Commandant James Fitzgerald, though he could not have been the killer as he had a cast-iron alibi – he had been at the wedding of Michael Noyk, a leading Jewish republican. Before long, though, the police learned that he had, at the very least, helped cover up the trail of the killers. It had been Fitzgerald who had taken the logs after the police asked for them and returned them with the relevant pages missing.[34]

Faced with a wall of silence from the military forces, the police continued to investigate Ernest Kahn's murder until, in 1924, a chance interaction in a Dublin court led to a breakthrough. A police sergeant, James Hughes, observed two men, Ralph Laffan and James Conroy, talking in the court. He recognized the two as similar to the pair wanted for the murder of Ernest Kahn. This was a sensational development given the identity of one of the men. While Laffan was private citizen, James Conroy was a senior figure in Free State Military circles and a veteran of the War of Independence. He had served in the Dublin Active Service Unit, and 'the Squad', Michael Collins' hand-picked group of IRA volunteers who targeted key British officials in Dublin during the War of Independence. He had also been with Collins at Béal na Bláth when he had been killed.[35]

The police initially focused their efforts on Laffan. He was arrested in December 1924 and quickly broke under the strain of interrogation. The police brought in David Miller, who bore the bullet wound on his shoulder from the night he had been shot alongside Ernest Kahn. On seeing Laffan, Miller immediately recognized him, saying, 'your face has haunted me since that night'.[36]

Confronted with such damning evidence and facing a potential death sentence, Ralph Laffan made a statement to the police revealing the sensational truth behind what had happened. He claimed that while he had driven the car, the actual killers of Ernest Kahn were his brother Fred Laffan and the distinguished republican veteran Commandant James Conroy.[37] Ralph Laffan absolved himself by arguing that Miller had confused him with his brother, Fred Laffan.

Before any further arrests could be made Fred Laffan and James Conroy fled Ireland for Mexico, and by 1925, the case against the two had stalled.[38] Ralph Laffan was nevertheless put on trial but he was acquitted – his defence, that he had been mistaken for his brother, was successful. Meanwhile, the two he named as the killers, his brother Fred, and Conroy, remained beyond the reach of the authorities in Mexico.

The matter would eventually come to a head in the early 1930s, when Conroy finally returned to Ireland. The authorities believed he had assurances from key witnesses that they would not testify against him. However, the Dublin Metropolitan Police which had been absorbed into the national police force, the Gardaí, nevertheless weighed up the evidence they had gathered on Conroy through informants and former soldiers to see if they could press ahead with a prosecution. The scale of Conroy's illegal activity they uncovered was astonishing. While the Gardaí were convinced that Conroy had been involved in the murder of Ernest Kahn and Bernard Goldberg, they had strong evidence to suggest he had also committed two armed robberies in Dublin over the summer of 1923, stealing over £1,000.

In terms of a motive for the murder of Kahn, in 1932 Garda intelligence reported rumours that Conroy had become enraged after a sex worker he was acquainted with had been assaulted by an unnamed Jewish dentist. This seems improbable, and begs the question as to why the dentist had not been targeted. Conroy's political affiliations in the 1930s suggest a more explicit anti-Semitism was the reason for the attacks. By 1934 he had become a member of the Blueshirts. Modelled on Mussolini's Blackshirts and Hitler's Brownshirts, this fascist organization provided a political home for an array of malcontents on the extreme right of Irish politics. With a strong emphasis on traditional values it was most similar to Spanish fascism and harboured several vocal anti-semites.

Ultimately the police decided against arresting Conroy. The passage of time had damaged the chances of securing a conviction. Fred Laffan, a key witness, was still living in Mexico. Ralph Laffan, the Gardaí believed, would retract his statement that Conroy had been involved. Meanwhile, David Miller, who had been with Ernest Kahn on the night in question, had served a short prison sentence after being involved in a fatal car accident. This would inevitably be used to undermine his credibility on the witness stand in any trial. Perhaps more significantly, the Gardaí believed Conroy would intimidate Miller if he attempted to testify against him.

While Ernest Kahn's family never saw justice, his killer received a military pension and eventually emigrated to the USA. When Conroy applied for this pension, Paddy Daly, Conroy's comrade in the Dublin IRA and the Free State Army, himself a man accused of involvement in the attack on the McCarthy sisters in Kenmare, described Conroy as a 'real good murderer'.[39] Few could argue with this.

To what extent the army officers who protected Conroy were aware of his activities never fully emerged. Their actions, nevertheless, underscored the complex and fraught situation in Ireland in 1923, as the island moved agonizingly from war towards peace. This transition was hampered by the bitterness emanating from the Civil War. Killings continued, with many considering the IRA assassination of Kevin O'Higgins in 1927 the last act in the conflict. The memory of these events, however, was not easily forgotten and would shape the political landscape in Ireland for decades to come.

CHAPTER 13

The Price of Progress

1928

Thou shalt neither vex a stranger nor oppress him;
for ye were strangers in the land of Egypt.
(Exodus 22:21)

From east to west, Europe in the early 1920s was a continent in turmoil. Although an armistice had brought an end to World War I on 11 November 1918, peace remained elusive. Ireland was not the only region consumed by a war of independence and riven by civil war; similar conflicts had erupted all across Eastern and Central Europe. Three of the world's great powers – the Russian, German and Austro-Hungarian Empires – had ceased to exist by 1918, and many of the new states that rose up in their wake were disputed territories. The post-war map of Europe now contained independent states such as Poland, Latvia, Estonia and Lithuania, which had previously been provinces of larger empires. Bloody conflicts, many of them fought over the borders of these emerging states, saw an estimated four million people killed in what was supposedly a time of peace, between late 1918 and 1923.[1]

The scale of death in some regions was even greater than during the world war – over 30,000 people, 1per cent of the population – died in Finland's bloody civil war in the opening months of 1919. This was fifteen times the number of fatalities from the Irish Civil War.

While many of these conflicts were rooted in the experience of defeat or revolution, nearly every single country across the Continent faced deep divisions of one kind or another. Even where borders were not contested, the perennial tensions over the distribution of wealth and resources found new expression in increasingly violent strikes and clashes between left and right. These had been fuelled by the sense among many that, given the immense cost the war had exacted, life would now improve. This hadn't been the case.

In 1925 when Jacob Kunz left his home in Bavaria, Southern Germany,[2] and travelled nearly two thousand kilometres to Ireland, he traversed a continent of dashed expectations. While his ultimate destination was Limerick on the west coast of Ireland, every step of the way he found signs of discontent. His own homeland was tentatively emerging from the chaos of the early 1920s but, with nearly two million Germans unemployed in the young Weimar Republic, a deep well of resentment remained.

Even in England, arguably the most stable country on the Continent in the 1920s, tensions were rising by 1925. Back in 1918 the British wartime prime minister, David Lloyd George, had famously promised 'Homes Fit for

Heroes' for the veterans of the war. By the middle of the decade that was a distant and broken pledge. As Jacob Kunz made his way north-westward through the Continent to Ireland, deep divisions were emerging between the trade-union movement in the UK and the British government over attempts to reduce wages. These would lead to the General Strike of 1926.

On a continent defined by division, Jacob Kunz's destination, the Irish Free State, appeared to outsiders at least to have fared far better than most. While the four years of conflict between the start of the War of Independence and the end of the Civil War had led to over four thousand deaths, this paled in comparison to the experience of other countries in Eastern Europe. Three thousand people had been killed in Riga following the occupation of the city by right-wing paramilitary forces in the summer of 1919. This was in a city which had already seen its population halved due to war and revolution over the previous two years.[3]

By 1925 the Free State also appeared to be finally emerging from its revolutionary turmoil. The government, now firmly in control, had emerged victorious and, despite its authoritarian tendencies, elections continued to be held. While the defeated side, represented by Sinn Féin, refused to take their seats in the Dáil, the country appeared more stable than it had been in a decade.

To many the government seemed dynamic compared to those of other countries. The Indian journalist Saint Nihal Singh, another visitor to Ireland in the mid-1920s, had nothing but praise for W.T. Cosgrave and his cabinet. In a series of articles published in the English *Daily Herald*, Singh time and again praised the fresh thinking of the leadership in the Free State – inspired at least in part, he thought, by their youth.[4] Many of the cabinet ministers were still in their thirties.

Singh was not the only one who held such views – the work that drew the German Jacob Kunz to Ireland in 1925, if anything, confirmed the sense that the leadership of the Irish Free State was nothing if not ambitious. He was one of several hundred German workers travelling to Ireland to work on what was one of the largest infrastructural projects in the world at the time – the Ardnacrusha hydroelectric dam. The project embodied the growing optimism and confidence Singh had observed in his meetings with the Irish Free State leaders.

The plan was remarkable – the Ardnacrusha dam, once completed, would harness Ireland's longest and largest river, the Shannon, to generate enormous amounts of electricity. If successful, the project had the potential to transform Ireland. In the mid-1920s Ireland's electricity generation was limited at best. Fuelled by coal imports, it was mostly used to power public street lighting. The plan for the Ardnacrusha dam, known as the Shannon Scheme, had the potential to vastly expand this, and would generate three times as much electricity as the existing network once complete.[5] This opened the potential to completely modernize the Irish economy. If successful, the Free State would a be a leader in the field. The potential of harnessing the hydroelectric power of the Shannon would allow the State to provide electricity for use in domestic and industrial settings – so ambitious was the project at the time that some critics questioned whether Ireland could even use all the electricity the dam would produce.[6]

The costs for the project were, unsurprisingly, astronomical. Coming in at around £5.2 million, this constituted around one-quarter of the government's entire annual budget. However, the planners had a bold vision: once operational, it would lead to nothing less than the electrification of rural Ireland, from towns and villages to the farms that remained the backbone of the Irish economy. The dam, in many respects, appeared to be a social and economic embodiment of Irish independence – a project planned in Dublin for the benefit of Ireland. This was all the more impressive given that Ireland had remained one of the most underdeveloped regions in Europe throughout the nineteenth century.

For Jacob Kunz, who came from one of the most fractured and divided countries in Europe, the support the project received from both left and right of the political spectrum suggested that Irish society had developed a degree of cohesion that other countries could only aspire to. The Labour Party and Trades Union Congress, which had often clashed with the government since Britain had withdrawn, welcomed the Shannon Scheme, claiming, 'it is of fundamental, and perhaps epoch-making, importance to the economic and social future of the country'.[7]

From its earliest days it was recognized that the Shannon Scheme would require international expertise. The scale of the groundbreaking project was beyond Irish engineering firms, and the German company Siemens-Schuckert, experienced in the field, was hired to oversee the construction of the dam. Under enormous pressure from the government once contracts were signed, Siemens wasted no time in starting work. While the majority of the workers would be Irish, a policy that would reduce unemployment, Siemens stipulated they would need to bring in workers with experience on such projects from Germany.

Among the first to arrive in Limerick had been Johann Kunz, Jacob's brother, who had started work in September. Three months later Jacob followed in his brother's footsteps as the German labour force on the project swelled to several hundred strong.

In the late summer the preparatory works – including the laying of sixty miles of railway to facilitate the project – had been carried out. The railway connected the site of the dam at Parteen, five kilometres north of Limerick, to the docks in the city. This facilitated Siemens bringing in heavy equipment directly from Hamburg in Germany.

Sizeable as the German workforce was, it was dwarfed by the huge numbers of Irish labourers hired to work on the project. As the preparatory works started in Limerick, Siemens also opened administrative offices in Dublin to manage the huge logistical task of hiring an army of 3,000 Irish workers.

To this end they had taken out adverts in September 1925, seeking 3,000 unskilled workers. The wages offered were thirty-two shillings, with accommodation, for a fifty-hour week. In a country where unemployment stood at around 90,000 in the mid-1920s,[8] the prospect of such large-scale employment drew praise in the international press. But by the time Jacob Kunz reached Limerick just three months later, the scheme was increasingly revealing that the Irish government was, in reality, failing to meet the expectations many had after the War of Independence. The implementation of the Shannon Scheme brought to the fore the deep ideological divisions over the direction of Irish society.

While the Irish trade union movement had welcomed the plans to build a hydroelectric dam, its attitude had soured once Siemens began works. Long before Jacob Kunz reached Ireland, it had clashed repeatedly with construction firms over their hiring policies. Initially, union branches around Limerick city had voiced concerns that their members were going to be ignored in favour of workers from Germany and other parts of the country.[9] While Siemens's plans to hire an enormous labour force of 3,000 workers could have allayed these fears, it led instead to a major confrontation with the Irish Transport and General Workers' Union (ITGWU).

While the dam was clearly an industrial project, Siemens used agricultural labourers' wages as a benchmark. The unions pointed out that agricultural wages were frequently supplemented by benefits in kind, which would not be available on the Shannon Scheme.[10] They also criticized the government for not consulting them before the contracts were signed. Negotiations failed, and within weeks the ITWGU initiated strike action. The union was in a powerful position, as it represented the Limerick dockworkers. In the autumn of 1925 the dockworkers refused to offload Siemens ships in the port, creating huge logistical problems.

As tensions were rising, Siemens took the controversial step of hiring former government minister Joseph McGrath as its Director of Labour. McGrath was a deeply divisive figure. A poacher-turned-gamekeeper, he had once been a union official himself. However, his actions during the Civil War and afterwards set the tone for how he would handle the strike. McGrath had overseen the Criminal Investigation Department (CID), which had executed political opponents of the Free State government after the Civil War had ended (see the case of Henry McEntee referenced in Chapter 12). To break the strike by the ITWGU, he hired former soldiers. Almost inevitably, the conflict soon turned violent. By the time Jacob Kunz arrived in Limerick in mid-December, the last clashes of the strike were taking place. The optimism that had marked Saint Nihal Singh's articles about the Irish Free State were now nowhere to be seen. Indeed, the strike had forced the mayor of Limerick to open what were in effect soup kitchens, to provide cheap food to the large numbers of destitute in the city.[11]

When Jacob Kunz started work on the project the conditions he found were appalling, and a deeply tense atmosphere prevailed across the enormous site that stretched miles along the Shannon. The German workers, frequently working in positions of authority, earned large sums of money compared to the Irish. Jacob Kunz was paid six pounds per week, nearly four times what the unskilled Irish workers earned. The Germans also availed of the limited free housing Siemens built at the site, but the promise that all workers would be accommodated was never met – many workers took board anywhere they could find it.

When a journalist from the *Irish Independent* visited the area in 1926 they found that 'the places in which men are living and sleeping are not at all fit for human beings'.[12]

Workers were sleeping in haybarns, stables and sheds. In one instance they described the bedding as 'old hay thrown on the floor with no suggestion of bed clothing'.[13]

Unable to eat at the site canteens because their wages were too low, the Irish workers built their own kitchens, but these were removed.[14] This situation was exacerbated by the Siemens policy of laying off workers with little justification and replacing them from the ranks of the unemployed. This practice, by design or intention, undoubtedly prevented the ITGWU from getting a foothold on the Shannon Scheme, but the fact that workers were being hired and fired at such speed put additional strain on the already struggling local infrastructure. Sacked workers frequently remained in the area in the hope of being rehired. Despite widespread press coverage the minister in charge, Patrick Gilligan, rejected calls to intervene, saying his priority was to not place any burden on Siemens that was not in the contract.[15]

The death toll on the project was high: the construction lasted for three and a half years, and forty-seven people were killed in workplace or related accidents.[16] The Irish government took Siemens to task while the company blamed Irish inexperience on major construction projects and demanded the right to hire more German labour, pointing out that Germans were dying at a lower rate.[17]

While the conditions were appalling, Siemens never had any issue finding cheap, willing labour, given the wider economic situation. Few political leaders had envied the position of the Irish Free State government in 1922. It had to try and establish a new state with few resources and, by the late 1920s, there was growing discontent about the policies it had decided on. While other countries facing similar financial constraints, notably Germany, often proclaimed a desire to develop a welfare state, the Free State government had pursued a different approach that pervaded all aspects of life. Similar to the extreme conservativism of its social policy (see Chapter 14), economically it implemented some of the most severe austerity in twentieth-century Irish history.

In an effort to balance the budget it cut the old-age pension by 10 per cent. The government refused to alter the structure of the Irish economy, instead desiring to maintain an agricultural sector geared toward cattle exports to England. In terms of industry the Free State was one of most underdeveloped regions in Western Europe but the government in the 1920s showed interest in changing this. Agriculture, not industry, was seen as the foundation of the Free State economy.

The Free State government considered large, wealthy farms to be the cornerstone of Irish society and the economy.[18] This was far removed from the reality of life. The minister for agriculture throughout the 1920s, Patrick Hogan, himself the son of a large farmer, somewhat absurdly equated the ordinary Irish farmer with a person who owned at least two hundred acres. In reality they were some 2 per cent of landowners.[19] Hogan saw big farmers as being one and the same as the 'agricultural community'.[20] Armed with this view, the government had used soldiers to break an agricultural labourers' strike for increased wages in 1923.

Meanwhile, conditions for the poor remained abysmal.

Little effort was made to improve the notorious working-class housing of the major cities. After a failed harvest in 1924, Hogan, himself from County Galway, dismissed widespread food shortages in the west, saying, '*there is always distress in the West*'.[21]

While poverty continued to drive people to the Shannon Scheme to find work, the low wages and poor conditions made it difficult for the unskilled workers to save money. As the project pushed on relentlessly, the construction was complicated by language differences between the German foremen and the Irish workers. Despite working at the site for four years, Jacob Kunz's brother Johann still required an interpreter as late as 1929.[22] In some instances, to communicate with workers who had come from Connemara in West Galway, they could need two translators – one from German to English, and a second from English to Irish.

Theft and robberies around the works were not unusual, given the large numbers of underpaid workers and unemployed in the surrounding area. In 1927 an auxiliary postman, William Cusack, was convicted of defrauding the German workforce by adding an additional charge of two shillings when he was delivering mail.[23] His defence pointed out that he was paid a meagre twenty-five shillings a week.[24] Amid such crime, Jacob and Johann Kunz had developed a somewhat strange practice with regard to their savings.

Each week, Jacob took responsibility for the money he and his brother saved. While they trusted some of their savings to a friend,[25] Jacob Kunz carried around large amounts of money on his person at all times. By 1928 this amounted to £80 in his pocket and over £400 sewn into the lining of his jacket. Surrounded by widespread poverty and deprivation this inevitably made him a target.

On 21 December 1928 Jacob Kunz left the works at Parteen, setting off on foot in the direction of his accommodation a few kilometres away at Ardnacrusha. Eager to return to his residence, he followed the fastest route along a trainline constructed for the project. This took Kunz through a countryside so churned by construction that it resembled a World War I battlefield.

In the darkness of that winter evening, and the noise of distant construction, Kunz had failed to notice a second man had followed him down the track. The German had not ventured far from Parteen when his pursuer silently approached him from behind. Kunz appears to have been oblivious to the approach of his assailant, who had armed himself with a heavy iron bar. Before he could defend himself, the man struck Jacob Kunz over the back of the head, knocking the German off his feet. The initial impact of the blow did not kill Jacob but left him unconscious on train line. As he lay motionless on the track his attacker rifled through his pockets, robbing him, before leaving his body on the line.

A short time later two more workmen coming from Parteen came across Kunz. He had regained consciousness and was sitting along the tracks with his head in hands. Approaching him, the workmen realized he had sustained serious injuries. When they tried to take him to a first-aid station at the works he resisted, revealing the motive for the attack by repeating two words in his heavy German accent, 'my monies, my monies'.

Although he was still clinging to consciousness, his injuries were dire. Taken to the nearby Limerick Hospital, he died later that night, having sustained a major brain injury and skull fracture. A motive for the attack was quickly ascertained. While the attacker had not realized Jacob had over £400 in the lining of his coat, he had stolen the £80 he carried in his pocket.

It did not take the police long to find a suspect. A few hours after the assault another worker on the Shannon Scheme, John Cox, was arrested. Cox had many reasons to resent Jacob Kunz. He had been replaced by Kunz in the position of foreman when Jacob had arrived and, in time, found himself working beneath the German. This dynamic was complicated further – John Cox was a veteran of the recent war against Germany and had sustained lifelong wounds in 1917.[26] Psychological reasoning aside, however, the direct motive for the attack was straightforward: money.

Earlier in the day John Cox had injured his hand, which meant an enforced week's leave of absence to allow the injury to heal. This left him in a difficult position as there was no sick pay provided to injured workers.[27] Later that day he was in Limerick, where he encountered a Garda he was acquainted with. He asked the Garda for money for a pint, and shared his financial woes. After drinking in a pub in the city he had taken a bus back to the works, where he visited the pay office around 5 p.m., to finalize details of his leave of absence. He was not spotted again until he reappeared in a pub back in Limerick city around two hours later.[28]

That two-hour window clearly provided ample time to commit the attack, and police suspicions grew when Cox changed details of his movements that day. Mud on an otherwise clean set of clothes, similar to that found at the crime scene, added further weight to the suspicions of guilt. The arrival of his wife Mary to the police station provided the Gardaí with an opportunity to trick the suspect into confessing.

Mary Cox had brought a parcel of supplies for her husband and after searching it, a Garda slipped a pencil with notepaper alongside the other items and wrapped it up. Handing it to back to her, he allowed her to give it to her husband.[29]

Naively, the prisoner believed the parcel had come directly from his wife. On seeing the pencil and paper, he took the opportunity to write a note for his wife. As Mary left, the police took the note to find that John had scribbled an address. This note took them to the ruins of a house where a search turned up the money that had been stolen from Jacob Kunz. While this proved his guilt in the eyes of many, the trick had put a successful prosecution at risk. When the trial, which was moved to Dublin, opened, the defence case focused on one issue – whether the note and money were admissible as evidence. The defence argued that they could not be used as evidence, given the subterfuge involved.[30]

The judge rejected this, and once the money and note were made admissible, John Cox's fate was sealed. The Dublin jury, however, was reluctant to convict him for murder, given that he faced the death penalty. It initially asked to be allowed to pronounce him guilty of manslaughter rather than murder but the judge ruled this out, stating it had only two options: to find John Cox guilty of murder, or acquit him. With little option, it passed a guilty verdict, although it did plead for clemency, stating somewhat bizarrely that Jacob Kunz may have had an abnormally thin skull, which contributed to his death.[31]

Ignoring this plea for clemency, the judge passed the death sentence, to take place on 11 April 1929. After a failed appeal John Cox was hanged by the English executioner Thomas Pierrepoint, who had continued to travel from England to carry out Free State executions after independence.

Jacob's brother, Johann Kunz, left Ireland after the trial in 1929, as the Shannon Scheme neared completion. On 22 July the Ardnacrusha dam was opened by W.T. Cosgrave, President of the Executive Council of the Free State. The dam was an incredible feat of engineering; the largest hydroelectric dam in Western Europe at the time – and another milestone in the consolidation of the Free State. At the opening ceremony there was little evidence of the suffering the workforce had endured. Dignitaries from across society in the Free State travelled to the Shannon to bear witness to what was unquestionably a historic moment. A special switch had been fitted to a slab of Connemara marble and after a brief speech, President Cosgrave flicked the switch. In an almost anticlimactic event, sluice gates on the Shannon slowly opened and water began the seven-mile journey to the dam downriver.

The ceremony in many ways captured Irish society in the late 1920s, not least in his closing act. The final word was given to a Catholic prelate – the Bishop of Killaloe, Dr Fogarty – to represent the Church, the moral guardians of the new state.

Meanwhile the presence of Éamon de Valera, the leader of Fianna Fáil, symbolized the increasing acceptance of the Free State across the political spectrum. Having opposed the Treaty, de Valera had taken the opposite side to the government in the Civil War. After spending over a year on the run he was arrested, and continued to contest the legitimacy of the Free State after his release. Even though he was elected to the Dáil, he at first refused to take his seat. In 1926 he left Sinn Féin and established a new party, Fianna Fáil. In 1927 de Valera and his colleagues dropped their abstentionism and took their seats. Those who denied the legitimacy of the Free State were growing increasingly marginalized and fewer in number.

Yet even as it stood as a beacon of the new state's successes, Ardnacrusha was also a testimony to the dashed expectations of many in Ireland. From the perspective of the labour movement, the Free State had fallen considerably short of even its most modest expectations. The death toll, pay and working conditions on the project had been abysmal, and revealed the continued status quo of inequality at the heart of Irish society.

CHAPTER 14

In Search of Public Morality

1936

> Unto the woman he said,
> I will greatly multiply thy sorrow and thy conception;
> in sorrow thou shalt bring forth children;
> and thy desire shall be to thy husband,
> and he shall rule over thee.
>
> (Genesis 3:16)

The New Year of 1922 got off to a less than auspicious start for Alice Brophy. On 2 January of that year, the forty-one year old was sentenced to a fortnight in jail; her most recent conviction of many, on prostitution-related charges. Knowing what to expect during her sentence in Mountjoy Jail was cold comfort. It wasn't her first time in prison and it would not, in all likelihood, be her last; but when Brophy left Mountjoy on 15 January 1922 she walked through the prison gates out to a changed Ireland, or so she was led to believe.

Few could deny these had been two momentous weeks

in Ireland. While she had been confined to her cell, the Anglo-Irish Treaty had been ratified by the Dáil and preparatory steps were underway to establish the Irish Free State. The day after her release the British authorities in the city formally handed over Dublin Castle to Irish republican forces. With an evacuation of British garrisons underway, the press voiced cautious optimism that this heralded a new era. There was no question but that the departure of the British Army was a significant development, but on a personal level, little had changed for Alice Brophy.

She quickly learned that, whether a subject of the United Kingdom or a citizen of the Irish Free State, life at the margins of Dublin society remained just as precarious. The authorities had always turned a blind eye to the sex trade in the brothels of the Monto, Dublin's red-light district, but if sex workers ventured beyond the district, they faced the full rigour of the law.

Brophy had accrued a litany of convictions for such offences. She first appeared in the prison records when she was convicted of soliciting three times back in 1917. This was followed by numerous convictions for public order offences between 1919 and 1921, legislation frequently used to prosecute sex workers. This trend continued seamlessly between administrations into the new era of 1922.

The near certainty of Alice Brophy's return to Mountjoy was borne out when she received another sentence for soliciting in early April 1922. Her sentence on this occasion, one calendar month, was her longest to date.

While the prison provided Alice with the essentials of

life, the Victorian jail was a loud, tense environment. Prisoners with young children brought the infants with them into the cells; their cries adding to an endless cacophony of noise. Violence between the inmates was not uncommon but for Alice Brophy the alternative – the life of a sex worker in the streets of Dublin – was no less dangerous. The sex trade was largely a business conducted after dark and while Dublin had been illuminated by electric lighting since the 1880s, Alice was arrested on numerous occasions soliciting in the Phoenix Park, a vast park with little passing traffic that could offer aid if needed.

Four weeks after entering Mountjoy, Alice left the prison, but this was the last time she passed through the gates of the jail. She would never return.

Although something of a regular fixture in the records of the institution over the previous five years, Alice Brophy, or at least the name 'Alice Brophy' never surfaced in the city again. What happened to her was something of a mystery. Her name did not reappear in the records of the living or the dead in Dublin after April 1922. It is possible she changed her identity; although her actual identity was never entirely clear.

Understandably, she had always been economical with the truth in her dealings with the police. She had sometimes gone by the name of Alice Clarke, while her details about her background were equally vague. When asked for a next of kin, she always said she had a brother, William, living in the town of her birth, Dunlavin, County Wicklow. There was, however, no record there of an Alice Brophy, or an Alice Clarke, or a William of either surname. Such was the way with many of Dublin's sex workers. They inhabited a transient world where it was accepted that people came and went. Few in positions of authority showed concern for their welfare. But the early 1920s was a particularly tumultuous time for sex workers in the city. That Brophy disappeared was little surprise.

From its inception, the government of the Free State adopted an increasingly hostile attitude towards discussions around sex, and sex workers in particular. There was no doubt that these women had always existed on the margins, but life became more uncertain and more difficult in the Free State.

Although it was forged in the heat of revolution, the Irish Free State was in no way, shape, or form a revolutionary society. Its break with the past was limited to the political sphere, and its leaders were proud of their conservative worldview. Kevin O'Higgins, the influential Minister for Justice, would describe himself and his government colleagues in 1923 as 'probably the most conservative-minded revolutionaries that ever put through a successful revolution'.[1]

When reflecting back on Irish society in the 1920s, a member of the Dublin Brigade of the IRA, Todd Andrews, recalled how 'the vestiges of Victorian morality still stank in the 1920s'.[2] This was particularly the case when it came to anything remotely related to sex or sexuality.

While the leaders of the Free State would rather have avoided discussing the subject at all, by the mid-1920s they were forced to tackle sex head on, when cases of venereal disease began to rise rapidly. As they set about forcibly addressing the problem, sex workers became the focus of their attention.

That venereal disease was a considerable problem in the mid-1920s was undeniable – one Dublin clinic had seen its case load double between 1920 and 1925.[3] This was deeply embarrassing for the moral conservatism of Free State leaders and contradicted what had been their simplistic analysis of social problems.

They had held that most problems in Irish society were merely symptomatic of a broader malaise arising from the British occupation of the island. Therefore, it stood to reason that these would dissipate after the British left. This was particularly the case regarding venereal disease, which was assumed to be associated with the large British garrisons on the island. By the middle of the decade the garrisons were gone, but venereal disease was on the increase. To address the issue, the government established an interdepartmental committee of inquiry to investigate the matter. When it reported its findings in 1926, the committee had decided on what would become central to official thinking in the Free State: all problems were ultimately related to the standards of public morality.

When it came to venereal disease, even though it may have been epidemiological in origin, the committee stated as fact that 'the incidence of venereal disease was a direct reflection of the moral situation'. The moral situation referenced in this case was the prevalence of sex outside the institution of marriage. Given this approach, it was somewhat inevitable that sex workers like Alice Brophy would find themselves subjected to vilification by what was an increasingly puritanical official stance.

While the committee was unequivocal that prostitution was not the cause of the increase in cases of venereal disease, it nevertheless went on to claim that a clampdown on the sex trade was key to resolving the crisis.

In its view, the problem was one of morality. Following this logic, it stood to reason that tackling the causes of what were regarded as low moral standards was the solution. This thinking would see the committee devote one of the nine pages of text in its report to the issue of prostitution,[4] a factor it had already accepted was not directly responsible for the surge in cases. While the committee's findings were never published, they reflected wider beliefs, and sex workers – increasingly viewed as a corrupting influence on society – became the target of public campaigns.

Throughout the early 1920s religious organizations had been actively campaigning in the Monto red-light district. The campaign adopted a crusading zeal. Night after night, members of the Legion of Mary campaigned in the Monto trying to convince sex workers to change their ways. While many women dismissed their entreaties, the campaign did enjoy considerable successes – and by 1923 sixty-one women had been removed from brothels and taken to hostels. But as the women were considered an immoral influence on society, their views were rarely taken into consideration. They were married off, with one historian later noting that the husbands were intended to provide the stability the brothel-keepers once had.[5]

This campaign culminated in a major raid on the Monto in 1925, after the religious organizations successfully enlisted the help of the Gardaí. The movement, which claimed to have shut down the notorious district, was widely acclaimed, but it was not as successful as was often asserted at the time. Another suppressed report from the early 1930s, this time into juvenile prostitution, revealed that the sex trade, although less visible, continued.[6]

It was into this maelstrom that Alice Brophy, or at least that identity, disappeared. Perhaps she resurfaced under another name. While it was possible that the reasons for her disappearance were nefarious, few in wider Irish society cared much about the fate of individual sex workers. They were a tiny minority of women who lived at the margins of life and had long been considered contemptible in the eyes of many. As they became less visible on the city streets, the improvement in perceived public morals was the overriding concern.

Yet while driving these women further to the margins of Irish society was lamented by few, the calcifying of the narrative, which linked sex outside marriage, immorality and wider public well-being, had catastrophic consequences far beyond the small number of women who were sex workers. An entire generation of Irishwomen, particularly single women, would find themselves targeted. The fate of Katie Kelly was emblematic of the deadly impact these policies could have.

Born in 1918, Katie Kelly's was the first generation of Irish people who knew no other country than the Irish Free State. They could, if the nationalist theory was to be believed, benefit fully from an independent Ireland free from morally bankrupt British influences.

The daughter of a labourer and a servant, Katie grew up in Youngstown, outside the town of Athy, County Kildare. Poor as her family was, her early years suggested that she had been born at a most opportune time for women. The 1918 election saw considerable numbers of women able to vote in a general election for the first time. That poll also saw Constance Markiewicz become the first woman to win a seat in the House of Commons. A few months later Markiewicz was appointed Minister for Labour in the revolutionary government during the War of Independence. During the revolution women became more active in Irish society than they had ever been able to before – Cumann na mBan, a women's revolutionary organization, for example, had a strong presence in most communities across the country.

But that was during the revolutionary era, and Katie Kelly, a woman with few memories prior to 1923, grew up in a society where the last vestiges of the optimism embodied in the revolution had all but disappeared. This was in no small part due to the complicated relationship between Irish Free State leaders and the hierarchy of the Catholic Church. Decades before the War of Independence, the Church had established itself as one of the most influential forces in Ireland. Several generations of Church leaders had built up strong links with successive British administrations. In return for its passivity in most political matters, the Church received considerable grants and was allowed more and more influence over education and healthcare.

Dogmatically conservative, Church leaders had been wary of the revolutionary movement, and in particular its more radical tendencies – but they had seen the potential advantages of an independent Ireland, in which they could exert great control over any government. Throughout the War of Independence they played what was a delicate hand extremely carefully. While the Church repeatedly condemned the IRA and excommunicated IRA volunteers, it never alienated the wider population, which was sympathetic to independence. When the British withdrew in 1922, the Catholic Church emerged as the uncontested and unquestioned moral authority over the vast majority in the Free State, given that some 90 per cent of the population were Roman Catholic.

Katie Kelly grew up in a society where political leaders were increasingly willing to defer to the Church to provide direction on a variety of social issues. Not only were those politicians by and large devout Catholics, some at least had a very limited understanding of the world of civilian affairs. Todd Andrews would later recall how his years as a revolutionary activist had left him 'emotionally immature in the matter of inter-sex relations', something he described as 'not uncommon' for his generation.[7] Andrews reflected that many of his generation had a one-dimensional view of women. He would later write, 'I knew nothing about women beyond their home-making functions and their ability to provide some of the services required to support the IRA military operation.'[8]

As the government was unwilling and unable to challenge the Catholic Church on key matters, the Church was able to heavily influence social policy. A close working relationship between Church and State was well established by the mid-1920s. When the cabinet discussed where to share the findings of the interdepartmental committee of inquiry on venereal disease, one suggestion was that the report should be circulated to clergymen and doctors.[9] The government also sought the views of the

Archbishop of Dublin on whether the report should be published.[10]

This governmental deference to Church on moral and social issues spoke volumes about the Free State of Katie Kelly's youth. While a doctor could treat a medical condition, it was considered essential to involve a cleric, who would improve standards of public morality. Although precise definitions of what constituted 'public morality' were often difficult to come by, young, single women in particular were often considered to be of dubious morality and bore the exacting gaze of both Church and State.

This question of their moral propriety had been clear to the committee. Although it determined that sex workers were not directly responsible for the spread of sexually transmitted diseases, it was unequivocal that women in general were the cause of the rising caseload. The committee's report stated that 'a class of girl who could not be regarded as a prostitute'[11] was responsible. Men were absolved of all culpability. The report labelled these single women 'amateurs' (as opposed to professional sex workers). This highlighted the ambiguity over the definition of a sex worker. The term 'amateur' implied they were similar, the only difference being that one was paid and the other wasn't. All were considered morally debased. Women who gave birth to children outside of marriage were treated as pariahs, becoming a living embodiment of this perceived immorality.

This was part of a policy that would see the aspirations of Katie Kelly's generation of young women diminish. Women were discouraged from having an active role in society. Political leaders increasingly fashioned a country where a woman's place was in the home. While by no means a new concept, successive Free State governments legislated to reverse the trend of the revolutionary era, which had seen women become more active in the public realm. A widely syndicated article in the national and local press in late 1924 outlined what was an increasingly prevalent criticism of women:

> Even in Ireland mothers were to be found who shirked or neglected their duty to their children. There were mothers who preferred the fashionable and crowded thoroughfare to their own quiet home; there were mothers who preferred talking on a platform or in a council chamber to chatting with their children in the nursery.

The column went on to critique women who engaged in 'convivial pursuits', counterposing this with their duty as mothers. It concluded with a warning to women to, 'Appear seldom on the promenade, and oftener by the cradle; come down from the platform and attend to the cot.' [12]

It was becoming clear when Katie Kelly reached adulthood in the mid-1930s that she would have fewer career options open to her, as the drive to force women from the public realm took legislative form. The 1924 Civil Service Act placed limitations on women working in the civil service, including the stipulation that they must resign upon marriage. Moves were also made to limit women to its lower ranks. This was followed by an attempt to remove women from juries two years later. These moves were not driven solely from the top down. Every Sunday most Catholics attended mass, where they were inculcated with similar ideas. This perhaps helps to explain the limited opposition to government policy.

Two general elections were held in 1927 and a new party, Fianna Fáil, entered the political landscape. Formed from the defeated side in the Civil War and led by Éamon de Valera, it won fifty-seven seats in the second election of that year.* Although it promised a less conservative economic policy, it supported the entrenched social policies of the Cumann na nGaedheal government.

While the early years of Katie's life saw diminishing opportunities for women in general, before she reached ten years of age she suffered a major setback on a personal level. The Kellys had always struggled financially, but when her father Christopher died from pneumonia at the age of forty-seven in March 1928, this plunged the family into dire poverty. Katie's mother Kathleen faced the prospect of raising a family on her own. Without any way to support her three children,[13] she placed Katie, then aged nine, and one of her sisters in an orphanage.[14] This was not a permanent arrangement, but chosen rather as a temporary measure in the unforgiving face of destitution.

While Katie Kelly spent the following eight years in care, Irish society became steadily more socially conservative. It goes without saying that she was afforded no sexual education whatsoever – this was one area where her generation were possibly less well educated than their parents. Even for the inquisitive it was extremely difficult to access material related to sex in any way, as the government

* Fianna Fail initially followed the republican policy of abstentionism but this was dropped in 1927, prompting the second election of the year.

censored material that it considered potentially damaging to public morals.

This censorship went to extraordinary lengths. Even though venereal disease was a well-recognized problem, a government committee on what was called 'evil literature' recommended prohibiting adverts relating to 'infirmity arising from or related to sexual intercourse'.[15] It also suggested banning literature related to contraception because it was a 'means of avoiding the consequences of sexual indulgence among the unmarried'.[16]

During the 1920s the quest for moral purity took on increasingly hysterical dimensions. Dance halls and jazz music, viewed as symptoms of moral decay and mere excuses for promiscuous sexual behaviour, came under fire. Fr John Flanagan, the parish priest in Fairview, Dublin, submitted his views to the Carrigan Commission investigating juvenile prostitution. Yet again conflating prostitution with sex outside marriage, he claimed that, 'conduct that in other countries is confined to brothels is to be seen without let or hindrance on our public roads'.

The Garda Commissioner, Eoin O'Duffy, described dance halls as 'orgies of dissipation'.[17] This was of course hysteria, as the Irish Free State ranked among the most conservative countries in Europe. Had Fr Flanagan or O'Duffy ventured inside the Eldorado nightclub in Berlin, described by a contemporary as a 'supermarket of eroticism',[18] they may have refined their ideas of what Flanagan called the 'growing evil' of 'public immorality'.

By the early 1930s the government had in effect shut down all public conversation around sex and sexual education. Literature referring to family planning and reproductive choices was banned.[19] The belief that morality was crucial to public well-being also had further, deeper detrimental impacts on society, impacts which would continue to haunt society for decades to come.[20] While the Carrigan Commission heard evidence about the extensive abuse of children, its findings were never made public, in a naive and counterproductive attempt to preserve public morality.

Katie Kelly remained in the orphanage as the Irish Free State witnessed its first change of government in 1932. This celebrated milestone of a peaceful transition of power, from Cumann na nGaedheal to their Civil War opponents Fianna Fáil, had limited impact in terms of policies towards women. The new leader of the Irish Free State, de Valera, and his cabinet colleagues were ideological products of the same society and imbued with similar ideas to their predecessors. Continuing the same approach, in December 1932 the Department of Education announced that female teachers would have to resign their posts if they married.[21]

Already difficult to access, contraception was formally banned in 1935. This had dire and reverberating consequences. By this time, due to governmental censorship of all kinds of sexual education literature, many in Katie Kelly's generation had little to no understanding of sex, or even of their own bodies.

By 1935, now sixteen, Katie finally returned to her family home, and the following year secured a job in domestic service in Grangecon House, a large stately home a few miles away in County Wicklow. While securing the job provided Katie with employment, the fact that she was taking up a similar position to that of her mother a generation earlier showed all too clearly the limitations of the Irish revolution and its impact on the lives of those living in its wake.

Stately homes like Grangecon in many ways harked back to what was increasingly a bygone era, yet while aristocratic families were leaving Ireland, Grangecon was a symbol of the new Irish elite. Katie Kelly's employer was Dermot O'Mahony, a government TD. The O'Mahony family had been involved in nationalist politics for generations and, after a time as a rancher in Patagonia,[22] Dermot O'Mahony returned to Ireland in 1921 and quickly adapted to life in the Free State. Joining Cumann na nGaedheal, he stood for the party in Wicklow in the June 1927 general election. Taking the seat, he was re-elected on several occasions in the following decade.

When Katie Kelly arrived at the house in May 1936 she joined a large staff of several maids and cooks, a valet and a governess. The house itself was a vast sprawling mansion dating back to the sixteenth century with twenty-four rooms including a wine cellar. As was the practice at the time, Katie was given a bed in the servants' quarters at Grangecon, sharing a room with another servant, Julia Mulreed. The work involved long hours as a domestic servant and Katie only returned to visit her mother every second weekend.[23]

Not long after her eighteenth birthday in September 1936, Katie returned to her mother's home for the weekend of Saturday the nineteenth. The following day her mother would accompany her back to Grangecon, later commenting that she hadn't noticed anything out of the ordinary with her daughter.

Two days later around 9 p.m., Katie was preparing hot-water bottles for the O'Mahony family[24] when she became seriously ill. Complaining of pains, she had to retire to her room early. Around two hours later, Mulreed returned to the bedroom she shared with Katie to find her condition had severely deteriorated. She was groaning in agony on the bed. Her cries would continue for around two hours until the cook, Bridie Palmer, who slept in a neighbouring room, was awoken by the sounds of Katie's distress. Such was Palmer's concern, she elected to wake Patricia O'Mahony, Dermot's daughter. Once Patricia O'Mahony saw Katie, she knew a doctor was urgently needed and left for Baltinglass, a town five miles away. It would take her over an hour to return with the doctor, but in that time, events at Grangecon House had taken an unusual course. The other servants of the house appeared deeply distressed. Katie Kelly was now in the servants' bathroom, the path from the bedroom marked by a trail of blood on the corridor.

It took Patricia O'Mahony some time to coax Katie from the bathroom, but when she emerged, she insisted that she was fine and was able to walk under her own steam. When the doctor examined her she was struggling to talk coherently, while bloodstains were discovered in her bed. It's unclear how extensive the doctor's investigation was, but he decided that the eighteen-year-old needed to be moved to Baltinglass hospital immediately.[25]

It was only the following morning that the full details of what had happened came to light. When the other servants set about cleaning her room, they found the remains of a newborn infant, which had been grievously harmed. Katie Kelly had given birth during the night and, in a state of severe mental anguish, had killed the child.

No one, including her mother or the staff in the house, had been aware she was pregnant.[26] It is unclear when she herself became aware of or understood what was happening. Having carried out several searches of the house, Gardaí found the murder weapon – a small blade. Katie was subsequently arrested at Baltinglass district hospital and charged with murder. She spent the following six months in prison. At a bail hearing in November the judge was willing to release Katie on bail, but this was set at two £100 sureties and it was unclear if anyone willing to support Katie had the money needed.

The case finally went before the courts in March 1937 when Katie pleaded guilty to a lesser charge of manslaughter. In her defence, her barrister claimed that she had been unaware that she was pregnant. Given the lack of education and public discussion around sex in general, this was entirely possible.

The truth of how she had become pregnant was never revealed, but the conception had to have taken place around January 1936. When she had started working in Grangecon, she was already five months pregnant. Her barrister, arguing in her defence, claimed Katie Kelly had killed her baby in 'a state of mental disturbance'. The lack of preparation, her limited attempts to conceal the crime, and the testimonies of eyewitnesses all supported this claim, and it was accepted by the judge.

While she was found guilty of manslaughter, Katie Kelly was not sentenced to prison. Instead, she was incarcerated in a Dublin 'home' for twelve months and bound over to keep the peace for the following three years. The specific Dublin home was not named, but it may have been one of the network of institutions in the city known as the Magdalene laundries. Operating since the eighteenth century, these 'asylums' operated by religious orders had originally functioned as hostels to help women in prostitution. However, at the turn of the twentieth century, many of the inmates were unmarried mothers, removed from wider society because of the threat they were deemed to pose to public morality. These institutions, supposedly charged with reforming the women, were little more than a prison to many, with regimes that could inflict severe punishments for minor infractions of regulations. The laundries meanwhile operated a commercial business which exploited the women as a source of free labour.

It is possible that Katie Kelly was sent to a different yet very similar institution – Our Lady's Home on Henrietta Street. Operated by the Sisters of Charity, a religious order of nuns, it accepted what were called 'better types' convicted of infanticide and similar offences.[27] It did not accept sex workers for fear of moral contagion[28]. Our Lady's Home, like the Magdalene laundries, was supported by a laundry, which the incarcerated women operated. Delegating the supervision of certain prisoners to the religious orders reflected the view that these women needed moral instruction and correction. This approach did little, if anything, to tackle the underlying causes that drove women like Katie Kelly to commit infanticide.

Tragic as Kelly's case was, she wasn't unique. Somewhat inevitably, there had been similar instances of infanticide before 1936 and they would continue to happen after her case. The specifics were so common that a probation officer, Evelyn Carroll, made the following generalization in 1941 about cases of infanticide that almost describes Katie Kelly's case word for word:

> The crime of infanticide may very often be traced to the fact that by some strange series of circumstances the girl's pregnancy has remained a secret up to the last. A large proportion of these crimes are committed in the residence of the girl's employer, who had failed to notice her condition.
>
> It is easy to see why a girl is driven to such a tragic act – extreme mental strain, a terrible fear of discovery, depression and the necessity for guarding her secret – all play their part. The girl, as one of them declared to me, may have no knowledge of her real condition for a considerable time, and having discovered it becomes bewildered, even desperate.
>
> Fearing instant dismissal if her condition becomes known, she says nothing and just carries on until the baby is born. Then in the frenzy of a moment and still trying to cover up her shame, she kills her child.[29]

What happened to Katie Kelly when she left the Dublin institution is unclear. She was yet another woman forced to the margins of Irish society.

CHAPTER 15

Servants of Empire

1940

I gave thee a king in mine anger, and took him away in my wrath.

(Hosea 13:11)

March 1940 was a tense anxious time in London. Scarcely two decades had passed since the end of World War I and Britain was again at war with Germany. Although war had been declared the previous September, Hitler had, in the first months of the conflict, directed his forces into Eastern Europe. This left Londoners in relative peace, but most knew this was only a reprieve. By early 1940, Germany and the Soviet Union had completed their dismemberment of Poland, and it was only a matter of time before the Nazi war machine focused its energies on Western Europe. Heavy snowfalls across the country only added to the sense of foreboding.

Against this backdrop, the Sikh immigrant Udham Singh ventured into the inclement weather and made his way across London. Having long desired to hold the British Empire accountable for one of the most notorious massacres of the 20th century, the chance had finally presented itself. Reaching the city centre, Singh made his way to Caxton Hall, a few hundred metres from the Houses of Parliament in Westminster, where the Royal Central Asian Society were hosting a meeting. Dressed in a sharp suit and a trilby hat, few took notice of Singh when he took a seat towards the back of the hall. All eyes were on the front row where various dignitaries were seated.

The topic for discussion that night was Afghanistan, although that was of no particular interest to Singh. A revolutionary, he had come to make a protest against the policies of the British Empire in his native India. Over the course of the evening several older white men – those seated in the front row – made contributions, each of them with decades of experience in service to the British Empire in Asia. It was when the meeting came to an end and the crowd began to dissipate that Singh made his move.

Standing up, he began to move rapidly through the crowd towards the front of the hall. As he neared the top of the room he drew a revolver and shouted, 'Make way, make way!' A few seconds later he would enter the pages of history, his life bound up with the fate of another immigrant of sorts in the hall that evening – the Irishman Michael O'Dwyer.

O'Dwyer and Singh may both have been immigrants in London but their experiences of Britain and the Empire were worlds apart. O'Dwyer, seventy-five years old in 1940, had once been among the most influential and powerful Irish men of his generation. Unlike Singh, he had no issue with the British Empire – in fact he had enjoyed a distinguished career in the civil service, and at one time served as one of the most powerful imperial administrators in India. But by 1940 history had left O'Dwyer an exile of sorts – although an Irish nationalist of a kind, the Ireland he yearned for had ceased to exist in 1922.

A marginal, even disreputable figure in some circles in Ireland in 1940, O'Dwyer was among a considerable minority of Irish people who were profoundly disillusioned by the aftermath of the War of Independence. These Irish men's and women's lives had been intertwined with the British Empire before the Treaty, and as opposition to British imperialism became a cornerstone of national identity in the Free State they were increasingly alienated from Irish society. Many, like O'Dwyer, lived in an historical cul-de-sac; struggling to adapt to life in the Free State and mourning a world that had passed with the withdrawal of the British garrison.

Some feared what post-independence held in store for them. Many Irish landlords, for example, having already sold their estates, transferred their capital out of the country and moved to England, where they often already had houses. Some were left with little alternative after their houses were burnt down in the War of Independence and the Civil War. When Olive Packenham-Mahon, the great-granddaughter of Denis Mahon, a landlord assassinated in 1847 (see Chapter 4) was asked about the foundation of the Free State, she said that many families like her own 'poured out of Ireland'. A unionist to the core, she was also a patriotic Irishwoman: unlike the others, she chose to stay.

Michael O'Dwyer was somewhat different. He did not come from Irish aristocracy like Olive Packenham-Mahon. The path in life that ultimately led him to Caxton Hall in 1940 was somewhat unusual – few people from his background attained the power and influence he did. The sixth son in a Catholic family of fourteen children, O'Dwyer had been born outside Tipperary town in 1864. His father was a well-to-do farmer, which shaped his son's generally conservative outlook on the world. With little interest in social change, the O'Dwyers had been targeted during the Land War.[1]

As was customary for a wealthy Catholic family, several of the O'Dwyer siblings entered the Church, but Michael chose another path. After attending St Stanislaus College in Tullamore, he pursued a career in the Empire, namely India. The Irish had long been drawn to India, ever since the conquest of the sub-continent had begun under the aegis of a private corporation, the East India Company. Most had served in the private army of the Company. By the time it was nationalized by the British government after widespread corruption, around 50 per cent of the soldiers serving in India had been recruited in Ireland.[2]

Michael O'Dwyer had greater ambitions than simply soldiering for the Empire, and he started out on a career in the Indian Civil Service (ICS). There was a tradition of educated Irishmen finding lucrative careers in India – 30 per cent of Trinity College Dublin engineering graduates had been working there in the 1860s[3]. While ostensibly offering a good bureaucratic career, the Indian Civil Service also offered the opportunity for great power and influence.

Originally, entrance to the ICS was limited to those

who had a personal recommendation, but by the 1880s this had changed to a merit-based system. The capable O'Dwyer took his exams in 1882, passed, and spent the following three years at Balliol College Oxford, where he received a first-class degree in jurisprudence. By 1885 he was on his way to India. From his initial posting in Shahpur in the Punjab Province, O'Dwyer rose rapidly. He held numerous positions in the Punjab, which straddles the modern Indian and Pakistani states.

By the early twentieth century O'Dwyer had come to the attention of Lord Curzon, the Secretary of State for the Colonies in London. In 1913 he appointed O'Dwyer to the position of Lieutenant-Governor of the Punjab. That same year his service to the Empire was recognized when he was knighted and became Sir Michael O'Dwyer. (He was not the only Irishman to achieve such a high position. The Kerryman Michael Keane would later become the Governor of Assam, while the Dubliner Loftus Otway Clarke held the position of Political Agent to the State of Manipur.)

O'Dwyer took up his position in what was a key period in Indian history. At the outbreak of World War I he faced the dual challenge of demands for troops from London on the one hand and rising Indian nationalism, with growing demands for Home Rule, on the other. O'Dwyer's enlistment drive proved enormously successful. One in every twenty-eight men in the Punjab would enlist in the British Indian Army.

Meanwhile in India, demands for Home Rule did not abate during the war. In 1915 Indian nationalists attempted to organize a major mutiny in numerous garrisons of the British Indian Army, an action which the planners hoped could be co-ordinated with a republican revolt in Ireland.* Ultimately, the authorities would learn of the revolt in advance while plans for co-ordination never moved beyond the aspirational stage.

Over the following years the histories of India and Ireland echoed each other. The end of World War I in November 1918 did not sate Indian demands for increased autonomy and democracy, no more than it eased the political tensions in Ireland. While these would develop into the Irish War of Independence through 1919, O'Dwyer was facing a similar movement in India. Indeed, in March 1919 the Imperial Legislative Council in India introduced the Anarchical and Revolutionary Crimes Act, which allowed the British authorities to hold suspects without trial. O'Dwyer, who positioned himself on the conservative end of all debates on India and opposed reform, was in general supportive of the harsh measures. But as was the case in his native Tipperary later that same year, the introduction of such measures had precisely the opposite effect to that intended, only serving to drive people towards revolutionary activity.

O'Dwyer's decision to arrest prominent Indian nationalists and incarcerate two them in the Himalayas provoked widespread protests and an outbreak of mass violence on 10 April. The British reaction was predictable, and remarkably similar to how they were attempting to handle the situation in Ireland. Rather than de-escalate the situation, O'Dwyer and the imperial authorities banned further

* Plowman, M.E., Irish Republicans and the Indo-German Conspiracy of World War I, 81.

demonstrations. Further protest was organized in the city of Amritsar, leading to an event that would frame how O'Dwyer was viewed across the world.

As the protest went ahead, people were gathering at Jallianwala Bagh, near the Golden Temple in Amritsar, to celebrate the spring harvest. In an event echoed on Bloody Sunday in Dublin a year and a half later, the British Army opened fire on large crowds of people. However, the loss of life at Jallianwala Bagh was catastrophic, and on a far larger scale than the horrors seen at Croke Park – hundreds were killed and thousands were injured. As is so often the case, a single incident would come to symbolize generations of mistreatment and undermine the entire British presence in India.

Michael O'Dwyer, while not present at the massacre, would become one of the most staunch defenders of the man directly responsible, the British commander Colonel Reginald Dyer. Although Dyer was removed from his position, O'Dwyer adopted a provocative and incendiary position, defending Dyer's actions. Even as the full details of the unprovoked massacre of innocent people came to light, O'Dwyer continued to back Dyer. He also enforced extremely draconian measures to quash the predictable outrage in reaction to the massacre at Jallianwala Bagh.

Martial law was declared in parts of the Punjab and this, as it would in Ireland a year later, led to flagrant abuses by soldiers. While O'Dwyer distanced himself from certain actions, saying that they were beyond his control, he did order the use of aeroplanes to attack crowds at Gujranwala. This act led to the deaths of at least twelve people, including children.

These events coincided with his planned retirement, but O'Dwyer might well have been removed from his position had he not left – he was later criticized by the Hunter Committee, which investigated the Jallianwala Bagh massacre. Although he had been a regular visitor to Ireland up until this point, when he returned from India it was little surprise that he did not choose to live there. The rise of Sinn Féin had alarmed O'Dwyer. From its earliest days, the party had been extremely critical of people like him. In 1908 the party in Wexford had distributed leaflets telling people, 'Sell your soul, your country and your God for the Saxon shilling. Join England's hireling murderers that hanged your forefathers. Your reward will be a life of immorality and a dog's death in the gaol or by the roadside. Go to India to murder women and children and shoot men who are fighting for liberty.'[4]

When he did finally return to Ireland in 1923, the country was a remarkably different place. In April 1920 the Dublin municipal council had criticized the prevalence of imperial street names: 'few cities in the civilised world where the names of governors, oppressors and despoilers have been honoured to the same extent'. Following the foundation of the Free State, Great Brunswick Street, named after an ancestral title of the British monarchs, was renamed Pearse Street in honour of Patrick Pearse.

Dublin began to change in other ways too, as monuments were removed or took on new meaning. An enormous arch had been built to commemorate the Dubliners killed in the Second Boer War, etched with the names of the battlefields of Colenso, Laing's Nek, Talana and Ladysmith. While it was left in place, it was increasingly referred to as Traitors' Arch.*

There was no question that the culture and political milieu that had produced the likes of Michael O'Dwyer was in rapid decline. It was an identity with no real purpose after the British withdrawal from the Free State in 1922: the twenty-six counties had left the United Kingdom and any reversal of this was increasingly inconceivable.

O'Dwyer and others like him were alienated by post-independence Ireland as British rule ebbed away. The regiments raised in the former Free State – the Royal Munster Fusiliers, the Connaught Rangers, the Prince of Wales's Leinster Regiment and the Dublin Fusiliers were disbanded. There had also been an exodus of British administrators and officials, something O'Dwyer mourned. In 1925, reflecting on the death of his brother, which he attributed to the strain of the Irish revolution, he said: 'The disappearance of old friends and the withdrawal of British troops had left the countryside dull and drab.'[5] This was true for a certain class. When talking about her life in the Free State, Olive Packenham-Mahon described the changes: 'fancy lives that people led, playing croquet and cards all night, that all changed, life became more realistic'.[6]

Yet this was very much the view of a select minority. While there were deep divisions about the direction Irish society took after the foundation of the Free State, the withdrawal of the British Army was widely celebrated. This for many was an immediate and recognizable benefit,

---

* An early reference to the name Traitors Arch appears in *The Kerryman*, 4 Sept. 1909.

something supporters of the Treaty were keen to point out. Indeed, O'Dwyer's reflections on Ireland in the opening chapter of his 1925 book, *India As I Knew It*, were poorly received. The *Irish Independent*, which praised the book as a whole, said: 'Sir Michael's reflections on Ireland were few in number. For his own reputation one could have wished them fewer.'[7]

O'Dwyer was not the only one to feel nostalgia for the old regime. In November 1924 tens of thousands would gather on College Green in Dublin to mark Armistice Day, the end of World War I. While the day was ostensibly to remember the dead, it was in reality a political event and would be increasingly contentious in the coming years as it became a rallying point for unionism in the Free State. The choice of location was symbolic: College Green was dominated by an enormous statue of William of Orange, a deeply divisive figure.

At the end of the proceedings, the crowd sang the English national anthem of the day, 'God Save the King'. It was little surprise that the event attracted protests from republicans and, after violence erupted at the periphery of the demonstration, it was subsequently moved to the Phoenix Park in 1925. On 10 November 1928, the evening before Armistice Day, the statue of William of Orange was blown up by the IRA. The stump was removed the following year.

Sir Michael O'Dwyer, for his part, chose to reside in London, where he was a regular commentator on Indian politics. He opposed reform, including the Chelmsford-Montagu Reforms, which proposed limited democracy in India. He described Mahatma Gandhi as, 'The biggest imposter who has ever fooled the credulity of people or frightened a cowardly government.'*

This position – opposition to extending democracy to India – was diametrically opposed to his views on Ireland. O'Dwyer was a deeply contradictory figure who struggled, like many Irish unionists, to feel at home on either side of the Irish Sea after the establishment of the Irish Free State. While staunchly loyal to the Empire, he had a somewhat nationalistic interpretation of Irish history prior to the late nineteenth century. A founding member of the Irish Genealogical Research Society, he challenged British interpretations of Irish history. In 1934 he wrote a detailed letter criticizing an article that had praised Oliver Cromwell.[8]

But given his own career and particularly his own record, he was not welcomed by many in the broader Irish community in Britain. After he joined the Gaelic Athletic Association in London, his subscription was returned when clubs from Ireland threatened to boycott an event in the city.[9]

The gulf between O'Dwyer and the direction Irish society was heading was starkly obvious by 1933 when he published a book, *The O'Dwyers of Kilnamanagh*. The book, which purported to trace his own family back through a thousand years of history, received a scathing review in the *Irish Press*. It brought up O'Dwyer's own career in the opening lines:

* *Time Magazine*, 25 Mar 1940.

> Sir Michael O'Dwyer was Governor of the Punjab at the time of the massacre of Amritzar; if he was not responsible, he did not deny responsibility; he did not resign. The suffering Indians rank him with the soldier who gave the order. It is, surprising, then, to find a man who has served the cause of freedom and humanity so ill, the author of a book of Irish history that reads like a patriotic chronicle.[10]

O'Dwyer responded to the newspaper with a veiled threat. Unrepentant, he described what had happened as the 'so-called massacre of Armritzar',* stating that the details were 'facts generally unknown in Ireland'.[11] He went on to point out that in 1924 he had successfully sued an Indian politician who made similar claims. One suspects that his point, that the British High Court of Justice had found in his favour, was not as convincing to readers in Ireland as he thought it was.

While his role in Jallianwala Bagh surfaced repeatedly in Ireland, it had left a searing mark in India, particularly in the Punjab, where it was viewed much as the 1916 Rising or Bloody Sunday were in Ireland – a radicalizing moment for many.

*

Born near Jallianwala Bagh in Amritsar in 1899, Udham Singh, who would finally meet O'Dwyer in Caxton Hall in 1940, was just one of the millions whose lives were interwoven with this event. Singh had been raised in a Sikh

* The Jallianwala Bagh massacre was initially known as the Amritsar Massacre.

orphanage. Having joined the British Army, he served as a soldier in the Middle East during the later stages of World War I. Although he does not appear to have been in Amritsar when the Jallianwala Bagh massacre took place, it had a profound impact on Singh. When he did to the city return shortly afterwards he immersed himself in the radical politics. Poverty forced him to emigrate for a second time in the 1920s, this time travelling to the USA, where he was involved in the Indian communist organization, the Ghadar Party. He returned to the Punjab in 1927 but was soon arrested and sentenced to five years in prison on firearms charges. For a detailed account of Singh's life see Anita Anand's *The Patient Assassin*.

Released in 1932, he emigrated to England. As tensions rose dramatically once more across Europe, India's demands for autonomy continued; and after the outbreak of World War II in 1939, the demands evolved and galvanized into calls for full independence. Udham Singh's fellow Sikh, the journalist Saint Nihal Singh, who had visited Ireland in 1924 (see Chapter 13), described the process at work: 'Independence has suddenly ceased to be merely a delusion of the dreamer in India. It has become a live issue, the issue of the day.'[12]

In London, Udham Singh, with a far more radical perspective on the world, decided to play his part by delivering a blow for independence at the meeting of the Royal Central Asian Society in Caxton Hall.

At the time, the Michael O'Dwyer was preparing to leave London for one of his regular visits home to his native Tipperary. Prior to his departure, he planned to attend a meeting of the Irish Genealogical Research Society in

London on 13 March but at the last minute, he changed his plans and instead went to Caxton Hall, for the Royal Central Asian Society talk on the situation in Afghanistan.[13] O'Dwyer felt obliged to attend, as he had promised to make a contribution on the subject. Seating himself at top of the hall, he was surrounded by other prominent imperial figures, including Brigadier General Percy Sykes, Lawrence Dundas, the Secretary of State for India and Burma, Lord Lamington, a former Governor of Bombay and Sir Louis Dane, O'Dwyer's predecessor in the Punjab. Meanwhile Udham Singh had slipped into the rear of the meeting unnoticed.

After the meeting started to break up, Singh pushed his way through the crowd. At the top of the room, the man from Amritsar came face-to-face with O'Dwyer, Sykes, Zetland, Lamington and Dane, and opened fire on them. He struck four of the men, leaving only Sykes unscathed. O'Dwyer was shot twice, once through the side, with a second bullet lodged in his body after hitting a rib. The seventy-five year old was killed instantly. The other three survived their injuries.

Singh, for his part, did not attempt to leave the hall. Instead, he waited to be arrested. When the police arrived he was taken into custody, where he gave his name as Mohamed Singh Azad, a carefully chosen *nom de guerre*. The three component names reflected the three major Indian religious traditions: Muslim, Sikh and Hindu. In his defence, he outlined how he had attacked the men as a political protest: ' I did not take the revolver to kill but to protest. I have seen people starving in India under British imperialism. I done it . . . I am not sorry . . . it was my duty.'[14]

Singh was tried at the Old Bailey in London. As World War II had started the previous year, the courts had been granted far-reaching powers. Little detail of the actual proceedings were reported in the press. Found guilty, Singh was sentenced to death and hanged in Pentonville Prison. His body was buried in the grounds of the jail, far from the Punjab and the people he had acted for.

In death, O'Dwyer and Singh would be remembered in very different ways. O'Dwyer, while mourned in the immediate aftermath of his murder, was increasingly regarded in Britain and Ireland as a man who belonged to another age. He had been a prominent figure in the British Empire but, in the later twentieth century, as it fell apart, few were willing to defend his actions, and for many he represented its worst excesses. In Ireland his memory was even more complex. In his native Tipperary, his obituary in the *Nenagh Guardian* defended his actions in 1919.[15] The *Irish Press* was far less forgiving. Alongside its obituary, it went to considerable lengths to point out his involvement in the Jallianwala Bagh massacre.

Singh, on the other hand, remained relatively obscure for a period after his death, having been executed behind prison walls while British society was focused on the new war on the Continent. After India gained independence in 1947, he garnered widespread recognition as a martyr. In 1974 Udham Singh's remains were exhumed and returned to his native India for cremation.

CHAPTER 16

Escaping Poverty

1965

> He sitteth in the lurking places of the villages; in the secret places doth he murder the innocent; his eyes are privily set against the poor.
>
> (Psalm 10:8)

In 1936 few people understood Dublin city or its problems better than Dr Matthew Russell. A shy man with a passionate interest in public health, the Dublin he knew was one that many citizens avoided at all costs – the slums and tenements. The physician had served as the city's Medical Officer of Health since 1921 and, over the intervening fifteen years, he had become intimately acquainted with the warren of back alleys and lanes that penetrated the city slums. Shocked by the abysmal conditions many Dubliners continued to live in, Russell had been a relentless advocate for government action over the appalling housing in the city.

When a housing inquiry was convened by the Department

of Local Government in 1936, Dr Russell was a key expert. The sixty-two year old painted a viscerally candid picture of the Dublin he knew, and many of those present would profess a shock verging on incredulity that such poverty continued to exist in the city where they lived and worked. Labelled as 'horrific' and 'shocking revelations', newspapers would report Dr Russell's testimony before the inquiry in detail. His descriptions of one street in particular, Marrowbone Lane, stunned those present. Marrowbone Lane's housing was dreadful and had been for decades. It had been labelled as 'squalid' even back in the 1890s and in the following half-century it had sunk further into a mire of poverty.[1]

In an effort to convey what life was truly like, Dr Russell gave specific examples. He described with disturbing candour what he found in Number 28, a six-roomed house that was home to twenty-six people. Each of the rooms of what had once been a spacious dwelling, now served as a home to an entire family. In one room, three generations – a grandmother, two parents and three children between the ages of three and ten – lived in wretched conditions. Basic utilities were non-existent. There was one shared outdoor toilet in the back yard, made from what Dr Russell described as 'rotten pieces of boards and corrugated iron'.[2]

The situation next door in Number 29 was arguably worse – a family of ten lived in what had been, in a different time, the drawing room of a family home. The houses were universally filthy; some were on the verge of collapse. Privacy was a luxury unheard of. At Number 22 there was no way to even lock the shared toilet in the yard.[3] In his concluding remarks, Dr Russell was clear about the solution. There was but one option – the houses had to be demolished.

While journalists proclaimed shock and dismay at the doctor's evidence before the inquiry, their outrage was in part at least performative. Dr Russell's so-called revelations merely confirmed what had been obvious to many Dubliners for decades. While few ventured inside the dilapidated buildings, the reality of how the poor lived had been well documented on numerous occasions. The collapse of two tenements in 1913 had prompted an inquiry. It too had recommended that some houses be knocked and an additional 14,000 new houses built for the city poor. That report had been shelved.[4]

In more recent years one of the more famous stage plays of the age, Seán O'Casey's *Juno and the Paycock*, had brought the realities of tenement life to theatres across the world, but the problems continued unaddressed and worsened each year. Generation after generation of working-class Dubliners lived and died in the tenements.

In 1936 the situation was somewhat different. Even the most cynical of Dubliners could not but be hopeful that things were finally about to change. In what would prove to be one of the great achievements of the Irish Free State, Fianna Fáil, after coming to power in 1932, had prioritized housing and slum clearance. By 1936 this was already leading to considerable changes in Dublin. As Dr Russell testified before the housing inquiry, demolition of some of the worst houses in the city was already underway.

Indeed, just over a year after Dr Russell refocused attention on the conditions in Marrowbone Lane, forty-eight families prepared to bid farewell to the houses that had stretched the definition of a home. They were moving to Emmet House on Watling Street, a new complex of flats, one of several built by Dublin Corporation.

Dubbed 'Moving Day' by the press, 29 November 1937 saw journalists flock to capture what they would later describe as the 'evacuation' of Marrowbone Lane. Throughout that afternoon a stream of Dublin Corporation lorries, donkey carts and even wheelbarrows hauled the belongings of the forty-eight families a few hundred metres through the streets to their new homes on Watling Street.[5] Photographers waiting at Emmet House captured the happy children outside their new flats. Their faces smiled out of the newspapers in the following days, but no picture or dramatic headline could capture the contrast between these families' new homes and their former dwellings. Moving house not only took the families through the streets of Dublin but history itself. In Marrowbone Lane the residents had to one degree or another been trapped in a time warp. The houses had been built back in the eighteenth century. Little maintenance had been carried out on them since the Acts of Union in 1800. By the 1930s they were relics of a bygone age. The architectural features of the original building were obscured by the wear and tear and dirt of several generations. Broken glass windows were not replaced, walls were rarely if ever repainted, doors fell off hinges and staircases rotted. Privacy did not exist given the overcrowding.

By contrast the short walk to Watling Street brought them into the twentieth century and some of the best public housing available in the city. Freshly painted walls, electricity, working appliances and a brand-new concept – privacy. No one had to share a front door with their neighbours.

Among the early residents in Emmet House were the plasterer Matthew Moore and his wife Mary. Matthew had spent his entire life in slum dwellings of one kind or another. As a child, he and his family had lived in a single room on Ardee Row. It was one of four rooms in the house shared by thirteen people in three families.

At Emmet House Matthew could plan a very different future for his children. Mary gave birth to a daughter, Bridie, in 1937 and she would grow up with no memory of the degradation her parents had endured in the slums. Although Bridie and her twelve siblings were raised in a comparatively small flat in Emmet House, the basic amenities they enjoyed were inconceivable in the tenements. Each flat had its own front door, running water and toilets. They also had unlimited electric lighting, charged at a flat rate per week.[6]

What was more impressive is that Bridie Moore and her contemporaries in Emmet House were not unique. In the 1930s and 40s an entire generation of working-class children was lifted from the squalor their ancestors had endured. In 1938 Dublin Corporation announced that it had identified 17,000 families who lived in buildings unfit for habitation. Crucially, it had also developed a five-year plan to build 12,000 houses at a cost of £7.5 million.[7] A separate plan, to build an additional 7,000 houses on the sites of former slums, which were due to be demolished, was also announced. The impact of these new living conditions was immediate and tangible – within a decade life expectancy in Ireland had dramatically increased. Bridie Moore could expect to live ten years longer than her grandparents. While this could not be attributed to housing alone, removing people from tenements – an ideal breeding ground for disease – played its part.[8]

While Emmet House and similar developments were symbols of the advances of the Free State, when they moved from Marrowbone Lane, families like the Moores brought many of the problems they had faced there with them. Matthew and Mary Moore had not lived in tenements by choice; they had lived there because they were poor. This poverty was not something they could leave behind on Marrowbone Lane. While they could raise their children in comparative comfort in their new flat, there was a growing degree of certainty that they would lose those same children to emigration once they were old enough to leave. For their daughter Bridie's generation, the cohort of children born between 1931 and 1941, 80 per cent would have no alternative but to seek a better life overseas.[9] This was not a recent development. As we've seen in previous chapters, emigration had been a constant feature of life since the nineteenth century and successive governments of the Free State had done little to stem the continuing exodus.

The Cumann na nGaedheal government that ruled the Free State until 1932 had demonstrated a willingness to accept emigration as a fact of life. In 1924, when the leader of the Labour Party Thomas Johnson raised the issue of unemployment, the Minister for Industry and Commerce Patrick Gilligan revealed a callous attitude towards the poor and their suffering. He stated in the Dáil that 'people may have to die in this country through starvation'. He went on to reject the notion that he or his government colleagues could be held accountable for poverty, saying, 'It is not any function of this Dáil to provide work, and the sooner that is realized the better.'[10]

But even those with jobs had reason to leave as incomes were in decline – rural farm labourers saw their wages fall by around 20 per cent between 1922 and 1931.[11] Despite the government maintaining that wider unemployment was comparatively low, the 1926 census indicated that this boast was a result of selective statistics rather than the reality of life in the Free State.[12]

The change in government in Dublin in 1932, which saw Fianna Fáil replace Cumann na nGaedheal, did not dramatically alter this trend. While the party promised a shift away from the austere conservative policies of Cumann na nGaedheal, its own economic strategy failed in the long term. A more assertive attitude toward Britain sparked a trade war that lasted throughout the 1930s and, while this ended in 1938 on relatively favourable terms for the Free State, the outbreak of World War II in 1939 posed new problems.

While the Free State remained neutral and was saved from the devastation of war, the conflict created economic turmoil. Shipping, essential to an island economy, was increasingly hard to acquire as the major powers diverted all resources to support their war economies.[13] Wage controls introduced in 1941 led to a 30 per cent decline in real wages. Emigration soared. Over 40,000 Irishmen and women enlisted in the British armed forces. They were only part of an exodus from Ireland that saw around

13 per cent of the adult population emigrate to Britain to work in the booming war economy.[14] After the war ended, the massive reconstruction programme that then began in Britain continued the huge demand for workers. The Free State economy, meanwhile, stagnated.

When Matthew and Mary's daughter Bridie reached her teenage years, emigration was reaching levels unseen since the Great Hunger. While Bridie found work in St Kevin's Hospital in Dublin after leaving school, there was little to hold her in the country in the long term. Along with the lack of economic opportunities, the stifling culture of the Free State was particularly unappealing for women. In August 1951 Éamon de Valera would proclaim life in Ireland to be 'infinitely better from the point of view of health and morals'[15] when referring to the emigrants. These words reflected a quest for moral superiority that set impossible standards for women, leading many to seek a better life overseas.

Irish society was particularly alienating for women like Bridie, who was described as 'a good girl who only wanted singing and dancing' by her mother. A young woman with a vivacious outgoing personality was frowned upon in a society which held that the ideal place for a woman was in the home as a mother. Inevitably, in 1958, at the age of twenty-one, Bridie Moore finally left Watling Street and her native Dublin in the hope of finding a better life overseas. She was one of the 400,000 people who emigrated from the Free State between 1951 and 1961: over 10 per cent of the 1951 population.

The one significant difference for Bridie Moore and her generation of Irish emigrants, in comparison to previous generations, was the destination. The United States had been the traditional choice for Irish emigrants but, for a range of reasons, it had become less popular since the 1920s. In 1924 the administration of US president Calvin Coolidge instituted sweeping immigration reform, and a new system allocated an annual immigrant quota to each country. This saw the Free State granted 29,000 visas per year, which was subsequently reduced to 18,000 in 1929. When the US economy collapsed after the Wall Street Crash, transatlantic emigration almost entirely ceased.[16] In 1931 only 800 Irish immigrants entered the US, as the Irish increasingly opted to travel to Britain instead. Although emigration to the US picked up again in the 1950s, by this time the overwhelming majority, like Bridie Moore, were moving east.

By 1961 683,000 people who had been born in the Irish Free State were living in England and Wales. As the Irish in Britain had long been subjected to racial discrimination, emigrants had congregated in large communities, most famously Cricklewood and Kilburn in North London.

By the time she arrived in London in the late 1950s, Bridie Moore found an Irish community that had established its own institutions. If she so wished, she could socialize almost entirely with Irish people in Irish pubs, dance in Irish dance halls and attend mass along with other Irish people in local Catholic churches. She could even watch a GAA match on Sunday afternoon.

She certainly appears to have gravitated towards the Irish community on arriving in Britain. She met and fell in love with another emigrant from Dublin, Michael O'Hara. And like most in the Irish communities, she remained in constant contact with home. An infrequent letter-writer, Bridie Moore rang her mother once a week and returned to Ireland on occasion.

For most of the Irish in Britain, even though they had been driven from Ireland by economic and social conditions beyond their control, homesickness was a constant companion.

In a reflection of their emotional attachment to home, Bridie Moore and Michael O'Hara came back to Dublin in September 1962 for their wedding, but the pair returned to England shortly afterwards.[17] During their trips home in the late 1950s and early 60s there were signs that Irish society was starting to change. Those who were able to afford it could return by aeroplane to the rapidly expanding Dublin Airport, although most opted for the cheaper ferry from Holyhead.

A more interventionist government, now led by Seán Lemass, was able to take advantage of the wider economic situation following World War II. Unemployment was falling and the 1960s saw a significant symbolic milestone. The 1966 census would record a 2.3 per cent growth in population – the first time the population had not fallen since the Great Hunger over a century earlier.

Renamed the Republic of Ireland in 1949, the country left the British Commonwealth the same year. By the 1960s, it was increasingly looking towards a future with continental Europe, and applied for membership of the European Economic Community in 1961.

It was around this period that migrants in Britain began to return home. By 1971, 32,000 children living in the Republic of Ireland had been born in Britain – but many didn't or couldn't return. For those who found the social conservativism too much to bear, there was no sign that the Catholic Church was loosening its grip. Their lives in Britain stood in stark contrast to Irish society at the time. Bridie Moore, for example, was able to access the contraceptive pill in Britain under the National Health Service after 1961. While this gave women far greater control over their own bodies, such measures were unimaginable in the Republic of Ireland, which remained extremely socially conservative. For others, the tentative signs of economic growth were still not enough to convince them to uproot families, break personal ties, or give up well-paid jobs in Britain.

There were also those for whom emigration had not been the success story they had expected when they left Ireland. Returning home under these circumstances was difficult. Although Michael and Bridie O'Hara returned to Ireland on occasion, it was apparent that their life in London was not what they had hoped for.

By 1964 the couple were living at Agate Road in Hammersmith and they faced difficulties on all fronts. The intensity of better times in their relationship, which had seen Bridie tattoo her husband's name, 'Mick', on her arm, were gone. Things had deteriorated to such a point that they spent the Christmas of that year apart. Financially, the couple were also in dire straits. Bridie struggled to escape the poverty that had defined her youth and, on occasion, turned to sex work to support her income. She was later described by Detective Inspector John Newman as a 'part-time girl who sold herself to pay the rent or for food'.[18]

She was arrested on several occasions on prostitution-related charges.[19]

Despite their difficulties, in the New Year of 1965, Bridie and Michael met in their home on 11 January. But after Bridie left the house later that evening to meet a friend, she did not return. Michael O'Hara would not hear from his wife again.[20] Given their strained relationship, he would only report her missing after several weeks, in early February. The fact that she had previously been arrested on prostitution-related charges, and lived what was regarded as a transient lifestyle, meant the police took little action. Yet Michael's fears that something had happened to Bridie were tragically well founded. On 16 February 1965, nearly five weeks after she had left her home in Hammersmith, Bridie O'Hara's remains were discovered on the Heron Trading Estate in North Acton. Her clothing had been removed and she had bruising on her face. She had clearly been murdered.

What had happened to Bridie O'Hara between the night she left her home and the day her body was found became the source of intense speculation in the following weeks. The case was highly unusual. A pathologist would later testify that the bruising on her face indicated she had been suffocated. Although she was found naked, the autopsy revealed that she had still been wearing some of her clothes at the time of her death. It also appeared that her body had then been stored for a few weeks in a warm, dry atmosphere, which delayed decomposition. At a later stage, the remainder of her clothing had been removed, and her corpse brought to the location where it had been discovered.

The aftermath of her murder was extremely distressing

for her family back in Ireland. While her mother flew to London for the inquest, in the end she did not attend it.[21] Indeed, the coroner would not be able to conclude the hearing for over a year, as Bridie O'Hara's murder was linked to that of five other young women. The police suspected that she had fallen victim to a serial killer operating in the Hammersmith area of the city. As all of the six women had at one time or another been sex workers, the police assumed this was related to why they were targeted.

Over the following year the police launched a major investigation, claiming they interviewed over 4,000 people and carried out over 120,000 inquiries.[22] Although Bridie O'Hara was seen leaving a local pub with a man, they never apprehended the killer. When the inquest reconvened in February 1966 and passed a verdict of murder by 'a person or persons unknown',[23] this only served to heighten the sensation around her case. The media, eager to draw parallels between the killer and the 1890s serial killer Jack the Ripper, coined the moniker Jack the Stripper. This coverage marginalized Bridie O'Hara and the other women, and saw the focus shift to endless surmising as to the identity of the killer.

As was common in such cases, the sexual aspects also dominated media coverage and the police investigation. While the murders do not appear to have involved sexual assault, the public discussion focused on the fact that the victims had all been sex workers. This prevented a broader analysis of other aspects of their lives, which may have been factors in their deaths.

All of the women had lived on the margins of London

society and ended up in sex work because of this. Bridie O'Hara was not targeted because she was an immigrant, but the fact that she was a struggling Irish immigrant had left her vulnerable. Her life had been a constant battle against poverty. She left her home and community in the hope that emigration would offer her an escape from it. In January 1965 her hopes were tragically and violently ended. Her case remains unsolved.

Few at home in Ireland took an interest in Bridie's case. Irish society had been exporting its young people for generations by the 1960s and the emigrants' value to the powers that be often lay in their financial value and the remittances they sent home. Bridie, as an emigrant and particularly a female emigrant who had struggled, was forgotten.

CHAPTER 17

The Troubles

1972

> The foxes have holes and the birds of the air have nests; but the Son of man hath not where to lay his head.
>
> (Matthew 8:20)

In July 1961 Basil Brooke, the Prime Minister of Northern Ireland, mounted the stage at Finaghy outside Belfast to address the annual Orange Order parade held to commemorate the Battle of the Boyne in 1690. The large crowd, decked out in orange sashes, the regalia of the Order, was thoroughly soaked, its mood tempered by unseasonally heavy rain.

In spite of the inclement conditions, the Orange Order had still mobilized tens of thousands to celebrate what was a significant milestone: 1961 marked the fortieth anniversary of the partitioning of Ireland and the foundation of the state of Northern Ireland. As keynote speaker, it fell to Brooke to deliver a State of the Nation speech of sorts, where he reflected on the successes of Northern Ireland and the challenges facing it.

In many respects the speech was typical of those given by politicians on such occasions. Brooke turned to history, recalling the violence of the 1920s and how an older generation, men like himself, had fought to establish Northern Ireland. He talked about the achievements of the northern state, making reference to the 'high living standards' and 'widespread prosperity' enjoyed by the people. Somewhat predictably, he went on to tell the sodden crowd before him that the best years were yet to come for what he called the 'freedom-loving community' of Northern Ireland.[1]

While such rhetoric was the stock-in-trade of politicians, predicting a rosy future was risky for Brooke in 1961. At times his speech had a somewhat defensive tone, perhaps betraying an awareness that he had strayed onto uncertain ground when speaking optimistically about the future. Northern Ireland had seen considerable economic problems over the previous decades, an experience that did not tally with Brooke's claims of 'widespread prosperity'.

The 1920s had seen Belfast's major employers, the shipyards and the linen industry, enter a period of decline. Unemployment soared to around 20 per cent in the 1920s. The 1930s and the Great Depression were worse still. Harland & Wolff, the famous Belfast shipyard that had turned out some of the world's best-known ships, started to see years when it produced no new vessels at all. Workman & Clark, the second major shipyard, closed in 1935.[2] While World War II had granted a temporary economic reprieve, the future remained deeply uncertain

– many in the crowd before Brooke that July had been on demonstrations the previous March, protesting the latest round of layoffs at Harland & Wolff.

The wider economic situation in Northern Ireland in July 1961 was equally bleak. A motion to the Irish Trades Union Congress the same month, in reference to Northern Ireland, described an 'unparalleled crisis in industry embracing every sector of the local economy'.[3] Just a few days after Brooke had painted an attractive future for Northern Ireland, the *Daily Herald* in England labelled it an 'unemployment blackspot'.[4]

The truth was, few in the rain-soaked crowd at Finaghy could say with any certainty that they would still have jobs in twelve months' time, let alone when they would march for the fiftieth anniversary in 1971.

Brooke's claim that people enjoyed 'widespread prosperity', to a crowd with a very different lived experience, spoke volumes as to the unique nature of society in Northern Ireland. But even in the face of the crisis gripping the region, there was still a sliver of truth in what he said; at least for those who had marched to Finaghy.

Although drawn from all ranks of society, the membership of the Orange Order was exclusively conservative and Protestant. Even in the face of uncertain economic conditions, conservative Protestants knew that their problems could be worse – they had fared far better than their Catholic neighbours in the past four decades. This had been the raison d'être of Northern Ireland after all, to establish a Protestant state. Whatever about its successes and failures in terms of employment, in this regard it had been successful.

Since the 1920s Northern Ireland had been a one-party

state, dominated by the Ulster Unionist Party, which ensured that Catholics were marginalized at every turn. The region was a democracy in name only. A careful restructuring of the electoral process led to a dramatic over-representation of Protestants. In Derry city, where Catholics constituted over 65 per cent of the population, twelve of the twenty seats on the local corporation were held by Protestants. In Dungannon Catholics could only win seven of the twenty-one seats, in a town where 53 per cent of the electorate was Catholic.[5]

Similar discrimination pervaded all aspects of life. By 1959, 95 per cent of all positions in the civil service were occupied by Protestants. While this level of bias was common across all public sector jobs, the private sector was little better. Catholics were over twice as likely to be unemployed than their Protestant neighbours, while those who could find work tended to have unskilled, poorer-paid jobs. By 1961 it had become a reality of life that when opportunity presented itself, Catholics were overlooked if Protestants expressed an interest.

As he reflected on the four decades of Northern Ireland in the summer of 1961, Basil Brooke did not ignore this situation. Following generations of Ulster Unionist leaders, he carefully used the plight of Catholics to allay potential criticism from less well-off Protestants about the economic situation. Although discreetly couched, Brooke's words pointed out the inevitability of the discrimination against Catholics provoking resistance, as it had in the past: 'Let us not delude ourselves that our opponents have accepted defeat. They return searching and probing for a weakness in our defences.'[6] Continuing with the use of militaristic language, he fell back on rhetoric employed by political leaders through the ages. He stripped the region's Catholics of individual identity, instead reducing them to a faceless threat: 'the tide of nationalism repulsed time and again will return'.[7]

Lest there be confusion that he might have been referring exclusively to the IRA, who had been involved in an ineffective armed campaign since 1956, he clarified that he was referring to all attempts to effect change coming from the Catholic nationalist community. He went on to say that, 'Whether they are propagandists or gunmen, we can deal with our enemies . . . let them not imperil the structure of the state.'[8]

These final words, 'the structure of the state', were key. Brooke was falling back on a tried-and-tested method to shore up Protestant support in the face of a very uncertain future. Given the highly unequal distribution of resources in the northern state, he heightened fears about what change could bring. From this viewpoint, for Protestant workers, the status quo was always the safest option.

While Brooke had carefully counterposed a bright future for Protestants with the threat posed by Catholics, there was another minority that had suffered appallingly under his government who were left out of his assessment of life in the region. The Traveller community had arguably endured the worst discrimination in the previous four decades, but Brooke did not even deign to mention their plight. While the Catholic minority of Northern Ireland had been the focus of constant governmental prejudice, the tiny Traveller population had been subjected to relentless oppression.

The Travellers, a people with a nomadic way of life, had not been targeted by the government of Northern Ireland solely because of their religion – while they were by and large Catholic, there were also some Protestant members. Although they had lived on the margins of Irish society for centuries, Travellers, who moved from place to place living in wagons and tents, had in times past provided essential skilled labour in the rural economy. But the mechanization of agriculture had stripped the community of its traditional place in the economy.[9] Travellers began to move to cities, where they were reduced to camping on wasteland. Now forced to the margins of urban society, hostility towards them had grown. Governments across Europe in the second half of the twentieth century increasingly refused to engage Travellers and other nomadic peoples on their own terms, instead opting for a policy of forced assimilation into the wider population. But the government of Northern Ireland chose an even more extreme strategy, one that appeared to be designed to remove Travellers, numbering just 1,012 in the North in 1948,[10] from the jurisdiction altogether. The authorities engaged in constant harassment and denial of the most basic amenities in an effort to force Travellers from the six counties.

The Belfast Medical Officer of Health confirmed that the city authorities operated a 'move them on' policy.[11] This meant that the few dozen Traveller families that lived in the city were constantly moved from campsite to campsite instead of being provided with a place to live. All arms of government in Northern Ireland worked in concert on this policy. Judges suspended custodial sentences for

Travellers on condition that they left the jurisdiction.[12] In one instance, a judge described Travellers as a 'running sore'.[13] In the face of such harassment the community went into rapid decline, nearly halving between 1948 and 1954. By the 1950s there were just 583 Travellers living in Northern Ireland.[14]

By the early 1960s that number had dipped below 300, although the pace of decline then slowed somewhat. This may have been due to the increasing official hostility towards Travellers in the Republic of Ireland, which forced some families back across the border. Although Basil Brooke had not attempted to blame such a small community for the stark problems facing Northern Ireland in the 1960s, his government continued to devote considerable energy to targeting what was by now just a few dozen families.

Belfast City Corporation began to organize what it called 'operations', invoking military terminology, when it cleared encampments. Using a self-fulfilling logic, the Minister for Home Affairs, William Craig, claimed that as the community was so small it did not need the facilities it regularly asked for.[15] In 1967 Omagh Town Council put up a notice banning Travellers from using the public toilets in the town.[16] Although the Traveller community had been forced to the brink of survival by the late 1960s, like the rest of Northern Ireland it would find life transformed when the discriminatory policies of the northern state finally pushed people to the breaking point and beyond over housing.

While Travellers had repeatedly called for a solution to their accommodation needs in the form of sites where they could camp, with running water and toilets, settled Catholics in Northern Ireland increasingly faced a housing crisis of their own.*

In the early 1960s the government of Northern Ireland had embarked on an impressive public house-building programme. Although thousands of homes were built, these, like all resources in the northern state, were allocated on the basis of religion rather than need. As is so often the case, a relatively minor local incident in October 1967 – the allocation of fifteen new publicly built houses in the village of Caledon in County Tyrone – proved decisive.

When these were given exclusively to Protestants, including one to a single nineteen-year-old who was secretary to a local Ulster Unionist politician, overlooking several large Catholic families, this sparked widespread protests. What started with the occupation of houses in Caledon spread across Northern Ireland in the following months. As it spread the housing campaign developed into a broader civil rights movement fuelled by decades of political disenfranchisement, unemployment and poor prospects. The violent and coercive reaction of the authorities, while effective in past decades, now proved counterproductive.

The violence of the Royal Ulster Constabulary (RUC) served as a catalyst to the growing movement. When the RUC attacked a civil rights demonstration in Derry city in October 1968, this led to several days of rioting. By the end of the year the protests had grown to such a scale that Terence O'Neill, who had replaced Basil Brooke as

---

* The term 'settled' refers to the non-Traveller community irrespective of background.

Prime Minister of Northern Ireland in 1962, proclaimed, 'Ulster stands at a crossroads,' that Northern Ireland was 'on the brink of chaos'. But in the absence of decisive action to alleviate the discrimination facing Catholics, his dramatic words had little effect.

The New Year of 1969 began much like the old. In January a civil rights march organized by a socialist organization, People's Democracy, was savagely attacked by a unionist mob at Burntollet Bridge outside Derry. The involvement of members of the Ulster Special Constabulary (commonly known as the B-Specials) in the mob violence added to the growing tension. It was amidst these increasing demands for equality that a potential for hope emerged for Northern Ireland's Traveller community.

By 1969 Travellers in Belfast had been continuously forced from encampment after encampment in the city. In the summer of 1969 some set up camp at Beechmount Avenue off the Falls Road. As had happened on countless occasions before, a petition from some residents was handed into Belfast City Corporation, demanding that the Travellers be moved on. But in the following days another petition, calling for the Travellers to be allowed to remain until the city council provided proper sites, secured 415 signatures from locals.

While the Travellers were moved on, and the issue continued to divide the settled community in the Falls Road area, this expression of support, modest as it was, indicated a softening of the hostility that had shaped relations in the city between settled and Traveller families for decades. As the Falls Road was a largely Catholic neighbourhood, the pressing nature of the housing crisis for Catholics may have provided a new understanding of the Travellers' plight. It also perhaps explains the actions of the Traveller community when Catholics in Belfast came under severe attack in the late summer of 1969, after the building tensions across the North erupted into major violence. While it quickly spread across Northern Ireland, the flashpoint which ignited the conflict was Derry.

Each year a Protestant fraternity in the city, the Apprentice Boys – a similar organization to the Orange Order – held a parade recalling the pivotal Siege of Derry in 1689. This was a demonstration of Protestant power in a city that was by now overwhelmingly Catholic, and always took provocative routes close to the Bogside, one of Derry's Catholic neighbourhoods. After the police forced back a counter-demonstration from the Bogside, unionist mobs began to attack Catholic homes in the area. This sparked four days of serious rioting in the city, known as the 'Battle of the Bogside'. The Catholic community erected barricades to prevent the unionists and the police from entering the area, which became known as 'Free Derry'.

Given the level of tension over the previous year, many unionists interpreted these events as evidence of what Basil Brooke had described in 1961 as 'searching and probing for a weakness'.[17] This led them to attack Catholic communities across the North, with levels of violence unseen since the 1920s.

One of the most serious incidents saw a large loyalist mob march on Bombay Street, a largely Catholic community in Belfast, on 15 August 1969. As had happened on numerous occasions over the previous century, the mob began to burn down houses, provoking a flight of Catholic families from the area. Having themselves faced eviction from hostile communities on countless occasions, the Traveller community offered to help evacuate the remaining houses on Bombay Street in the face of the violent mob. Driving across the city, they rescued the possessions of many of the families trying to flee the violence. While this act of solidarity helped some families, the spiralling violence was creating an unparalleled crisis across the North.

By September 1969, 1,800 families, 1,500 Catholic and 300 Protestant, had fled their homes as a result of the intercommunal violence. It claimed the lives of sixteen people that year, killed by the police or in riots and street clashes. The number of deaths in 1970 remained comparatively low – twenty-six people were killed – but the nature of the conflict rapidly began to change. The British Army had arrived in the summer of 1969 to support the government of Northern Ireland and the IRA, which had been in decline up to that point and uncertain how to respond, became more active.

In December 1969 the republican movement split into what became known as Provisional and Official wings. While both maintained their paramilitary capability, the Provisional IRA adopted a much more aggressive attitude to the escalating situation. These developments resulted in a more clear-cut military conflict, albeit an asymmetrical one, which saw republican paramilitaries fight the British Army, RUC and unionist paramilitaries: 171 people were killed in 1971 – of these, eighty-four were killed by the Provisional IRA, forty-five by the British Army, seventeen by the Ulster Volunteer Force (a unionist paramilitary group) and ten by the Official IRA. The percentage being killed during riots was in decline.[18]

The escalating war became a series of points of no return. The August 1971 murders of eleven unarmed civilians by the Parachute Regiment of the British Army, in the Catholic community of Ballymurphy in West Belfast, was decisive in Northern Ireland. On an international level, a similar massacre a few months later by the same regiment, of thirteen unarmed civilians on a civil rights demonstration in Derry, was another defining moment. The 30th of January 1972 would become known as Bloody Sunday, the second British atrocity in Ireland of the twentieth century to earn the name (the first taking place in Croke Park, Dublin in 1920 – see Chapter 10).

The emerging conflict was considerably more complex than the War of Independence had been five decades earlier. The republican position, similar to that of their predecessors in the 1920s, demanded a British withdrawal, which was opposed by the unionist majority of the population of the North. The unionist position, of essentially continuing with the status quo, was unsustainable in the face of a major insurrection. The British establishment, which had a similar view to the unionists, was unwilling to take decisive steps to implement reform. With no clear solution, all semblance of normality in Northern Ireland evaporated in 1972.

And yet, even though 480 people were killed that year, life continued. People still had to survive as best they could. On 1 March 1972 four young Travellers arrived in Belfast to look for scrap metal, one of the ways the community had begun to make a living as its traditional trades became obsolete. The four, Patrick Maughan, his younger brother John, Patrick Michael Connors and Michael McDonagh, spent the day driving around the city, loading metal into the back of their van.

It was after 11 p.m. that night before the boys finished their work, and finally went to look for a shop to get some food. The four were in the van, parked on Church Lane in the city centre, when an RUC constable approached.

As the van had been stolen a few months earlier, the boys panicked. Patrick Maughan, in the driver's seat, put the vehicle into gear and drove off before the constable could stop them. Asking no questions, British Army soldiers positioned on the street immediately opened fire on the van as it sped away. Patrick Maughan then heard moaning from the back of the van and so drove straight to the Royal Victoria Hospital on the Falls Road. When he and Michael McDonagh went into the back of the van there, they discovered that John Maughan, just sixteen years of age, and Patrick Michael Connors, just fourteen, were both dead. Panicking, the pair fled the scene on foot, leaving the van outside the hospital.

A few minutes later, when blood was seen dripping from the back door of the vehicle, hospital staff discovered the bodies of the two boys in the back. In a well-established pattern, seen previously in Ballymurphy in 1971 and Derry a month before, the authorities immediately tried to claim that the boys had links with republican paramilitaries and had fired first. This version of events would unravel before sunrise the following morning, as the security forces issued two contradictory statements on the incident.

The British Army initially claimed that the soldiers had

opened fire when one of the occupants of the van was seen reaching for a gun. This was contradicted a few hours later by a police statement, which said that the constable had approached the vehicle and ordered the occupants to get out, that the van pulled away, and four shots were fired at the policeman. The police statement claimed that it was at this point that the soldiers had returned fire, leading to the deaths of the two boys. Subsequent investigations indicated both statements were false. No evidence of gunfire from the van was produced, nor were weapons or ammunition found.[19]

In the following days, newspapers reported that the soldiers had fired several rounds into the back of a moving van as it drove away from them, directly into the vehicle rather than making any attempt to demobilize it. One of the boys had been shot in the head and the other, according to a security forces spokesman, was 'riddled with bullets'.[20]

Both families denied that either boy was a member of a paramilitary organization.

John Delany, the uncle of fourteen-year-old Patrick Michael Connors, stated of his nephew: 'I want to state that the shooting and killing of my nephew, Paddy Connors, was a foul and despicable deed. The child's only crime was that he was young and a man of the Travelling people in the wrong place at the wrong time.'[21] While it seems unlikely that the soldiers could have identified the boys as Travellers, there is no doubt that, as Northern Ireland descended into violence, those living at the margins were at greatest risk. People who did not have the luxury of remaining behind closed doors after dark were more vulnerable.

The way the boys' families were treated in the aftermath of their murders was unquestionably influenced by the fact that they were Travellers. When journalists visited their campsites the following day the families had still not been officially notified that their sons had been murdered.[22] This was hardly surprising, as the government of Northern Ireland had time and again illustrated its hostility to their community. The reactions of wider society, where the families might expect to receive support, were mixed.

The Liberal MP Sheelagh Murnaghan, a long-time campaigner for Travellers' rights, condemned the murders. In the Republic of Ireland (the Maughan and Connors families had originally come from counties Mayo and Wexford) the Labour TD Brendan Corish called for a full inquiry into their deaths.[23]

Meanwhile, reactions within the broader republican movement varied. Official Sinn Féin, the more radical faction of the split in 1969, aided the family. John Maughan's family were too poor to bury their son so the Official wing of the local republican movement in Armagh, forty miles south-west of Belfast, paid for the funeral and provided a grave in the republican plot of St Patrick's Cemetery for the teenager. Spokesman Seamus Trainor* made it clear that this had been done because of the dire circumstances John's family faced, and he reiterated that the boys were not IRA members.[24]

Such solidarity with the Traveller community was unusual at the time, and the reaction of the more conserv-

* Trainor would later leave the Officials and join the Provisionals in the mid 1970s.

ative Provisional faction of the movement more accurately reflected the sentiments of contemporary Irish society. The *Sligo Champion* carried a Provisional IRA statement on the murder that took a different tone. It not only distanced the Provisional IRA from the boys but from the entire Traveller community. Issued under the usual name of P. O'Neill,* it said: 'I can openly say there is no man in the IRA unless he is a sworn man. Those itinerants were never in the IRA because it is my conscientious belief they would not be taken.' [25]Indeed, in the following weeks, the murders of John Maughan and Patrick Michael Connors were quickly forgotten. A Fianna Fáil councillor in Sligo, Willie Farrell, asked if the lack of expressions of sympathy, common at the time when people were killed in Northern Ireland, was because the boys were Travellers.[26]

No soldiers were ever held accountable. The fact that the victims were Travellers left many ambivalent about their memory – an early indication of how Northern Ireland's Traveller community would fare in the coming decades of conflict. Having been forced further and further towards the margins of society, they were not accepted on either side of the divide in Northern Ireland. In the following weeks the news cycle quickly moved on as the conflict raged. The boys were just two of sixty-seven people killed in February and March 1972.

A fortnight after the murders the British government announced that it would take direct control of security in the North. The unionist government in Belfast, now led

* P. O'Neill was the traditional name used by the Provisional IRA when issuing statements.

by Brian Faulkner, resigned in protest, and the region was then ruled directly from Westminster, bringing to an end fifty years of unionist governance. However, the security situation did not improve.

Throughout 1972 opinion on all sides hardened. While the Ballymurphy massacre and Bloody Sunday left an enduring legacy in nationalist communities, an increasingly cavalier and reckless disregard for civilian life in IRA operations hardened unionist opposition to their nationalist neighbours' demands for equality.

On 21 July, a day that became known as Bloody Friday, the Provisional IRA detonated nineteen bombs across Belfast. While ostensibly targeting infrastructure, the tragically high casualty rate was predictable – nine people were killed and over one hundred injured. An observation by Sir Nevil Macready, the commander-in-chief of British forces in Ireland during the War of Independence, to the effect that the larger the casualties, the more elusive peace becomes, was taking effect.

While Macready's statement is true of any armed conflict, there were other factors at work in Northern Ireland – not least a deep sense of historic injustice and animosity to those who were responsible for past wrongs. The Provisional IRA's operational commander on Bloody Friday was Brendan Hughes, whose great-uncle Owen Hughes had been murdered with impunity by Buck Alec Robinson in 1922 (see Chapter 11). One of the victims of Bloody Friday was William Irvine. His neighbour David Ervine would cite Bloody Friday as one of the reasons for his joining the Ulster Volunteer Force.[27]

While the cycles of violence gave the conflict its own

momentum, the underlying causes – including the discrimination that shaped government in Northern Ireland – remained. Attempts to establish a power-sharing government in 1974 floundered in the face of opposition from unionists who refused to share power and republicans who rejected any partitionist arrangement.

It would be nearly twenty-five years before a lasting peace was forged. Republicans would drop their demand for a British withdrawal, while unionists accepted reforms that Basil Brooke would undoubtedly have seen as 'imperiling the structure of the state' in 1961. This saw the highly sectarian police force, the RUC, disbanded and replaced by the Police Service of Northern Ireland in an effort to make the force more inclusive to Catholics.

A process was initiated that saw most republican and unionist prisoners released. Perhaps most crucially, large amounts of money were invested in the region, which was reeling from three decades of warfare. While problems remained, the system of government that had discriminated against Catholics was dismantled.

Meanwhile, the Traveller community, which had suffered constant discrimination, was largely ignored as the northern state changed shape. Travellers' experience of the war had been complicated. Having fallen to 300 people in the early 1960s, the community in Northern Ireland endured. By 2001 it had grown to 1710, a much higher rate of growth than the wider population.

Still, their living conditions remained abysmal. In the 1980s the British government described these as 'the worst of any group in the United Kingdom'. The growth of the community in Northern Ireland, in spite of these shocking conditions, was amongst other things an indictment of the experience of Travellers in the Republic of Ireland, where life was little better.

An Irish government report in the 1960s indicated that 10 per cent of all Traveller children died before they were two years of age.[28] While 15 per cent of the general population lived past the age of sixty, fewer than 3 per cent of Travellers did.[29] A 2007 study showed that life expectancy among Travellers in the Republic still lingered at levels unseen in the wider population since the 1940s.[30]

Despite the dramatic changes to life throughout Ireland, the words of the Traveller Missie Collins provide a stark example of how her community had been left behind: 'To be an old Traveller means that you're only over forty, an age when most settled people are starting off their lives.'[31]

CHAPTER 18

At a Crossroads

1982

> Let love be without dissimulation. Abhor that which is evil; cleave to that which is good.
>
> (Romans 12:9)

In 1995 Tony Kushner's Broadway play *Angels in America* arrived in Ireland for a run in the Abbey Theatre in Dublin. The widely acclaimed play, celebrated as ground-breaking at the time, would find itself plunged into the middle of a bitter conflict in Ireland.

Throughout the early 1990s Ireland had become increasingly divided over what was known as the 'liberal agenda'. This had seen key battlegrounds emerge over the future direction of society, defined by one journalist as 'divorce, abortion, contraception, and legalising homosexual acts'.[1] The very fact that rights which other countries took for granted were being debated spoke to the deeply conservative nature of Irish society – yet the trajectory of events in the early 1990s increasingly alarmed Irish conservatives.

In 1990 the feminist and outspoken supporter of gay rights, Mary Robinson, had been elected president, the first woman to hold the office. The 1992 general election had seen the centre-left Labour Party double its seats, although it remained only the third-largest party. Two fractious referenda in 1992 had seen women win the right to leave the State to have an abortion, illegal in the Republic. In 1993 homosexuality was decriminalized and a referendum to remove the constitutional ban on divorce was due to take place later in 1995.

When *Angels in America* opened in the Abbey it was inevitable that the play, set in New York's gay community, would get drawn into the wider debate on Irish societal values. After the opening weekend it was the topic of discussion on the *Sunday Show* on State broadcaster RTÉ's Radio 1, leading to an incendiary debate.

The show's panel included the conservative government backbencher Brendan McGahon. Not satisfied with critiquing the play, he launched into a vicious tirade against the gay community. Labelling homosexuality as 'unnatural' and 'disgusting'[2] he went on to proclaim that, controversial as his views may have been, he was speaking for the ordinary people of Ireland. McGahon stated: 'Liberals and left-wing trendies in Dublin 4 may well support homosexuality but they are totally out of touch with the opinion of ordinary people.'[3]

Offensive as this outburst was, in 1995 it was very difficult to state with any certainty where the majority of Irish people stood on one of the key issues of the day. Progress up to then had been extremely limited in scope. Abortion was still illegal – the 1992 referenda had only granted women the right to travel and the right to access information on abortion services overseas. Homosexuality was decriminalized by a parliamentary vote on the back of a judgment in the European Court of Human Rights (ECHR), which had ruled against the Irish laws. The opinion of the electorate had not been required or sought.

There was also ample evidence that the country had limited desire for change. Fianna Fáil, strident opponents of the 'liberal agenda', had been returned as the largest party in every election since 1932. Public debate pivoted around extremely conservative talking points: whether homosexuality should be legal or not, whether women had the right to leave the State to have an abortion or not, and whether contraception should be freely accessible or not. It was difficult to decipher what, if any, further changes the public wanted.

Five months after the McGahon outburst provoked by *Angels in America*, wider public opinion was tested on a key issue of the so-called 'liberal agenda' – divorce. A referendum was held on whether the constitutional ban should be removed. After a bitter campaign, the result provided little clarity. The vote on 24 November 1995 saw the ban on divorce removed, but only by the narrowest of margins: 1.6 million people voted, but just over 9,000 votes separated the two sides. Almost half of the electorate had voted to keep the ban in place.

An unedifying jibe from Úna Bean Mhic Mhathúna, a leading conservative campaigner, labelling those in favour of removing the ban as 'wife-swappin' sodomites', reflected the fact that society was increasingly polarizing into two camps. Many of those who favoured social change on a given issue in the 'liberal agenda' usually also supported broader liberalization. In terms of wider Irish public opinion, it would take the benefit of hindsight before one could state with certainty the direction that it was moving in. Indeed, few in 1995 could have foreseen the extent of the radical change in societal attitudes that was beginning to unfold.

Twenty-three years after Brendan McGahon's homophobic tirade on RTÉ Radio 1 in 1995, another panel discussion took place that embodied what had been a seismic shift in public opinion over the previous decades. This time the discussion was part of a series called *Pantisocracy*, hosted by and named after one of the most prominent members of Ireland's gay community, the drag performer Rory O'Neill, whose stage name was Panti Bliss.

In an episode broadcast on 7 August 2018, O'Neill's five guests were all members of the LGBTQ+ community. Entitled 'Legally Gay!', the episode celebrated the twenty-fifth anniversary of the decriminalization of homosexuality in the Republic and the changes that had taken place in Irish society since. The community's right to exist was no longer a matter of public debate. By 2018 Dublin's Pride Parade, attended by 60,000 people, was the second-largest parade in the city's calendar after St Patrick's Day.

The defining moment had been in 2015, when a constitutional referendum on same-sex marriage was held. The ballot, viewed by many as a wider test of public attitudes towards the LGBTQ+ community, had passed easily – 62 per cent voted in favour. Three years later, just ten weeks before the recording of 'Legally Gay!', a second referendum was held.

The issue this time was women's reproductive rights.

On that occasion 68 per cent voted to remove the constitutional ban on abortion, paving the way for terminations in Irish hospitals. While LGBTQ+ rights and women's reproductive choices were separate issues, the change in attitudes to both underlined the fundamental shift in societal views in the Republic.

While 'Legally Gay!' was an upbeat reflection on these changes, there was an inevitably sombre subtext to the conversation. The progress between the 1980s and 2010s had been hard won and laced with pain and suffering. For many, the violence and discrimination suffered by the LGBTQ+ community was not something that could be forgotten. At one point in the discussion, host Rory O'Neill and two of his guests, Tonie Walsh and Izzy Kamikaze, reflected on the changes that they had witnessed and experienced. The three had come out in the late 1970s and early 80s, in a very different Ireland.

Throughout most of the twentieth century, fear, prejudice and bigotry had defined life for the community. O'Neill recalled being a nineteen-year-old who had to root out small classified adverts to find the semi-clandestine events of the gay community. Kamikaze spoke of the similar experiences of lesbians in Dublin. She came out in the early 1980s, a time when the community was, in her words, 'coded' and 'secret'. She described finding other lesbians as 'quite a challenge'. The secrecy that prevailed was driven by fear.

Homosexuality was illegal in Ireland at the time, and punishable with a custodial sentence. Between 1962 and 1972, 455 men were convicted because of their homosexuality.[4] People were frequently imprisoned. Between

1940 and 1978, an average of thirteen men a year were jailed for offences such as 'indecency with males' and 'gross indecency'.[5] While the State enacted legislation, the key opinion-shaper in Irish society – the Catholic Church – deemed homosexuality a sin. This fuelled public prejudice and found expression in the 1980s notion that AIDS was a punishment from God on gay men. The possibility that the stringent regulation of the sale of contraceptives made safe sex difficult was not considered.

Forced to the margins, the LGBTQ+ community was vulnerable to attack. Physical assaults were common; murders not infrequent. For the majority of the community – those who were not openly out – there was a constant fear of being outed. Meeting a potential partner involved overcoming the very real concern that they might be a criminal intent on blackmail.

Socially, the community was also marginalized. Explicitly gay bars did not exist, and so the community gathered in pubs that were friendly. Dublin pubs such as Davy Byrne's, the Dawson Lounge and Bartley Dunne's were among the handful of establishments that were supportive and welcoming.[6]

For those who could not afford to drink in pubs, or feared identification if they frequented those known to be friendly to the community, one alternative was cruising. This saw gay men meet for casual and often anonymous sexual encounters in locations such as public toilets and parks, such as the Phoenix Park and Fairview Park. But this was by no means risk-free either. They often fell victim to thieves, who targeted them knowing their victims were unlikely to contact the authorities; a court case would potentially raise the reasons why the victim had encountered their assailant in the first place.

Even those who were openly gay struggled to fight for the most basic human rights for their community. Although there were a few small organizations, no gay newspapers or magazines were published in Ireland. Attempts to import the British *Gay News* saw occasional seizures of the magazine by customs officers at Irish ports.[7] Tonie Walsh, a long-time gay activist, historian and archivist, compared society's attitude towards the LBGTQ+ community at the time to the Taliban.[8] The struggle to change these views as well as government policy – a struggle which was all too often a matter of life and death – proved to be a gargantuan challenge.

Ireland's movement for LGBTQ+ rights became increasingly visible in the 1970s. A handful of groups started operating in the country and in 1979 the National Gay Federation established the Hirschfeld Centre on Fownes Street, in Dublin city centre. Named after Magnus Hirschfeld, an early advocate of LGBTQ+ rights in Weimar Germany who was forced into exile by the Nazis, the Hirschfeld Centre served as a meeting space and social centre. As well as running a nightclub, Flikkers, considerable energy was devoted to political campaigning. The sale of pink triangle badges, which homosexuals were forced to wear in the Nazi concentration camps, conjured a sense of the history of their struggle.[9]

At this early stage, the emerging movement also began to chip away at the intolerance it faced from wider society. In 1980 Rose Robertson, the founder of Parents Enquiry, an English organization, was invited to Dublin to speak at a public meeting. Robertson, a former Special Operations Executive agent who had first encountered the family problems of young gay men when working with the Resistance in Nazi-occupied France, helped parents who struggled to deal with their sons' and daughters' homosexuality.[10] Meanwhile, Bernard Keogh, the secretary of the National Gay Federation, regularly wrote to the newspapers, challenging the prejudice that was frequently propagated in Irish media.

In 1980 the openly gay Trinity College lecturer David Norris initiated legal action against the Irish State, arguing that the discrimination he faced contravened his rights under the Irish constitution. The challenges facing the nascent movement were underlined when this lawsuit was rejected. Ireland's accession to the European Economic Community in 1973 had changed the State's legal framework, and Norris expressed his determination to bring a case to the ECHR if necessary. But this would take years; in the meantime, homophobia remained a feature of everyday life.

In 1982, when Norris was chosen to promote Irish tourism in the US because of his expertise as a Joycean scholar, public criticism resulted in the academic giving an undertaking that he would not mention his views on homosexuality. A member of the Cork/Kerry Tourism Board, Paddy Linehan, said he was horrified by Norris's selection to represent Ireland, describing it as disgraceful.[11]

The community remained so marginalized at this time that it was scarcely visible. While gay organizations had over a thousand members by 1980, there were still no Pride parades. From 1979 the community began to organize events for Gay Pride Week, but these were small gatherings. In 1980 pink carnations were distributed in Dublin city centre and in 1981 2,000 balloons were released from St Stephen's Green. But it was a tragic, harrowing and violent event in September 1982 that would prove to be a defining moment in bringing about real change.

Declan Flynn was born in 1951, in the Dublin suburb of Whitehall. Although his early years were a time of growing optimism in Ireland, as the economy and population grew throughout the 1960s, this had evaporated by the time Flynn reached adulthood.

By 1982 Fianna Fáil had ruled the country for thirty-nine of the previous fifty years. While it could point to the clearance of the slums in cities and the completion of electrification in 1978 as major achievements, the Republic struggled economically. A sharp economic downturn saw unemployment increase from 5.7 per cent in 1973 to 14 per cent ten years later.[12]

Despite these difficulties, Flynn managed to find various jobs. He worked as an auxiliary nurse in St Brendan's Hospital in Grangegorman, and subsequently with his father as a sign manufacturer. Around 1980 he secured a position in Aer Rianta, the company which managed Dublin Airport, one-way travel from the country being one of the few booming industries.

In the face of a deepening recession, Ireland was yet again haemorrhaging its population. Emigration returned to levels unseen since the 1950s. Increasing numbers of Irish people were once more travelling en masse to the US, only now as illegal immigrants. Working in the airport,

Flynn continued to live at home, where he enjoyed a close bond with his family.

But it was another part of his life, one he didn't share with his family, that would put him centre stage in Irish history in September 1982. As a gay man, Declan Flynn was a familiar face in the Hirschfeld Centre on Fownes Street, where he volunteered. While the centre provided a sanctuary for the community, wider Irish society remained extremely homophobic. Throughout the summer of 1982 there had been several attacks on gay men in Fairview Park in Dublin. At least one member of the community had brought the matter to the attention of the Gardaí, but no action was taken.[13]

This left many oblivious to the dangers and, on the evening of 9 September, Flynn made his way through the park after spending an evening with friends. Unbeknownst to him, a local gang, the Rollers, responsible for the string of attacks over the previous weeks, had arrived before him. By this time the gang had already viciously assaulted around twenty gay men, who they referred to as 'steamers'.

On the evening in question, they adopted their usual strategy. One sat on a bench while four others lay hidden, the idea being that a single man on a bench might draw the attention of a gay man cruising in the park.

How the attack on Declan Flynn began is unclear. In one version of events, he sat down on the bench; others have questioned whether Flynn, an extremely shy and retiring person, would have had the confidence to approach someone in this manner.

In any case, the four members of the gang who had been hidden emerged. Flynn, sensing the danger, started running in the direction of central Fairview. A few metres from the park entrance and safety, he was tripped up and the gang set on him, beating him savagely with sticks. A detective would later state that these weapons were heavier than Garda-issue truncheons.[14] The injuries Flynn sustained were horrific. He suffered several serious wounds to his head and was bleeding profusely.

Shortly after the gang fled into the darkness of the park, two people out walking came across the gravely injured Flynn. He was still alive when paramedics reached the scene, but was pronounced dead in the early hours of the morning, shortly after reaching hospital.

Although many in the gay community suspected that this was the latest in the string of homophobic attacks in Fairview Park, the initial press coverage did not ascribe a motive. A murder investigation was initiated by the Gardaí and in three days, all five members of the gang, ranging in age from fourteen to eighteen, had been arrested. While the fourteen-year-old was not identified because of his youth, the remaining four were. Two of them, Robert Armstrong and Tony Maher, both aged eighteen, were serving soldiers in the Irish Army. Colm Donovan, seventeen, and Patrick Kavanagh, eighteen, were unemployed. Armstrong admitted under questioning 'we were all part of a team to get rid of queers from Fairview Park'.[15] In his statement, Maher said: 'A few of us had been queer-bashing about six weeks and had battered twenty steamers. We used to grab them. If they hit back, we gave it to them.'[16]

With such admissions, all five were charged with murder – but a subsequent deal with the Director of Public Prosecutions saw the four older members plead guilty to the lesser charge of manslaughter. The fifth, the unnamed fourteen-year-old, entered a not guilty plea and so went to trial. Although he admitted to being present, he claimed that he was not involved in the administering of the fatal wounds.

When his trial opened on 1 March 1983, the full details of the homophobic nature of the attack emerged. The hearing lasted just over three days and the jury retired on 4 March. But in a sign of what was to follow, before the jury left the courtroom for their deliberation the judge, Justice Sean Gannon, removed murder as an option. Instead, he instructed them that they could only consider the lesser charge of manslaughter. It took the jury over three hours to find the boy guilty of manslaughter, but they urged the judge to treat him with leniency.

The following week Justice Gannon reconvened the court to sentence all five of the gang for manslaughter. What followed provoked outrage. He passed down the sentences, ranging from twelve months to five years, but suspended all of them. None of those involved in the killing of Declan Flynn would serve any further time in prison.

Faced with the fact that Flynn's killers had escaped with near-impunity, the fallout from the killing proved a decisive moment for the LGBTQ+ community and, in time, broader Irish society. Among the groups to condemn the sentence was the Cork Gay Collective. Its spokesperson Kieran Rose described the verdict as outrageous, pointing out that it endangered the lives of all gay people.[17] In the Dáil, Proinsias De Rossa of the Workers' Party echoed this view: 'The only reasonable interpretation that can be drawn from the sentencing policy adopted in this case is that the life of a person who was alleged by his attackers to have been a homosexual . . . was considered in some way to be of less value than the life of any other person.'[18]

Fearing the judge's decision would be interpreted as a licence to attack members of the community, gay organizations were determined to make a stand, and organized a protest march to Fairview Park. Although small by later standards, several hundred people participated. This was one of the first public protests to assert the rights of the community, and certainly the largest ever seen in Ireland. It was a milestone in what would be a long struggle to emerge from the dangerous margins of Irish society, in which it had previously been practically invisible.

Three months later the annual Gay Pride Week took place in Dublin, from 20–26 June. In 1983 this had a more defiant tone compared to previous years. While many events echoed the major celebration it would become in later years, a march 'to demand basic human rights' on 25 June was the key event of the week. Several hundred people marched through the streets of Dublin to a rally outside the GPO. This building, heavily associated with the 1916 Rising, was a traditional focal point for demonstrations in the city.

While its reaction to Declan Flynn's murder was a defining moment for the community, the broader political ambivalence, and the refusal to decriminalize homosexuality, underlined the monumental challenge ahead. In 1983 there were signs that Ireland was, if anything, as socially conservative as it had ever been.

*

In recent years Irish conservatives had become alarmed by the course of international events. Increased abortion access in the USA, which stemmed from the Supreme Court's Roe v Wade decision, concerned them. Fearing a similar judgement could allow abortion access in Ireland in the future, the Pro-Life Amendment Campaign lobbied for a constitutional amendment that would close off this possibility.

This could only be passed by referendum, and the Eighth Amendment to the Irish constitution was voted on in September 1983. Backed by the Catholic hierarchy and Fianna Fáil, the amendment passed by nearly 70 per cent.

Irishwomen suffered another setback three years later, when an attempt to relax the constitutional ban on divorce was emphatically defeated in a 1986 referendum by a similar alliance of conservative political forces and the Catholic Church. With conservative power in Ireland seemingly unassailable, the prospects for change on LGBTQ+ rights looked desperately limited.

But the seeds of a diverse social movement that would transform Ireland were already being planted. A feminist movement for gender equality in the workplace had gained traction throughout the 1970s. While Ireland's accession to the European Economic Community in 1973 gradually forced the government to change many sexist laws, women continued to be viewed by a lot of men as second-class citizens.

The establishment of Women's Aid and Ireland's first Rape Crisis Centre drew attention to the archaic laws that remained on the Irish statute books. Up until 1981 a man could sue someone who had an affair with his wife on the grounds that they had devalued his property. Marital rape was not considered a crime until 1990.

Although the Eighth Amendment and divorce referenda of the 1980s had been crushing defeats, the various groups marginalized by Irish society increasingly supported each other. The demonstration protesting the murder of Declan Flynn included a representative of the Rape Crisis Centre and a member of the feminist Greenham Common Women's Peace Camp.[19] In 1983 the Gay Pride leaflets outlined the alliance of those who supported the community's demands, which as well as those campaigning against the Eighth Amendment, included trade unions and left-wing political parties.

But the limited victories of the 1980s took place against the backdrop of relentless discrimination. In 1987 David Norris was successfully elected as a senator from the constituency of Trinity College graduates. The following year he was finally victorious in the ECHR, which found that Irish laws criminalizing homosexuality were a breach of his human rights. And yet, homophobia remained rife – when Norris was asked to open a local festival in Birr, County Offaly, a local councillor protested on the grounds that 'he's gay and that's out for me'.[20]

Furthermore, the Fianna Fáil government of the day refused to act on the ECHR ruling. It would take six years and a coalition government that did not involve Fianna Fáil before homosexuality was finally decriminalized in 1993. Pride that year, which saw one thousand people participate, included the chant: 'What did we want? Gay rights! When did we get them? Yesterday!'

Broader changes in Irish society in the 1990s provided

space for the LGBTQ+ movement to build on decriminalization. Most significant of all were the crises that wracked the Catholic Church. It had been one of the main obstacles to change in Irish society, but began to lose influence in the 1990s. In 1992 it emerged that the Bishop of Galway and Kilmacduagh, Eamonn Casey, had a secret family with an American woman, Annie Murphy. Two years later another high-profile cleric and a regular commentator in the Irish media, Father Micheal Cleary, had his secret family revealed shortly after his death. Both men had taken vows of celibacy and publicly defended the conservative Church teaching on sex.

However, the anger fuelled by this hypocrisy was overshadowed by the revulsion and outrage that followed a series of child sexual abuse scandals that emerged over the following years. Revelations that children had been abused for decades in Church-run institutions, and that paedophile priests had been protected by the Church hierarchy, destroyed the faith of many Irish Catholics. Mass attendance began to decline rapidly, falling from 85 per cent in 1990 to 65 per cent in 1997.[21] Even more concerning for Church leaders was the fact that around two-thirds of those aged fifteen to thirty-four in urban areas were no longer attending mass.[22] The Catholic Church had lost its influence as moral arbiter over a considerable swathe of society.

As the architecture of conservative Ireland collapsed, space for the LGBTQ+ community grew. Change took the form of an increasingly visible community, the opening of gay bars, but most importantly in countless personal conversations, as LGBTQ+ people came out to friends, family and co-workers. This was having an impact in a myriad of ways as early as the mid-1990s. In December 1994 *Fair City*, one of the most popular soap operas produced in Ireland, announced it was introducing its first gay character. The show's executive producer, Declan Eames, commented: 'Soap is a reflection of everyday life and many people have friends and relatives who are gay.'[23]

Yet *Fair City* avoided depicting a gay kiss. Two years later a new Irish-language soap, *Ros na Rún*, featured a gay couple in its opening season. The following season in 1997 showed a gay kiss, a first for Irish television. There was added significance in this, as *Ros na Rún* was set in a small rural village (*Fair City* was set in Dublin). In a further sign of changing attitudes Seán Ó Tarpaigh, who played the gay character Tom in *Ros na Rún*, noted in 1999 that 'there hasn't really been any complaints about my character'.[24]

It would be a further eighteen years after that kiss before the wider Irish population was given the chance to express its views. A referendum proposing changes to the constitution that would redefine marriage to explicitly include same-sex unions was held in May 2015.

When the ballot passed comfortably, those who had been involved in the campaign for a Yes vote were not as surprised as some commentators. It had been their decades of tireless activism that delivered the change, and their lived experience had been a litmus test of that change before the referendum. When asked about the result, Rory O'Neill reflected: 'It's not that Ireland has changed today, but that Ireland has confirmed the change that we already knew had happened.'

In September 2022, four decades after Declan Flynn's brutal murder, hundreds of people returned to Fairview Park to commemorate the man whose death had been such a pivotal moment. While most remembered the legacy of his tragic and violent death, his brother Paul paid tribute to the Declan he knew: 'He was a quiet man. He loved pop music, and family celebrations. He was particularly loving to his parents and to his younger brother Greg who had Down syndrome. His gentle nature was in stark contrast to the brutality that abruptly ended his life.'[25]

Acknowledgements

This book was written with the invaluable support of friends and family, but there are a few people who deserve special mention, without whom I would not have been able to complete this book.

At the outset of the project I approached Finbar Cafferkey to edit and provide feedback on early drafts of the book. A shared understanding of the past and present, not to mention his command of language shaped the final draft. Tragically Finbar did not live to see the publication of the book. It is dedicated to his memory.

The support of my partner Shirley, who encouraged and supported me at every step, was integral. She also helped shape the book through her insightful perspectives on the subject matter. Her superior command of the English language was also invaluable when my own reached its limitations.

I was lucky to have great people to help in the research phase of the book. A debt of gratitude is owed to three in particular. Liam Costello spent more time than anyone should reading inquest reports when helping with the background to the cases. Stewart Reddin and Sam McGrath provided invaluable research on particular areas of expertise. Finally I would also like to thank the team at HarperCollins who have been fantastic and a joy to work with, in particular Stephen Reid whose editorial skills brought colour and life to the past.

The end notes in this section include primary sources and abridged secondary sources. A corresponding, unabridged list of the secondary sources, along with governmental reports, can be found in the References section that follows.

Notes

CHAPTER 1

1 National Archives of Ireland (NAI) CSO/RP/SC/1821/785.

2 *Belfast Commercial Chronicle*, 3 Dec. 1821.

3 *The Examiner*, 2 Dec. 1821.

4 *Louisville Public Advertiser*, 23 Feb. 1822.

5 *The Calcutta journal of politics and general literature*, 10 May 1822.

6 *Windsor and Eton Express*, 27 Aug. 1821.

7 Holton, K. '"All our joys will be complated": the visit of George IV to Ireland, 1821'.

8 *Freeman's Journal,* 1 Nov. 1821.

9 *Donnelly, J., Irish Peasants: Violence and Political Unrest, 1780–1914, 64–8.*

10 J.G. Kohl, 'Travels in Ireland', 32.

11 *Saunders's News-Letter*, 9 Nov. 1821.

12 NAI CSO/RP/SC/1821/785.

13 *Clonmel Advertiser,* 24 Nov. 1821.

14 NAI CSO/RP/SC/1821/494.

15 *Belfast Commercial Chronicle*, 3 Dec. 1821.

16 NAI CSO/RP/SC/1821/494.

17 NAI CSO/RP/SC/1821/494.

18 NAI CSO/RP/SC/1821/287.

19 Ibid.

20 Ibid.

21 NAI CSO/RP/SC/1821/287.

22 NAI CSO/RP/SC/1821/785.

23 James Kelly, *Food Rioting in Ireland in the Eighteenth and Nineteenth Centuries*, 52.

24 *Carlow Morning Post*, 13 Mar. 1822.

25 *Finns Leinster Journal*, 1 Sep. 1827.

26 James Kelly (ed), *The Cambridge History of Ireland*, Vol. III, 1730–1880, p.99.

27 Brian Jenkins, *Era of Emancipation: British Government of Ireland, 1812–1830*, 101–2.

CHAPTER 2

1 Lewis, S. (1837), *A Topographical Dictionary of Ireland*, 376–377.

2 *Roscommon & Leitrim Gazette*, 11 Oct. 1834.

3 *Newry Telegraph*, 31 Mar. 1835.

4 Ibid.

5 Ibid.

6 McMahon, R., '"A Violent Society"? Homicide Rates in Ireland, 1831–1850', 17.

7 National Library of Ireland (NLI) MS 490, 171. 'The Murder of Stanhope Fleming at the Clare Hill near Moira'. A second ballad from the nineteenth century, 'Young Flemond's Murder

near Moira', is a sectarian telling of the story. However this appears to have been written by someone unfamiliar with the story – the name Fleming is for example incorrect.

8 Curran, D., *The Rise and Fall of the Orange Order During the Famine: From Reformation to Dolly's Brae*, 20.

9 Ibid., 11.

10 Blackstock, A., *Tommy Downshire's Boys: Popular Protest, Social Change and Political Manipulation in Mid-Ulster 1829–1847*, 142.

11 NAI CSO/RP/OR/1831/1578.

12 NAI CSO/RP/OR/1831/475.

13 *Northern Whig*, 4 Aug. 1834.

14 *Belfast Commercial Chronicle*, 16 Mar. 1835.

CHAPTER 3

1 *Cork Examiner*, 2 Nov. 1846.

2 Cormac Ó Gráda, *Ireland: A New Economic History of Ireland*, 120.

3 *Freeman's Journal*, 27 Oct. 1845.

4 Ibid.

5 Ibid.

6 House of Commons (HC) Debate, 5 May 1846, Vol 86. 134.

7 *Dublin Weekly Register*, 12 Sep. 1846.

8 *Ballyshannon Herald*, 25 Sep. 1846.

9 *Saunders News-Letter*, 22 Sep. 1846.

10 Ibid.

11 NAI OR/Waterford/1846

12 Ibid.

13 Ibid.

14 Ibid.

15 Ibid.
16 Ibid.
17 Ibid.
18 Ibid.
19 *The Pilot*. 28 Oct, 1846.
20 *Cork Examiner*, 26 Mar. 1847.
21 *Waterford Chronicle*, 17 Apr. 1847.
22 HC debate, 8 Feb. 1847, Vol 89, 945.

CHAPTER 4

1 *Freeman's Journal*, 25 Aug. 1847; *Nenagh Guardian*, 23 Oct. 1850.
2 *Cork Examiner*, 10 Nov. 1847.
3 *Dublin Weekly Register*, 13 Nov. 1847.
4 *Cork Examiner*, 10 Nov. 1847.
5 *Dublin Evening Post*, 9 Nov. 1847.
6 *Cork Examiner*, 10 Nov. 1847.
7 Reilly, C., *Strokestown and the Great Irish Famine*, 101.
8 Ibid., 84.
9 Ibid., 20–21.
10 Ibid., 59.
11 Ó Gráda, C., *Black '47 and Beyond*, 129.
12 Ibid.
13 Ibid.
14 Royal Commission of Inquiry into the State of the Law and Practice in Respect of the Occupation of Land in Ireland HC XIX 1845, 21
15 Strokestown Park Archive (STR) 1A/105
16 Bulik, M., *The Sons of Molly Maguire: The Irish Roots of America's First Labor War*, 97.

17 Reilly, C., *Strokestown and the Great Irish Famine*, 54.

18 Trevelyan, C. *The Irish Crisis*, 1.

19 Ibid.

20 Donnelly, J. S., 'The Great Famine and its interpreters, old and new', *History Ireland*, autumn 1993.

21 Reilly, C., *Strokestown and the Great Irish Famine*, 62.

22 *Freeman's Journal*, 30 Jun. 1847.

23 Reilly, C., *Strokestown and the Great Irish Famine*, 83.

24 *Cork Examiner*, 5 Nov. 1847.

25 Bulik, M., *The Sons of Molly Maguire: The Irish Roots of America's First Labor War*, 98.

26 *Cork Examiner,* 5 Nov 1847.

27 Military Archives of Ireland (MAI), Bureau of Military History (BMH), Patrick Mullooly Witness Statement (WS) 1087, 6.

28 Fahey, J., Olive Hales Pakenham Mahon, Strokestown (1982) – *Looking West*, RTÉ Radio.

CHAPTER 5

1 Central Relief Committee, Transactions of the Central Relief Committee of the Society of Friends During the Famine in Ireland, in 1846 and 1847,178

2 David Keane to Michael Neile, letter, 21 March 1848 New York Historical Society. Manuscripts Collection.

3 Ó'Gráda, C., 'School Attendance and Literacy before the Famine: A Simple Baronial Analysis', 4.

4 Minutes Clogheen Board of Guardians, (CBoG), 8 Aug. 1842.

5 Ibid., 24 Apr.1843.

6 Ibid., 10 Apr. 1843.

7 Ibid., 24 Apr. 1843.

8 Ibid., 4 Aug. 1845.

9 Ibid., 11 Aug. 1845.

10 Ibid.

11 Ibid., 6 Dec. 1846.

12 Griffith, Richard., *General Valuation of Rateable Property in Ireland, Parish of Shanrahan County Tipperary*, 77.

13 Minutes, CBoG 4 Dec. 1847.

14 *Waterford News and Star*, 28 Jun. 1861.

15 *Freeman's Journal*, 24 Jul. 1862.

16 *Nenagh Guardian*, 26 Jul. 1862.

17 *Freeman's Journal*, 24 Jul. 1862.

18 *Clonmel Chronicle*, 10 May 1862.

19 *Nenagh Guardian*, 26 Jul. 1862.

20 Ibid., 23 Jul. 1862.

21 Ibid., 26 Jul. 1862.

22 Ibid.

23 NAI MFGS 51/1–163.

CHAPTER 6

1 Marx, K., *Karl Marx: Collected Works Vol II*, 641.

2 McGee, O. *The IRB: The Irish Republican Brotherhood, from the Land League to Sinn Féin*, 63.

3 Eleventh Annual Report of the Registrar General of marriages of births marriages and deaths in Ireland, HC [C-1495], 108.

4 Dooley, T., *Sources for the History of Landed Estates in Ireland*, 8.

5 Pat Finnegan, *Lough Rea, That Den of Infamy: the Land War in Co. Galway, 1879–82*, 21.

6 Ibid.

7 Ibid., 30.

8 Ibid., 26.

9 Ibid., 30.
10 *Dublin Weekly Nation*, 28 Aug. 1880.
11 *Northern Whig*, 26 Aug. 1880.
12 Ibid., 21 Sep.1880.
13 *Dublin Daily Express*, 20 Sep. 1880.
14 *Freeman's Journal*, 7 Nov. 1888.
15 *Freeman's Journal*, 7 Nov. 1888.
16 Irish Loyal and Patriotic Union,'A verbatim copy of the Parnell Commission report: with complete index and notes', 105.
17 *Freeman's Journal* 1763–1924, 14 May 1881.
18 Albano, D., 'Funeral customs in nineteenth century Ireland', 182
19 *Freeman's Journal*, 7 Nov. 1888.
20 *Sligo Champion*, 10 Mar. 1883.
21 Finnegan, *Lough Rea, That Den of Infamy*, 88–95.
22 Ibid.
23 Ibid., 100.
24 *Irish Examiner*, 1 Aug. 1883.
25 Michael Davitt, *The Fall of Feudalism in Ireland, or the Story of the Land League Revolution*, xi.

CHAPTER 7

1 Shiels, D., *The Irish in the American Civil War*, 7.
2 *Cincinnati Enquirer*, 27 Apr. 1984.
3 Connolly, S., *On Every Tide*, 285.
4 Ó Gráda, *Before and After the Famine*, 169.
5 *Cincinnati Enquirer*, 26 Apr. 1894.
6 *Ibid.*
7 *Ibid.*
8 Ibid.

9 Ibid.
10 Ibid.
11 Ibid.
12 *Cincinnati Enquirer*, 27 Apr. 1894.
13 Ibid.
14 *The Cincinnati Enquirer*, 26 Apr. 1894.
15 Ó Gráda, *Before and After the Famine*, 161.
16 *Cincinnati Enquirer*, 26. Apr 1894.
17 Ibid.
18 Ibid.
19 Ibid.
20 *The Cincinnati Enquirer*, 27 Apr. 1894.
21 *The Cincinnati Enquirer*, 26. Apr 1894.
22 Ibid.
23 *The Cincinnati Enquirer*, 27 Apr. 1894.
24 *The Cincinnati Enquirer*, 26. Apr 1894.
25 *Cork Constitution*, 26 Apr. 1894.
26 *The Cincinnati Enquirer*, 26 Apr. 1894.
27 *The Cincinnati Enquirer*, 27 Apr. 1894.
28 Ibid.
29 Ibid., 19 May 1894.
30 Ibid., 11 Oct. 1894.
31 Ibid., 20 Apr.1895.
32 Ibid., 27 Nov. 1895.
33 Ibid., 28 Nov. 1895.
34 Ibid., 12 Jun. 1898.
35 Ibid., 23 Nov. 1899.
36 Local 12 News, 'Detectives, Historians Solve Murder by Priest from 1894.

A Lethal Legacy

CHAPTER 8

1 *Wexford People*, 16 Jul. 1890.
2 Census of Ireland 1891: Area, Population and Number of Houses; Occupations, Religion and Education volume I, Province of Leinster. HC [C-6515], 359
3 Ginnell, L., *Land and Liberty*, 30.
4 Fortieth Report of the Inspectors of Lunatics (Ireland) HC [C 6503] 1890–1891, 5.'
5 Walsh, B., 'Life Expectancy in Ireland since the 1870s'
6 1851 Census of Ireland Report on the Status of Disease – Part III HC [1765], 66.
7 Kelly, B., *Hearing Voices: The History of Psychiatry in Ireland*, 294.
8 Ibid., 253.
9 Fortieth Report of the Inspectors of Lunatics (Ireland) HC [C 6503], 3.
10 Ibid., 5.
11 Katherine Fennelly. 'Out of sound, out of mind: noise control in early nineteenth-century lunatic asylums in England and Ireland', *World Archaeology*, Vol. 46, No. 3
12 Fortieth Report of the Inspectors of Lunatics (Ireland) [C 6503], HC 1890–1891, 139.
13 *Freeman's Journal*, 12 Jul. 1890.
14 Ibid.
15 Ibid.
16 Ibid.
17 Ibid.
18 Fortieth Report of the Inspectors of Lunatics (Ireland) HC [C 6503], 1890–1891, 82
19 *Freeman's Journal*, 15 Jul. 1893.

CHAPTER 9

1 *Waterford Standard*, 1 Nov. 1910.
2 *Waterford News*, 2 May 1919.
3 Dorney, J., 'The Belfast Dockers and Carters Strike of 1907.'
4 *The Irish Times*, Evening edition, 21 Sep. 1914.
5 Ibid.,11 Aug. 1914.
6 Ibid.
7 Waterford City & County Council, Waterford from 1914–1918.
8 *Waterford Star*, 3 Jun. 1916.
9 *HC debate, 3 May* 1916, Vol 82, 30–9
10 *Irish Independent*, 15 May 1916.
11 *Waterford Star*, 13 May 1916.
12 *Freeman's Journal*, 31 Mar. 1917.
13 P. McCarthy, *The Irish Volunteers and Waterford Part II 1916–1919: The Resistible Rise of Sinn Féin*, 254.
14 Ibid.
15 *Freeman's Journal*, 18 Mar. 1919.
16 *Waterford News*, 2 May 1919.
17 Ibid.
18 Ibid.
19 Ibid.

CHAPTER 10

1 Ghose, A.K., 'Food Supply and Starvation: A Study of Famines with Reference to the Indian Sub-Continent', 397.
2 *Dublin Daily Express*, 1 Jun. 1897.
3 *Donegal Independent*, 25 Jun.1897.
4 NAI Calendar of Wills and Administrations 1858–1920, 1896
5 HC Debate, 2 May 1906, Vol. 156, 570–1.

6 Campbell, F., *Land and Revolution Nationalist Politics in the West of Ireland*, ll98.
7 Ibid., 91.
8 RTÉ Doc on One, Higgins, O. & Blake, S. (2019) 'Reprisals – the Eileen Quinn Story'
9 Campbell, F., *Land and Revolution: Nationalist Politics in the West of Ireland 1891–1921*, 254.
10 *Irish Independent*, 25 Apr. 1919.
11 *Tuam Herald*, 3 Apr. 1920.
12 Ibid., 28 June 1919.
13 MAI, BMH, Seamus Babington WS1595, 22.
14 Hopkinson, M. *The Irish War of Independence*, 60.
15 Dáil Éireann debate, 29 Jun. 1920 Vol. F, No. 15.
16 Hopkinson, M. *The Irish War of Independence*, 60–61.
17 Robinson, L., *Lady Augusta Gregory Journals 1916–30*, 111.
18 Ibid.
19 Ibid.
20 *Galway Observer*, 6 Nov. 1920.
21 *Westminster Gazette*, 16 Nov. 1920.
22 Ibid.
23 HC Debate, 8 Nov. 1920 Vol 134, No.43.

CHAPTER 11

1 Gregory, I. et al., *Troubled Geographies: A Spatial History of Religion and Society in Ireland*, 63.
2 Black, A.&C., *Black's Guide to Ireland*, 109.
3 Lynch, J., *Harland And Wolff: Its Labour Force And Industrial Relations 1919*, 47.
4 Black A.&C. *Black's Guide to Ireland*, 108
5 Ibid.

6 *Belfast Telegraph*, 22 Mar. 1913.

7 Report of the Departmental Committee into the Housing Conditions of the Working Classes in the City of Dublin (1913) [HC 7273], 23.

8 Report of the Belfast Riots Commissioners HC [4925], 5.

9 Gregory, I & Cunningham, N., *Troubled Geographies: A Spatial History of Religion and Society in Ireland*, 81.

10 Ibid.

11 Radford, M., 'Closely Akin to Actual Warfare', History Ireland, Vol 7, No. 1, 1999.

12 Report of the Belfast Riots Commissioners HC [4925], 5.

13 *Irish Independent,* 14 Jul. 1919.

14 *Larne Times*, 17 Jan. 1920; *Belfast News-Letter*, 26 Feb. 1920.

15 MAI, BMH, John McCoy WS492 pp.5–6

16 Fanning, R., 'Anglo-Irish Relations: Partition and the British Dimension in Historical Perspective', 12–13.

17 Hopkinson, *The Irish War of Independence*, 159.

18 Murphy, R., *Walter Long and the Making of the Government of Ireland Act, 1919–20* (1986), 86.

19 *Dublin Evening Telegraph*, 13 Jul. 1920.

20 MAI IRA Nominal Rolls, Belfast Brigade, RO/402.

21 Halpin, E & O'Corrain, D. The Dead of the Irish Revolution, 548.

22 *Northern Whig*, 25 Nov. 1921.

23 *Belfast News-Letter*, 13 Apr. 1922.

24 Ibid.

25 Moloney, E. *Voices from the Grave: Two Men's War in Ireland*, 61.

26 O'Connell, S., 'Violence and social memory in twentieth century Belfast', 741.

27 *Belfast Telegraph*, 7 Apr. 1927.

28 Moloney, E. *Voices from the Grave: Two Men's War in Ireland*, 61.

CHAPTER 12

1 Ryan, M., *The Real Chief: Liam Lynch*, 11.
2 O'Higgins, K., 'Three Years Hard Labour', 7.
3 Ó'Gráda, C., 'Settling in: Dublin's Jewish immigrants of a century ago', 2.
4 Ibid.
5 NAI 2007/56/153.
6 Hanley, '"The Irish and the Jews have a good deal in common": Irish republicanism, anti-Semitism and the post-war world', 60.
7 Ibid.
8 *Dublin Daily Express*, 26 Aug. 1914.
9 *Evening Irish Times*, 17 Aug. 1914.
10 *Londonderry Sentinel*, 18 Aug. 1914.
11 *Irish Independent*, 9 Feb. 1915.
12 O'Connor, E., 'Agrarian unrest and the labour movement in Co. Waterford, 1917–1923', 40.
13 Ó Corrain, D. & O'Halpin, E., *The Dead of the Irish Revolution*, 27.
14 Ibid., 41.
15 *Belfast News-Letter*, 24 Mar. 1920.
16 *Freeman's Journal*, 4 Dec. 1920.
17 *Irish Times*, 18 Nov. 2003.
18 NAI MFGS 51/1–163.
19 Gannon, S.W., 'Revisiting the "Limerick Pogrom" of 1904'.
20 *Northern* Whig, 11 Jan. 1922.
21 O'Connor, E., 'Agrarian unrest and the labour movement in Co. Waterford, 1917–1923', 41.

22 Ferriter, D., *Between Two Hells – The Irish Civil War*, (2022).
23 *Freeman's Journal*, 11 Aug. 1923.
24 Ibid., 18 Aug. 1923.
25 Connolly, L., 'Sexual Violence in the Irish Civil War: a forgotten war crime?', 136.
26 Ibid., 136–137
27 Ibid.
28 *Freeman's Journal*, 3 Nov. 1923.
29 NAI 2007/56/153.
30 NAI 2007/56/153.
31 Ibid.
32 NAI 2007/56/153.
33 *Irish Independent*, 17 Nov. 1923.
34 NAI 2007/56/153.
35 IMA, Military Service Pensions Collection (MSPC), James Patrick Conroy W24SP80 pension application.
36 *Cork Examiner*, 27 Mar. 1925.
37 NAI 2007/56/153.
38 NAI 2007/56/153.
39 IMA, MSPC, James Patrick Conroy W24SP80 pension application.

CHAPTER 13

1 Gerwarth, R., *The Vanquished: Why the First World War Failed to End*, 1917–1923, 23.
2 *Irish Independent*, 27 Dec. 1928.
3 Gerwarth, R., *The Vanquished: Why the First World War Failed to End, 1917–1923*, 167.
4 *Daily Herald*, 12 Jan. 1925.
5 McCarthy, A., 'The Irish National Electrification Scheme', 545.

6 Bielenberg, A., *The Shannon Scheme and the Electrification of the Free State,* 41.
7 Thirty-first annual report of the Labour and Trade Union Congress 1925, 26.
8 NAI TSCH S 4278 A.
9 *Kerry News*, 18 Sep. 1925, 3.
10 Bielenberg, *The Shannon Scheme and the Electrification of the Free State*, 41.
11 *Limerick Leader*, 9 Dec. 1925.
12 *Irish Independent*, 29 Jun. 1926.
13 Ibid.
14 Bielenberg, A., *The Shannon Scheme and the Electrification of the Free State*, 58.
15 *Irish Independent*, 12 July 1926.
16 McCarthy, M., *High Tension: Life on the Shannon Scheme*, 110.
17 Ibid., 113–5.
18 McCabe C., *Sins of the Father*, 75.
19 Lee, J.J., *Ireland 1912–1985: Politics and Society*, 115.
20 Ibid.
21 Dáil Éireann Debate, 13 Feb. 1925, Vol. 10, No. 3.
22 *Limerick Leader*, 11 Mar. 1929.
23 Ibid.
24 *Limerick Leader*, 5 Mar. 1927.
25 *Cork Examiner*, 24 Dec. 1928.
26 Ibid., 14 Mar. 1929.
27 Bielenberg, A., *The Shannon Scheme and the Electrification of the Free State*, 109.
28 *Limerick Leader*, 16 Mar. 1929.
29 Ibid.
30 Ibid.

31 Ibid.

CHAPTER 14

1 Dáil Éireann Debate, 1 Mar. 1923 Vol. 2 No. 35.
2 Andrews C.S., *Man of No Property*, 178.
3 Ibid., 3.
4 Ibid., 10.
5 Luddy, M., 'Sex and the Single Girl in 1920s and 1930s Ireland', 88.
6 NAI TAOI S 5998.
7 Andrews, C., *Man of No Property*, 48.
8 Ibid.
9 NAI TSCH 4183.
10 Ibid.
11 Ibid.
12 *Frontier Sentinel*, 1 Nov. 1924.
13 *Nationalist and Leinster Times*, 31 Oct. 1936.
14 *Irish Press*, 2 Mar. 1937.
15 The Report of the Committee on Evil Literature 16
16 Ibid., 14.
17 Carrigan, W., Report of the Committee on the Criminal Law Amendment Acts (1880–1885) and Juvenile Prostitution.
18 Evan, R. *The Coming of the Third Reich*, 125.
19 Beaumont, C. Women, citizenship and Catholicism in the Irish free state, 1922–1948, 566
20 Ibid.
21 O'Leary E., 'The Irish National Teachers' Organisation And The Marriage Bar For Women National', 47.
22 *Cork Examiner*, 22 Apr. 1960.
23 *Nationalist and Leinster Times*, 10 Oct. 1936.

24 Ibid.

25 *Frontier Sentinel*, 1 Nov. 1924.

26 Ibid., 17 Oct 1924.

27 Carroll, E.M., 'Memorandum re: women and girls who come before the central criminal court on serious charges – and other relevant matters', 201.

28 Ibid.

29 Ibid.

CHAPTER 15

1 O'Dwyer, M., *India as I Knew It*, 8.

2 Gannon, S.W. '"The Green Frame of British Rule?" – Irish in the Indian Civil Service'.

3 Benson, C., *Nabobs, soldiers and imperial service: the Irish in India.*

4 Campbell, F., *Land and Revolution Nationalist Politics in the West of Ireland*, 116.

5 O'Dwyer, M., *India as I Knew It*, 10.

6 Fahey, J., Olive Pakenham Mahon, Strokestown (1982) – Looking West, RTÉ Radio 1.)

7 *Irish Independent*, 8 Jun. 1925.

8 *Cork Examiner*, 6 Oct. 1934.

9 *Irish Independent*, 6 Apr. 1931.

10 *Irish Press*, 26 Jun. 1933.

11 *Irish Press*, 7 Jul. 1933.

12 *The Baltimore Sun*, 2 Jun. 1940.

13 *The Derby Daily Telegraph* 21 Mar. 1940.

14 *The Derby Daily Telegraph Mar. 21 1940*

15 *Nenagh Guardian*, 6 Apr. 1940.

CHAPTER 16

1 *Evening Herald*, 29 Oct. 1892.

2 Ibid

3 *Irish Press*, 27 Oct. 1936; *Irish Press*, 28 Oct. 1936.

4 Report of the Departmental Committee into the Housing Conditions of the Working Classes in the City of Dublin (1913) [HC 7273], 20.

5 *Irish Press*, 30 Nov. 1937.

6 *Irish Press*, 30 Nov. 1937.

7 *Evening Herald*, 31 Jan. 1938.

8 Walsh, B., 'Life Expectancy in Ireland since the 1870s.'

9 Dunne, C., *An Unconsidered People*, 11; *Delany, E. Demography, State and Society: Irish Migration to Britain, 1921–1971*, 226.

10 Dáil Éireann Debate, 30 Oct. 1924, Vol. 9, No. 6.

11 Lee, J.J., *Ireland, Politics and Society 1912–1985*, 115.

12 Ibid., 126.

13 Bartlett, T., *The Cambridge History of Ireland, Volume IV, 1880 to Present*, 370.

14 Girvin, B., *The Forgotten Volunteers of World War II.*

15 Delaney, E., *Demography, State and Society: Irish Migration to Britain, 1921–1971*, 63.

16 Connolly, S., *On Every Tide*, 333; Daly, M., 'The Irish Free State and the Great Depression of the 1930s: the interaction of the global and the local', 24–25.

17 *Evening Herald*, 17 Feb. 1965.

18 Kirby, D., *Laid Bare: The Nude Murders and the Hunt for 'Jack the Stripper'*, 157.

19 Ibid.

20 *Shepherds Bush Gazette & Post*, 17 Feb. 1966.

21 *Evening Herald* 19 Feb. 1965.
22 *Shephard's Bush Gazette and Post*, 17 Feb. 1966.
23 Ibid.

CHAPTER 17

1 *Belfast Telegraph*, 12 Jul. 1961.
2 Ó'Gráda, C., 'The Irish economy during the century after partition'.
3 *Belfast Telegraph*, 10 Jul. 1961.
4 *Daily Herald*, 21 Jul. 1961.
5 The Campaign for Social Justice in Northern Ireland, *Northern Ireland: The Plain Truth*.
6 *Belfast Telegraph*, 12 Jul. 1961.
7 Ibid.
8 Ibid.
9 Kelly, M. & McNeela, 'Assimilation policies and outcomes: Travellers' experience', 15.
10 *Belfast Telegraph*, 2 Nov. 1967.
11 Ibid., 26 Nov. 1963.
12 *Irish Weekly and Ulster Examiner*, 31 Mar. 1962.
13 *Belfast Telegraph*, 24 Oct. 1967.
14 Ibid., 6 Dec. 1965.
15 Ibid., 12 Nov.1967.
16 Ibid., 24 Feb. 1967.
17 *Belfast Telegraph*, 12 Jul. 1961.
18 Based on the sutton index of deaths available at cain.ulster.ac.uk
19 *Belfast News-Letter*, 2 Mar. 1972; *Evening Herald*, 2 Mar. 1972; *Irish Press*, 3 Mar. 1972.
20 *Belfast News-Letter*, 2 Mar. 1972.
21 *Irish Independent,* 3 Mar, 1972.

22 *Evening Herald*, 2 Mar. 1972.
23 Ibid.
24 *Irish Press,* 3 Mar 1972; *Irish Independent* 3 Mar, 1972.
25 *Sligo Champion*, 10 Mar. 1972.
26 *Sligo Champion*, 10 Mar. 1972.
27 Molony, E., *Voices from the Grave*, 201.
28 *Evening Herald*, 23 Dec. 1965.
29 Report of the Commission on Itinerancy, 49.
30 Brack, J. & Monaghan, S., 'Travellers' Last Rights: Responding to Death in a Cultural Context', 563.
31 Ageing for Travellers redefined as 40+ years due to low life expectancy, Paveepoint.ie, accessed 19 Feb. 2023.

CHAPTER 18

1 *Irish Independent*, 27 Nov. 1995.
2 Ibid., 10 Jun. 1995.
3 Ibid.
4 Ferriter, D., *Occasions of Sin*, 392.
5 Ibid.
6 Ferriter, D., *Occasions of Sin*, 393.
7 *Sunday Press*, 13 Mar. 1983.
8 Murray, P., *The Case I Can't Forget: The Killing of Declan Flynn.*
9 *Irish Press*, 1 May 1979.
10 *Irish Independent*, 19 Jun. 1980.
11 *Irish Examiner*, 5 Mar. 1982.
12 Cenrtal Statistics Office (CSO) Ireland and the EU 1973–2003, Economic and Social Change.
13 *Irish Press*, 9 Mar. 1983.
14 Murray, P., *The Case I Can't Forget: The Killing of Declan Flynn.*

15 *Irish Press*, 9 Mar. 1983.

16 Ibid.

17 *Irish Examiner,* 10 Mar. 1983.

18 *Cork Eaminer* 11 Mar. 1983

19 *Sunday Independent*, 20 Mar. 1983.

20 *Irish Press*, 16 Aug. 1988.

21 Donnelly, J.S, 'A Church in Crisis'

22 Ibid.

23 *Evening Herald*, 20 Dec. 1994.

24 *Sunday Tribune*, 11 Apr. 1999.

25 Linehan, A., 'Hundreds gather in Fairview Park to remember Declan Flynn.', GCN.ie, 12 Sep. 2022.

References

Albano, D., 'Funeral Customs in Nineteenth Century Ireland', [Thesis], Trinity College (Dublin, Ireland). Department of History, 2012,' Tara.tcd.ie, Accessed 13 Dec 2022.

Andrews, C. S., *Man of No Property*. Dublin: The Lilliput Press, 2001.

Annand A., *The Patient Assassin: A True Tale of Massacre, Revenge and the Raj*, London, Simon & Schuster, 2019.

Bartlett, T., *Cambridge History of Ireland Vol 3 1880 to the Present*. Vol. 4. Cambridge: Cambridge University Press, 2018.

Beaumont, C., 'Women, Citizenship and Catholicism in the Irish Free State, 1922–1948'. *Women's History Review*, Vol. 6, No. 4, 563–85.

Bielenberg, A., *The Shannon Scheme: And the Electrification of the Irish Free State*. Dublin, Lilliput Press, 2002.

Black (Firm), A. & C., *Black's Guide to Ireland*. Edinburgh, 1912.

Blackstock, A., 'Tommy Downshire's Boys: Popular Protest, Social Change and Political Manipulation in Mid-Ulster 1829–1847'. *Past & Present*, No. 196 (2007), 125–72.

Brack, J., *Travellers' Last Rights: Responding to Death in a Cultural Context*, Parish of the Travelling People, 2007.

Bubb, A., 'The Life of the Irish Soldier in India: Representations and Self-Representations, 1857–1922', *Modern Asian Studies* 46, No. 4 (2012), 769–813.

Bulik, M., *The Sons of Molly Maguire: The Irish Roots of America's First Labor War*, Fordham University Press, 2015.

Burke, T., '"Poppy Day" in the Irish Free State'. *Studies: An Irish Quarterly Review* 92, No. 368 (2003), 349–58.

Campbell, F., *Land and Revolution : Nationalist Politics in the West of Ireland 1891–1921*, Oxford, Oxford University Press, 2008.

Carrigan, W., 'Report of the Committee on the Criminal Law Amendment Acts (1880–1885) and Juvenile Prostitution.' Dublin, Stationery Office.

Carroll, E.M., 'Memorandum Re: Women and Girls Who Come before the Central Criminal Court on Serious Charges – and Other Relevant Matters', *Irish Probation*, Vol. 11 (2014), 196–207.

Census of Ireland 1891, Area, Population and Number of Houses; Occupations, Religion and Education Volume I, Province of Leinster, HC [C-6515].

Central Relief Committee of the Society of Friends, *Transactions of the Central Relief Committee of the Society of Friends During the Famine in Ireland, in 1846 and 1847*. Dublin, Hodges and Smith, 1852.

Clark, S. & James S. Donnelly Jr., *Irish Peasants: Violence and Political Unrest, 1780–1914*. University of Wisconsin Press, 2003.

Connolly, L., 'Sexual Violence in the Irish Civil War: A Forgotten War Crime?' *Women's History Review* 30, No. 1 (2 January 2021), 126–43.

Connolly, S., *Catholicism and Social Discipline in Pre-Famine Ireland*, New University of Ulster, 1977.

Connolly, S., *On Every Tide: The Making and Remaking of the Irish World*. First edition. New York, Hachette Book Group, 2022.

Connolly, S., *Belfast 400: People, Place and History*. Liverpool University Press, 2012.

Connolly, S., *Priests and People in Pre-Famine Ireland, 1780–1845*. Dublin, Four Courts Press, 2001.

Cook, S., 'The Irish Raj: Social Origins and Careers of Irishmen in the Indian Civil Service, 1855–1914'. *Journal of Social History,* 20, No. 3 (1987), 507–29.

Cowman, D & Brady D., *The Famine in Waterford, 1845–1850: Teacht Na Bprátaí Dubha*. Dublin, Geography Publications, 1995.

Crowley, J., Smyth. W.J., & Murphy, M., *Atlas of the Great Irish Famine, 1845–52*, Cork, Cork University Press, 2012.

Curran, D., *The Rise and Fall of the Orange Order During the Famine From Reformation to Dolly's Brae*, Dublin, Four Courts Press, 2021.

Daly, M., 'The Irish Free State and the Great Depression of the 1930s: The Interaction of the Global and the Local'. *Irish Economic and Social History,* 38 (2011), 19–36.

Davitt, M., *The Fall of Feudalism in Ireland*. 1st edition, London, Harper & Brothers, 1904.

Delaney, E., *Demography, State and Society: Irish Migration to Britain, 1921–1971*, Liverpool, Liverpool University Press, 2000.

Donnelly, J.S., *Captain Rock: The Irish Agrarian Rebellion of 1821–1824*, Wisconsin, University of Wisconsin Press, 2009.

Donnelly, J. S., 'The Great Famine: Its Interpreters, Old and New'. *History Ireland* 1, No. 3 (1993), 27–33.

Donnelly, J. S., *The Great Irish Potato Famine*, Cheltenham, The History Press, 2002.

Dooley, T. *Sources for the History of Landed Estates in Ireland*, Dublin, Irish Academic Press, 2000.

Dorney, J., 'The Belfast Dockers and Carters Strike of 1907', theIrishstory.com, accessed 20 May 2023.

Dorney, J., *The Civil War in Dublin: The Fight for the Irish Capital, 1922–1924*, Newbridge, Merrion Press, 2017.

Dorney, J., *Peace after the Final Battle: The Story of the Irish Revolution, 1912–1924*, Dublin, New Island, 2014.

Dunne, C., *An Unconsidered People: The Irish in London*, 2nd edition, Dublin, New Island, 2021.

'Eleventh Annual Report of the Registrar General of Marriages of Births Marriages and Deaths in Ireland HC [C-1495]'.

Evans, R., *The Coming of the Third Reich*, London, Penguin, 2003.

Fahey, J., *Looking West Olive Pakenham Mahon (Strokestown)*, 1981, RTE Sound Archives.

Farrell, R., et al., *Roscommon: History and Society*, Dublin, Geography Publications, 2018.

Fanning, R., 'Anglo-Irish Relations: Partition and the British Dimension in Historical Perspective', *Irish Studies in International Affairs* 2, No. 1 (1985): 1–20.

Fennelly, K., 'Out of Sound, out of Mind: Noise Control in Early Nineteenth-Century Lunatic Asylums in England and Ireland', *World Archaeology* 46, No. 3 (2014), 416–30.

Ferriter, D., *Occasions of Sin: Sex and Society in Modern Ireland*, London, Profile Books, 2010.

Ferriter, D., *A Nation and Not a Rabble: The Irish Revolution 1913–23*, London, Profile Books, 2015.

Ferriter, D., *Ambiguous Republic: Ireland in the 1970s*, London, Profile Books, 2013.

Ferriter, D., *Between Two Hells: The Irish Civil War*, London, Profile Books, 2021.

Ferriter, D., *Judging Dev: A Reassessment of the Life and Legacy of Eamon de Valera*, Dublin, Royal Irish Academy, 2007.

Ferriter, D., *The Transformation of Ireland, 1900–2000*. London: Profile Books, 2004.

Finn, D., *One Man's Terrorist : A Political History of the IRA*, London, Verso, 2019.

Finnegan, P., *Loughrea: 'that Den of Infamy' during the Land War in Co. Galway, 1879–82*, Dublin, Four Courts Press, 2014.

Fitzpatrick, D., *Irish Emigration 1801–1921*, Dublin, Economic and Social History Society of Ireland, 1984.

Fortieth Report of the Inspectors of Lunatics (Ireland), HC [C 6503].

Gannon, S., '"The Green Frame of British Rule?": Irish in the Indian Civil Service', theIrishstory.com, accessed 7 Jan. 2023.

Gerwarth, R., *The Vanquished Why the First World War Failed to End, 1917–1923*, London, Penguin Random House, 2016.

Ghose, A. K., 'Food Supply and Starvation: A Study of Famines with Reference to the Indian Sub-Continent', *Oxford Economic Papers* 34, No. 2 (1982), 368–89.

Gibney, J., *The United Irishmen, Rebellion and the Act of Union, 1798–1803*, Barnsley, Pen & Sword Books, 2019.

Ginnell, L., *Land and Liberty*, Dublin, Duffy & Co., 1908.

Girvin, B., 'The Forgotten Volunteers of World War II', *History Ireland*, Vol.6, No.1, 1998.

Gmelch, S., *Nan: The Life of an Irish Travelling Woman*, Illinois, Waveland Press, 1991.

Gregory, I., et al., *Troubled Geographies: A Spatial History of Religion and Society in Ireland*, Bloomington, Indiana University Press, 2013.

Gregory, A., *Lady Gregory's Journals, 1916–1930*, London, Macmillan, 1947.

Hanley, B. & Millar, S., *The Lost Revolution: The Story of the Official IRA and the Workers Party*, Dublin, Penguin, 2009.

Hanley, B., *The Impact of the Troubles on the Republic of Ireland, 1968–79*, Manchester, Manchester University Press, 2019.

Hanley, B., *The IRA, 1926–1936*, Dublin, Four Courts Press, 2002.

Hanley, B., '"The Irish and the Jews Have a Good Deal in Common": Irish Republicanism, Anti-Semitism and the Post-War World'. *Irish Historical Studies* 44, No. 165 (May 2020), 57–74.

Hanley, B., 'Poppy Day in Dublin 1920s and 30s', *History Ireland*, Vol. 7, No.1, 1999.

Helleiner, J., *Irish Travellers: Racism and the Politics of Culture*, Toronto, University of Toronto Press, 2000.

Holton, K., '"All Our Joys Will Be Complated": The Visit of George IV to Ireland, 1821'. *Irish Historical Studies* 44, No. 166 (Nov. 2020), 248–69.

Hopkinson, M., *Green Against Green – The Irish Civil War: A History of the Irish Civil War, 1922–1923*, Dublin, Gill & Macmillan, 2004.

Hopkinson, M., *The Irish War of Independence*, Dublin, Gill & Macmillan, 2002.

Hoppen, K. T., 'An Incorporating Union? British Politicians and Ireland 1800–1830', *The English Historical Review* 123, No. 501 (2008), 328–50.

Howlin, N. & Costello, K., *Law and the Family in Ireland, 1800–1950*, London, Palgrave, 2017.

Ireland and the EU 1973–2003, Economic and Social Change Dublin, Central Statistics Office, 2004.

Jeffery, K., *An Irish Empire?: Aspects of Ireland and the British Empire*, Manchester University Press, 1996.

Jenkins, B., *Era of Emancipation: British Government of Ireland, 1812–1830*. Belfast, McGill-Queen's Press, 1988.

Jordan, D., *Land and Popular Politics in Ireland: County Mayo from the Plantation to the Land War*, Cambridge, Cambridge University Press, 1994.

Joyce, N., *My Life on the Road: An Autobiography*, Dublin, Gill & Macmillan, 1985.

Kelly, B., *Hearing Voices: The History of Psychiatry in Ireland*, Newbridge, Irish Academic Press, 2016.

Kelly, J., *The Cambridge History of Ireland, 1730–1880*, Vol. 3, Cambridge, Cambridge University Press, 2018.

Kelly, J., *Food Rioting in Ireland in the Eighteenth and Nineteenth Centuries: The 'Moral Economy' and the Irish Crowd*, Dublin, Four Courts Press, 2017.

Kennedy, F., 'The Suppression of the Carrigan Report: A Historical Perspective on Child Abuse'. *Studies: An Irish Quarterly Review* 89, No. 356 (2000), 354–63.

Keogh, D., *Jews in Twentieth-Century Ireland: Refugees, Anti-Semitism and the Holocaust*, Cork, Cork University Press, 1998.

Kinealy, C., *A Death-Dealing Famine: The Great Hunger in Ireland*, London, Pluto Press, 1997.

Kinealy, C., *The Great Irish Famine: Impact, Ideology and Rebellion*, London, Bloomsbury, 2017.

Kirby, D., *Laid Bare: The Nude Murders and the Hunt for 'Jack the Stripper'*, Cheltenham, The History Press, 2016.

Kostick, C., *Revolution in Ireland: Popular Militancy, 1917 to 1923*, London, Pluto Press, 1996.

Larkin, E., *The Pastoral Role of the Roman Catholic Church in Pre-Famine Ireland, 1750–1850*, Dublin, Four Courts Press, 2006.

Lacey, B., *Terrible Queer Creatures: Homosexuality in Irish History Dublin*, Dublin, Wordwell, 2008.

Lee, J.J., *Ireland, 1912–1985: Politics and Society*, Cambridge, Cambridge University Press, 1989.

Lewis, S., *A Topographical Dictionary of Ireland*, London, S. Lewis & Co., 1837.

Luddy, M., *Prostitution and Irish Society, 1800–1940*, Cambridge, Cambridge University Press, 2007.

Luddy, M., 'Sex and the Single Girl in 1920s and 1930s Ireland', *The Irish Review*, No. 35 (2007), 79–91.

Lynch, J., 'Harland And Wolff: Its Labour Force And Industrial Relations, Autumn 1919'. *Saothar* 22 (1997), 47–61.

Marx, K., *Karl Marx: Selected Works in Two Volumes*. London, International Publishers, 1949.

Maguire, M., 'Civil Service Trade Unionism in Ireland (Part I), 1801–1922', *Saothar* 33 (2008), 7–21.

Maguire, M., 'Civil Service Trade Unionism in Ireland (Part II), 1922–90'. *Saothar* 34 (2009), 41–60.

Maguire, M. 'The Carrigan Committee and Child Sexual Abuse in Twentieth-Century Ireland', *New Hibernia Review / Iris Éireannach Nua* 11, No. 2 (2007), 79–100.

Maxwell, N., 'A Church in Crisis', *History Ireland*, Vol. 8, No. 3, 2000.

Mac Suibhne, B., *The End of Outrage: Post-Famine Adjustment in Rural Ireland*, Oxford, Oxford University Press, 2017.

McCabe, C., *Sins of the Father*, Dublin, The History Press, 2011.

McCarthy, A. J. P., 'The Irish National Electrification Scheme', *Geographical Review* 47, No. 4 (1957), 539–54.

McCarthy, M., *High Tension: Life on the Shannon Scheme*, Dublin, Lilliput Press, 2004.

McCarthy, P., *The Irish Revolution, 1912–23: Waterford*, Dublin, Four Courts Press, 2015.

McCarthy, P., 'The Irish Volunteers and Waterford Part II, 1916–1919: The Resistible Rise of Sinn Féin'. *Decies*

Waterford Archaeological and Historical Society, No. 61, 2004, 245–67.

McCready, C. T., *Dublin Street Names Dated and Explained*, 2nd edition, Vol. 1, Dublin, Carraig Books, 1987.

McDonagh, P., *Gay and Lesbian Activism in the Republic of Ireland, 1973–93*, London, Bloomsbury, 2021.

McGarry, F., *Eoin O'Duffy: A Self-Made Hero,* Oxford, Oxford University Press, 2008.

McGee, O., *The IRB: The Irish Republican Brotherhood, from the Land League to Sinn Féin*, Dublin, Four Courts Press, 2005.

McMahon, C., *The Coffin Ship: Life and Death at Sea during the Great Irish Famine*, New York, New York University Press, 2021.

McMahon, R., '"A Violent Society"? Homicide Rates in Ireland, 1831–1850', *Irish Economic and Social History* 36 (2009), 1–20.

McMahon, R., *Homicide in Pre-Famine and Famine Ireland*, Oxford, Oxford University Press, 2013.

Mokyr, J., *Emigration and Poverty in Prefamine Ireland*, Centre for Economic Research, University College Dublin, 1982.

Mokyr, J., *Why Ireland Starved: A Quantitative and Analytical History of the Irish Economy, 1800–1850*, revised edition, London, Allen & Unwin, 1985.

Moloney, E., *Voices From The Grave: Two Men's War In Ireland*, London, Faber & Faber, 2010.

Murphy, R., 'Walter Long and the Making of the Government of Ireland Act, 1919–20', *Irish Historical Studies* 25, No. 97 (1986), 82–96.

Nolan, W. & McGrath, T., *Tipperary: History and Society*. Dublin, Geography Publications,1987.

Nolan, W. & Power, T., *Waterford History & Society: Interdisciplinary Essays on the History of an Irish County*, Geography Publications, 1992.

O'Brien G., *Coming Out: Irish Gay Experiences*, Dublin, Currach Books, 2003.

O'Connell, S., 'Violence and Social Memory in Twentieth-Century Belfast: Stories of Buck Alec Robinson', *Journal of British Studies* 53, No. 3 (2014), 734–56.

O'Connor, E., 'Agrarian Unrest and the Labour Movement in County Waterford 1917–1923', *Saothar* 6 (1980), 40–58.

O'Dwyer, M., *India as I Knew It, 1885–1925*, London, Constable, 1925.

O'Grada, C., *Ireland before and after the Famine*, New York, Manchester University Press, 1988.

Ó Gráda, C., *A Rocky Road: The Irish Economy Since the 1920s*, Manchester, Manchester University Press, 1997.

Ó Gráda, C., *Black '47 and Beyond: The Great Irish Famine in History, Economy, and Memory*, Princeton, Princeton University Press, 2000.

Ó Gráda, C., *Ireland: A New Economic History, 1780–1939*, London, Clarendon Press, 1994.

Ó Gráda, C., *Jewish Ireland in the Age of Joyce: A Socioeconomic History*, Princeton, Princeton University Press, 2016.

Ó Gráda, C., *Settling in: Dublin's Jewish Immigrants of a Century Ago*, Dublin, Field Day Publications, 2005.

Ó Gráda, C. & O'Rourke, K., 'The Irish Economy during

the Century after Partition', *The Economic History Review* 75, No. 2 (2022), 336–70.

O'Halpin, E. & Ó Corráin, D., *The Dead of the Irish Revolution*, New Haven, Yale University Press, 2020.

O Higgins, K., 'Three Years Hard Labour: An Address Delivered to the Irish Society of Oxford University', 31 Oct. 1924.

O'Leary, E., 'The Irish National Teachers' Organisation and the Marriage Bar for Women National Teachers, 1933–1958', *Saothar* 12 (1987), 47–52.

O'Riordain, E., *Famine in the Valley*, Galty Vee Valley Tourism, 1997.

Pakenham, T., *The Year of Liberty: The Great Irish Rebellion of 1798*, London, Times Books, 1998.

Prior, P., *Asylums, Mental Health Care and the Irish: 1800–2010*, Newbridge, Irish Academic Press, 2017.

Plowman, M.E., 'Irish Republicans and the Indo-German Conspiracy of World War I', New Hibernia Review / *Iris Éireannach Nua*, Vol. 7, No. 3, (2003), 80–105.

Radford, M., 'Closely Akin to Actual Warfare', *History Ireland*, Vol. 7, No.4, 1999.

Redmond, J. & Judith H., '"One Man One Job": The Marriage Ban and the Employment of Women Teachers in Irish Primary Schools', *Paedagogica Historica* 46, No. 5 (2010), 639–54.

Regan, John M., *The Irish Counter-Revolution, 1921–1936: Treatyite Politics and Settlement in Independent Ireland*, Dublin, Gill & Macmillan, 1999.

Reilly, C., *Strokestown and the Great Irish Famine*, Dublin, Four Courts Press, 2014.

Royal Commission of Inquiry into the State of the Law

and Practice in Respect of the Occupation of Land in Ireland HC XIX 1845.
Report of the Belfast Riots Commissioners [HC 4925] 1887.
Report of the Commission on Itinerancy, Dublin, Stationary Office, 1963.
Report of the Committee on Evil Literature, Dublin, Stationary Office, 1927.
Report of the Departmental Committee into the Housing Conditions of the Working Classes in the City of Dublin [HC 7273] 1913.
Report of the Disorders inquiry committee 1919–1920, Calcutta Superintendent Government Printing, India, 1920.
Ryan, M., *The Real Chief – Liam Lynch*, Cork, Mercier, 1986.
Shiels, D., *The Irish in the American Civil War*, Cheltenham, The History Press, 2013.
Special Commission to Inquire into Charges and Allegations Against Certain Members of Parliament and Others, *A Verbatim Copy of the Parnell Commission Report: With Complete Index and Notes*, London, Irish Loyal and Patriotic Union, 1890.
Trevelyan, C., *The Irish Crisis*, London, Longmans, 1848.
Vaughan, W. E., *Murder Trials in Ireland, 1836–1914*, Dublin, Four Courts Press, 2020.
Vaughan, W. E., *Landlords and Tenants in Mid-Victorian Ireland*, London, Clarendon Press, 1994.
Vaughan, W. E., *A New History of Ireland Vol V Ireland under the Union*, Oxford, Oxford University Press, 1976.

Vesey, P., *The Murder of Major Mahon, Strokestown, County Roscommon, 1847*, Dublin, Four Courts Press, 2008.

Walsh, B., 'Life Expectancy in Ireland since the 1870s', *The Economic and Social Review* 48, No. 2 (2017), 127–43.

Walsh, M., *Bitter Freedom: Ireland in a Revolutionary World 1918–1923*, London, Faber & Faber, 2016.

Whelan, F., *Dissent into Treason: Unitarians, King-Killers and the Society of United Irishmen*, Dublin, Brandon, 2010.

White, J., *My Clonmel Scrapbook County Tipperary Famous Trial, Romances, Sketches, Stories Ballads Etc.* 3rd edition, Dundalk, Dundalgan Press, 1995.

Woodham-Smith, C., *The Great Hunger: Ireland 1845–1849*, London, Penguin, 1991.

1851 Census of Ireland Report on the Status of Disease, Part III [HC 1765]. HMSO, 1854.

Online Sources

'Ageing for Travellers Redefined as 40+ Years Due to Low Life Expectancy', paveepoint.ie, accessed 30 Jan. 2023.

Gannon, S., 'Revisiting the "Limerick Pogrom" of 1904', theIrishstory.com, accessed 20 May 2023.

Glennon, K., 'The Dead of the Belfast Pogrom – Counting the Cost of the Revolutionary Period, 1920–22', therishstory.com, accessed 5 Dec. 2022.

Glennon, K., 'The Dead of the Belfast Pogrom – Addendum', therishstory.com, accessed 5 Dec. 2022.

Higgins, O. & Blake S., 'Reprisals: The Eileen Quinn Story', *Doc on One*, RTÉ.ie, Accessed 20 Aug 2022.

'Hundreds Gather in Fairview Park to Remember Declan Flynn', GCN.ie, accessed 30 Oct. 2022.

Kohl, J.G., 'Travels in Ireland', Celt.ucc.ie, accessed 20 Jan. 2023.

Murray, P., 'The Case I Can't Forget: The Killing of Declan Flynn', 2022. RTÉ.ie, accessed 17 Feb. 2023.

Ó'Gráda, C., 'School Attendance and Literacy Before the Famine: A Simple Baronial Analysis'. *SSRN Electronic Journal*, 2010.

O'Neill, R., 'Legally Gay!' Pantisocracy, Season 6, Episode 3, pantisocracy.ie, accessed 7 Jan. 2023.

Shiels, D., How Many Irish Fought in the American Civil War?', irishamericancivilwar.com, accessed 20 Apr. 2023.

'Waterford City & County Council: Waterford 1914–1918'. www.waterfordcouncil.ie, accessed 19 Jan. 2023.

Index